TASMAN BAY

Canoe Bay

Abel Head

Brereton Cove

b

n

Tonga Saddle

Shag Harbour

Onetahuti Bay

Tonga Island

a William Welby Hadfield
~~now~~ Bill Hadfield
~~Wo~~odhouse Hadfield
~~Wa~~ters
~~b~~ank
~~Awaroa~~ School 1
~~Awaroa~~ School 2
~~Awaroa~~ School 3
g Awaroa School 4
h *Venture*
i Perrott (Silver Point)
j Fred and Jessie Hadfield
previously Ricketts
k Welby and Laura Hadfield
l Cemetery
m Cunliffe, Cracknell,
Nicholls
n Baigents Mill
o Waiharakeke Mill, Brown
p Gilbertson, Samuels
q Thompson
r Black, Sigley, Bruning

AWAROA LEGACY

The story of the Hadfield family

OTHER BOOKS BY CAROL DAWBER

FICTION

BACKTRACK

EARTHWORK

SOUNDS EASY

NON-FICTION

BAINHAM - A HISTORY

COLLINGWOOD TO THE HEAPHY TRACK

THE JACKSONS OF TE AWAITI

NORTH OF KAHURANGI, WEST OF GOLDEN BAY

GUIDES ALIVE, THE NELSON STORY

INHERITING THE DREAM

FERNTOWN TO FAREWELL SPIT

LINES IN THE WATER

AWAROA LEGACY

The story of the Hadfield family

by
CAROL DAWBER
&
LYNETTE WILSON

First published October 1999
Second edition April 2005

published by October Enterprises Ltd t/a
River Press
<riverpress@xtra.co.nz>

for
Abel Tasman Wilsons' Experiences
P O Box 351
Motueka
<info@AbelTasman.co.nz>
www.AbelTasman.co.nz

Cover design by: Melissa Middleton
Printed and bound by:Times Offset, Malaysia

ISBN 0-9598041-6-1

For my great-grandmother
Adele
and all the Adeles who came after her

This is the story of the Hadfields of Awaroa, whose descendants own and operate Abel Tasman Wilsons' Experiences. We invite you, our visitors and guests, to share our family history as you walk and kayak around the Abel Tasman National Park and enjoy the hospitality of our Torrent Bay Lodge and Meadowbank Homestead - Awaroa.

The legacy of the Hadfields is the story of pioneer men and women who came to a new and untamed land and set out to support themselves and raise their children, depending on their own resources and each other. Meadowbank Homestead - Awaroa is filled with memories of the earlier Meadowbank homestead, built by William and Adele Hadfield in 1884, and of the children who grew up within its walls.

Awaroa today is a place apart, a place where the seabirds call a welcome and the stars hang heavy in the sky. It's a place to take time out, to consider the world from a different perspective and to enjoy the simple peace of beach, bush and solitude as the first settlers did nearly a hundred and fifty years ago. This is our Awaroa legacy.

Haere mai ra, e te manuhiri tuarangi – welcome to all our guests

ABOUT THIS BOOK

When I was a little girl I used to visit my grandparents at Awaroa. I loved those visits, and I asked a lot of questions. In recent years I became aware that if the family history was to be preserved their stories must be written down, so this book is an attempt to record the lives and loves of my branch of the family, the Hadfields of Awaroa.

Over the years I have gathered information from photographs, diaries, notes and letters, and from the stories my mother, grandparents, aunts and uncles told me. The task fell to me partly because I am the senior member of my generation, perhaps because I and my husband and children are now custodians of the property where William and Adele chose to raise their family, most importantly because I became fascinated by the rich vein of history we share.

It was not until very recently that my great grandmother Adele's second marriage and subsequent murder was talked about. It was the family tragedy, yet the more I uncovered about this remarkable woman the more I wanted her story to be told. She is part of our heritage, a powerful personality who is still a strong presence at Awaroa, and the many years she and my great grandfather William Welby Hadfield spent there together are acknowledged and celebrated in this book.

I am grateful to my husband John and all those members of the family who have supported and encouraged my efforts. I would also like to thank the Winters, the Glasgows, the Nalders, the Gibbs and other friends who have allowed me to add their photographs and memories to this rich store of information. Photographs not otherwise credited have come from our own family collections.

My family has been at Awaroa for 136 years and six generations now. We look forward to sharing its beauty with William and Adele's descendants and with our visitors into the new millenium.

Lynette Wilson
Riwaka, August 1999

AUTHOR'S NOTE

To be invited into someone else's family history is a rare privilege for any writer, and this project has given me the opportunity to go right back into the affairs of some of our earliest settlers. The task was a big one as we sifted and assembled material from letters and diaries, family memoirs and stories handed down through the years.

We are grateful particularly to Bernard Hadfield whose publications *Hadfield* and *The Newth Snow Hadfield Connection* provided a starting point, to Beryl and Gordon Murphy for information on the Ricketts family and to Palmerston North City Library archivist Ian Matheson. The Nelson Provincial Museum, Alexander Turnbull Library, National Archive, *Manawatu Standard* and *Nelson Evening Mail* have all been valuable sources of information, as has earlier work by Ella Flower, Jenny Vidgen and Yvonne Primmer. I was privileged to interview Lynette's aunts and uncles Nelson, Muriel, Bill, Ada and Joan and Bethany, and I thank them for their trust and cooperation.

The nature of this book is such that the authors cannot guarantee the accuracy of all the information in its pages. To the best of our knowledge the stories and events are true. Any errors or omissions are regretted.

Carol Dawber
Picton, August 1999

CONTENTS

HADFIELD FAMILY MEMBERS WHO LIVED AT AWAROA: 1863 - 1999

1858 - Frederick and Ann HADFIELD came to NZ with their children

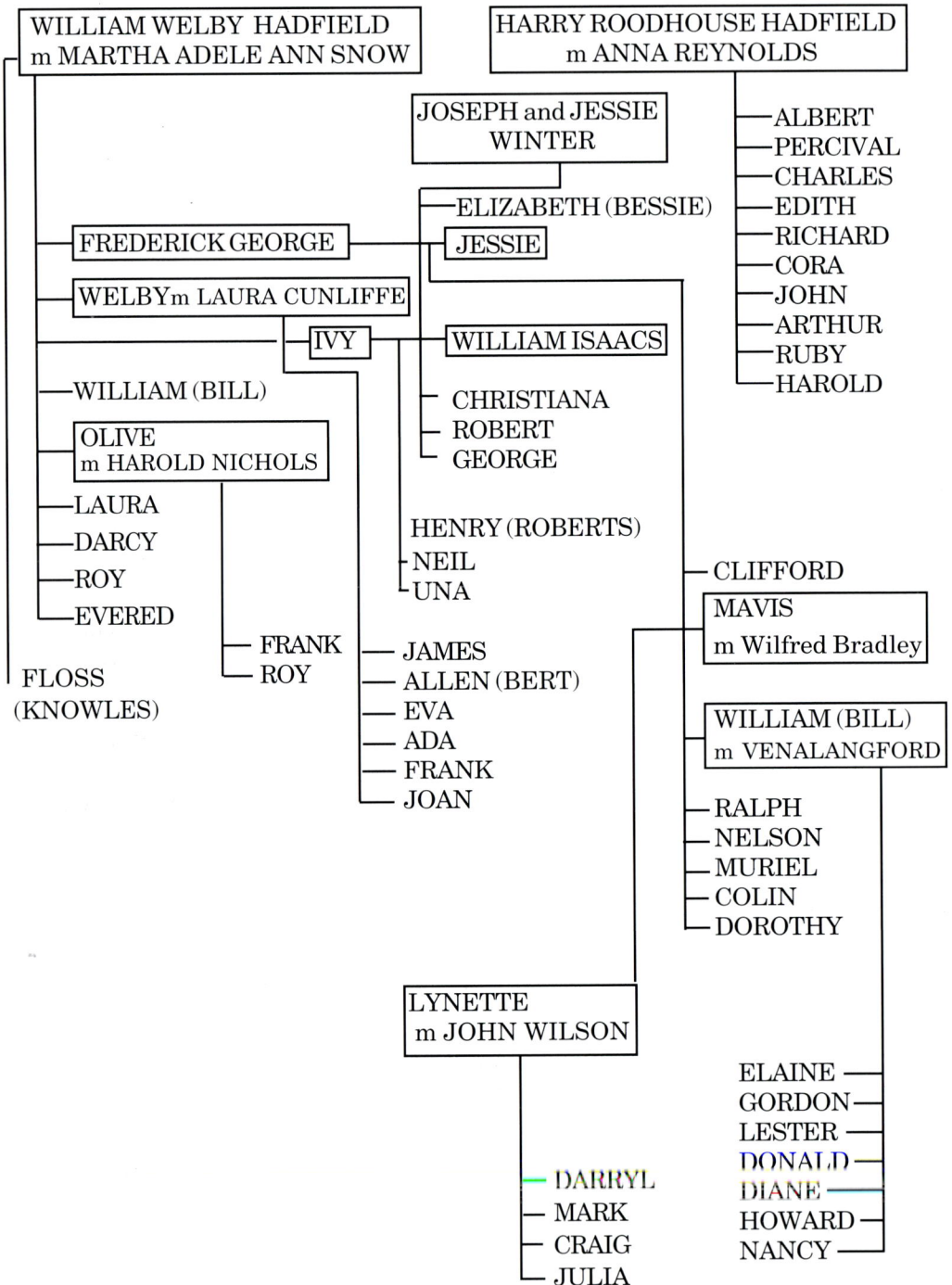

WILLIAM WELBY HADFIELD
m MARTHA ADELE ANN SNOW

HARRY ROODHOUSE HADFIELD
m ANNA REYNOLDS

JOSEPH and JESSIE WINTER

- ALBERT
- PERCIVAL
- CHARLES
- EDITH
- RICHARD
- CORA
- JOHN
- ARTHUR
- RUBY
- HAROLD

ELIZABETH (BESSIE)

FREDERICK GEORGE

JESSIE

WELBY m LAURA CUNLIFFE

IVY

WILLIAM ISAACS

- CHRISTIANA
- ROBERT
- GEORGE

WILLIAM (BILL)

OLIVE
m HAROLD NICHOLS

- LAURA
- DARCY
- ROY
- EVERED

HENRY (ROBERTS)
- NEIL
- UNA

- CLIFFORD

MAVIS
m Wilfred Bradley

- FRANK
- ROY

- JAMES
- ALLEN (BERT)
- EVA
- ADA
- FRANK
- JOAN

FLOSS
(KNOWLES)

WILLIAM (BILL)
m VENA LANGFORD

- RALPH
- NELSON
- MURIEL
- COLIN
- DOROTHY

LYNETTE
m JOHN WILSON

ELAINE —
GORDON —
LESTER —
DONALD —
DIANE —
HOWARD —
NANCY —

- DARRYL
- MARK
- CRAIG
- JULIA

PROLOGUE :

1906

A DISCARDED NEWSPAPER lay on the seat of the railway carriage, headline uppermost. Church Street Tragedy. Husband Remanded in Custody. Fred Hadfield averted his eyes. He had read the paper slowly and reluctantly, compelled to face the horror contained in the printed columns. Now he wanted the whole thing to be over as quickly as possible.

The steam locomotive clanked and hissed as it slowed towards the station. Bush-covered hills and dark gullies had given way to more open country and the young man in the carriage looked with interest at the sheep chewing their way through green pasture, their wool creamy and curled with a summer's easy food. He was glad of the distraction and he watched a man working his dog close by the train, keeping his little flock moving as the sudden whistle from the engine made them skitter and jump.

Then he sighed and gathered his things together. He checked the watch at his waistcoat. Ten o'clock, and a difficult day to get through before he could leave this strange and alien part of the country.

The station was busier than Fred had expected, porters bustling with the luggage wagon and patient horses stamping in their shafts. He started towards the ticket office to ask directions, stopped when he saw the newspaper hoarding. Accused Served in South Africa, the headline read. A frown crossed the man's face and he squared his shoulders, turning away from a second billboard which said Husband On Trial For Murder.

A group of women gathered around it, their faces pink and wattled like young turkeys.

"They say she was no better than she should be," one was saying.

"They say he kissed her afterwards, there in the gutter while she lay dying."
A gasp of indrawn breath, delicious scandal.

"It's the poor motherless children I feel sorry for."

"But who would have them now? I mean, a murderer for a father."

"They're burying her today, I hear."

The women turned and noticed him then, a well-built man approaching thirty, moustaches neatly trimmed in the fashion of the day. His clothes were plain and serviceable, the suit a Sunday one, his working boots well polished and his ruddy skin betraying his years outdoors.

He brushed past them, collected his small leather suitcase and began to walk down from the platform, ignoring the waiting cabs, striding out towards the far end of the street. A watcher would have seen him consult a paper in his pocket, hesitate, ask directions from an old man leaning against the striped pole of a barber's shop. If the observer were keen-eyed he or she would have noted the tension in the man's fit frame, the determination in his step and the resolute cast to his jaw. But in Palmerston North in 1906 strangers were noted and categorised by their business, not their emotions, and this one was obviously a farmer come to town, a sight so common no one wondered where he farmed or what his purpose was.

He found the church and braced himself to face the stares, but there were few. Men and women stood stiffly, sang, sat down, and stood again. The words were simple, the procession to the graveside short. The minister looked more like a football player than a man of God, Fred thought privately, but the service was respectful and he felt his mother would have liked it.

He stared down at the plain coffin, adorned with few flowers, and his eyes were dry and hard, his few words courteous but curt. He kept his thoughts to himself and the other mourners, a sombre group of older uncles, aunts and cousins, muttered their condolences and soon moved away.

May Slyfield and her husband Ray were there from Wanganui. Hers was a familiar face and her few words strengthened him. His grandparents were there too, frail and old-looking, and he shook hands solemnly with his grandfather, embraced Grandmother Snow with awkward formality and answered their questions about his brothers and sisters. He refused their suggestions of hospitality and further conversation as politely as he could, explaining that he had business to attend to.

The house he wanted was a mile from the centre of town and Fred was uncomfortably hot by the time he turned up the path, but he didn't take his coat off. He stood for a moment, looking at the wide front door, not noticing young frightened eyes watching from a window. When he knocked the watcher disappeared, and the door was opened by a woman in the black and red uniform of the Salvation Army who led him through to her husband.

The eyes that faced him across the parlour table were compassionate and that disconcerted him more than anything had yet. He sat stiffly, spoke grimly, and drank the proffered tea as gingerly as if it had been served in the finest bone china instead of in plain serviceable institution cup and saucer. He declined scones and biscuits, avoided the compassion and waited.

The door opened and a young boy came in. Two pairs of eyes surveyed each other anxiously, the likeness between them stamped so clearly the watchers were taken aback although they had expected it. Then the visitor stood, carefully putting his cup and saucer back on the starched cloth with a hand that hardly trembled. He moved towards the boy, held out a hard, work-roughened hand, waited until the boy's small pink hand stole into it for a formal handshake.

"Evered, do you remember who I am? I'm your brother Fred. I've come to take you home."

"How do you do, sir?" The boy replied stiffly. Then his lip trembled and he bit it to stop the tears. "Oh Fred, Mother's gone to heaven and she can't come back."

"I know, Evered. That's why I've come for you. I'm going to take you home to Awaroa."

"Will Mother be there at Awaroa? Is that where she's gone?"

Fred looked stern. "No, Evered, Mother has gone to heaven, as you were told, and she won't be coming back to Awaroa. We won't discuss her any more now. You'll stay here with the Clarkes for a few days, and then I'll come back to get you."

He glanced up at the woman and stood stiffly as the boy was led away.

Fred spent the next three days at a boarding house near the centre of town, and every morning he went to the courthouse. He took his dinners alone, and every evening he went out and walked the streets, speaking to no one. His route varied, but each time it took him along the same section of Church Street.

Finally the case he was waiting for was called, and William Knowles stood in the dock. The courthouse was crowded, and their eyes met only once, but that was enough for the older man who quickly lowered his, shaken and distressed. He was formally committed to trial and led away.

Fred's business was nearly over, and only one small task remained before he was free to go home. He settled with his landlady, left his bag at the station and headed for the Salvation Army captain's home once more.

"We're going back to Wellington on the train, so you can go with Mrs Clarke and get your things and say your goodbyes while I finish my business," he told young Evered. There were papers to be signed and bills to be paid but the business did not take long. The Salvation Army captain said his words of comfort and condolence but he was new to the district and had not known those involved. He was too wise to assume a familiarity where there was none.

The woman with the compassionate eyes came back into the room and waited but said little, trying to gauge the calibre of the stranger in front of her. She had prayed long and hard that morning, as they all had, because there was a problem to be resolved.

If it was God's will, this young man would play a part. If not? She sighed. She had already worked out how to play her own part in the most honest way she could, the rest was up to Him.

"Perhaps we could go to the children's room and find Evered now?" she suggested softly. "He will be there with Reginald and Florence."

Fred frowned. "Could he not be sent for again?"

"He's only a little boy, Mr Hadfield. Just nine years old. He might be finding all this a little difficult, as we all are. He's a very good boy and we'll be sorry to see him go."

"Very well then."

She rose and led the way down a short hallway to the nursery, a big airy room where several children played with blocks and dolls under the supervision of a young woman in a black work apron. Evered was at one end with a little boy half his age, holding his hand very tightly, and a younger child rocking on a rocking horse before them. Fred hesitated, frowning at the woman beside him but she had moved away to speak to her own children, her back turned to him.

He stood there, ill at ease, not wanting to approach the little group but knowing that he had to.

"Evered," he called gruffly. "It's time to go."

But the boy turned to him with puzzled eyes. "Reg and Flossie are not ready, sir. Their bags are not packed, and Flossie still has her indoor clothes on."

"They're not coming with us, Evered," he said gruffly. "Now say goodbye."

The little boy with Evered was four, his face still plump from babyhood. He stared at the stranger with big round frightened eyes, his world already shattered beyond his understanding. He looked to the woman for reassurance and she came to him, her arms around him, and spoke to the older child.

"Evered, Reginald is going to a different home now. He will have a new Mama and Papa all of his own, and he will be very happy. They will come for him after you have gone, so you must give him a kiss and say goodbye now and go with your brother."

The two children looked solemnly at each other, the younger boy's face crumpled in tears, and the other woman led him away to play with some of the other children. He was easily distracted, as four year olds are, and Evered stood staring up at his brother.

"Will Flossie have a new mother too?"

"Yes, God will send her a new mother."

"And will her new mother come today?"

The grownups hesitated and boy's tone grew strong and challenging.

"You're not going to give her one, are you?"

"Evered." Fred's voice was harsh. "Say goodbye to Captain and Mrs Clarke and come with me now."

"No. I shan't. You shan't make me." He picked the little girl up from the rocking horse and held her clumsily in his arms, reeling from the weight of her. "Flossie's my sister and Mother said I was always to look after her. You have to bring her too."

Fred looked to the woman beside him for help but her eyes were downcast. Captain Clarke watched him sombrely, his expression unreadable. Fred was angry, and reached out to tear the little girl out of his brother's arms. She looked up at him and her pouty little mouth creased up into a laugh as she stretched her own arms out to him. Her weight was thrown forward and Evered would have overbalanced if Fred hadn't caught the child up from him. He held her stiffly, seeing her properly for the first time.

Solemn grey eyes regarded him. Big, proud eyes. His mother's eyes.

"She'll be treated kindly here," the Salvation Army officer said softly. "We won't be very likely to find her a home, but lots of girls go to orphanages and the Army is about to open its own orphanage in Wellington. She will be fostered out with some family until then and she will grow up under the care of the Army until she can go into service. She can be a scullery maid when she's 14, or something like that. She'll never know family life, of course, poor wee thing, but perhaps some charitable folk will take her in and be kind to her."

There was a silence, the laughter and chatter of the other children in the room stilled suddenly. Evered stood as if he was stone, tears tracing lines down his young cheeks, and Fred frowned down at the little girl's grey eyes still fixed on his. Then a plump hand reached for his watch chain, the mouth crumpled to laughter again.

"Be good enough to pack her things too," he said abruptly. "She'd best come home with us to Awaroa."

He set the child down and turned on his heel to leave the room.

It was a long journey home. The man, the boy and the little girl were silent in the railway carriage, the children soon lulled to sleep by the rhythmic rocking of the train. Fred spent the long hours staring at the girl, wondering at his own impulsive action. Then, finally, after they had reached the boarding house and the children had been fed and put to bed, the girl in a rough cot and the boy beside him under crisply-ironed sheets, he gave way to his own emotions. It was to be the last and only time he wept for his mother.

Fred Hadfield was no stranger to small children. The eldest of nine, he had cared for young brothers and sisters all his life and his hands were gentle as he washed and changed the little girl and packed her things and helped her and Evered to brush their hair and tidy themselves. A bowl of porridge at the landlady's table and a settling of the bill and they were off again, striding through the streets of Wellington to the wharf, embarking on the Union Steam Ship Company's steamer *Penguin* for the long passage to Nelson via Picton.

It was a typical Wellington day, blustery and wet, and by the time they were safely on board and heading out of the harbour the boat was already dipping and rolling in the swells. Fred felt better with the deck beneath his feet. He nodded to acquaintances, sniffed the sea air and pointed out dolphins dancing in the deep waters.

The crossing was rough and Everard was frightened when they came into the rough waters of Cook Strait, so Fred took the children below where they slept and woke again, refreshed. At Nelson they took a horse-drawn cab to Olive's house and young Evered greeted his older sister with grave pleasure, comfortable in her company.

Olive stared at Florence.

"She has Mother's eyes," she said, looking at Fred keenly. "What will become of her?"

Fred watched the little girl play with Olive's own child. Francis Nicholls had just had his first birthday and was struggling to pull himself upright, trying to walk and falling over at every step while little Flossie, bigger and more sure footed, laughed and enticed him with a toy horse she kept pulling just out of reach. Evered sat close by, watching the children anxiously, ready to intervene if they annoyed the adults.

"The sooner the boy gets back home the better," Fred said gruffly. "He needs colour in his cheeks."

Olive was heavily pregnant again, her movements awkward as she handled the big teapot. She was hoping for a girl this time and watched little Flossie avidly. "I have some cloth I'll give you for Laura to sew," she told her brother. "She will need a pinafore for the farm."

"She has clothes."

"She's growing fast. How old is she, Fred? Two years? Two and a half? When is her birthday?"

Both were silent. Neither knew, and the awareness descended between them like a weight. Brother and sister eyed each other gravely and it was the man who turned away first.

It was late the next evening when the *Wairoa* drew abreast of Awaroa. The travellers were on deck, Fred waiting with the confidence of habit, the children solemn and shivering in the May night air. The stars hung heavily above them, the sky far brighter and richer than the sea below, and a beam of light flashed from the north every 60 seconds.

"That's the Farewell Spit lighthouse," Fred told Evered, pointing. "Do you remember?" But the boy shook his head, awed by the pitch black strangeness of it all.

Fred waited with the little girl in his arms, seeing the soft light in the window at Meadowbank, the fainter light against the hill that he knew was Jessie's house. He wouldn't have picked it out at all if he hadn't known exactly where to look. He wondered what she would say, how she would look at the child and at him. The thought of her sharp, wise eyes gave him strength.

There was a shout and a shape loomed out of the darkness, a lantern low on the port side, a splash of phosphorescence as an oar was shipped. A sailor hurled a rope and Fred took Evered's hand and moved the children forward to the little pile of stores and suitcases waiting on the deck.

"Shall we take the boy first, Captain Hadfield?"

"Yes please," he said and watched as a rope was secured fast around Evered's chest and under his arms. Strong arms lowered the boy from sight, an answering shout told him he was safe in the dinghy. Then the sailors looked questioning at the little girl in his arms but he shook his head. "I'll carry her. Give me the rope."

Swiftly and surely he looped it around the child and himself. She was crying softly, fearfully, but he didn't stop to calm her. She would learn about boats, and the sooner the better. He nodded at the handful of passengers who had braved the cold to come out on deck and watch the transfer, and there was a swift handshake with the captain who had left his post to offer the courtesy of a personal farewell.

And a last glance at the child they'd all be talking about, Fred thought cynically as he tightened his grip on Flossie and let them guide him down the ladder and into the void between the steamer and the smaller boat.

Rough hands caught his legs and guided them, strong arms steadied him as he sat down quickly in the stern sheets. Oars were used, shouts exchanged and the big dark bulk of the steamer moved away into the night, the deep thrum of the motor fading gradually away. There was silence then, the silence of a vast and empty sea, and the dinghy rocked gently in the steamer's wake.

The old man raised a lantern and by its dim light he studied the passengers he'd collected.

"You've brought the girl home then?" he said at last.

"It was for the best."

No more to be said then, and Fred sat still in the stern while the old man rowed. Evered huddled against his brother, shivering with tiredness and cold, and little Florence trembled in his arms.

Fred Hadfield slept soundly that night, at home in his own bed again with the sound of the sea gentle above the soft sighing of his brothers in the room they all shared. If he dreamed at all it was of Jessie Winter, the wise-eyed Welsh woman he hoped to share his life with.

In the house under the hill Jessie was wakeful, pleased he was home again, wondering how he had fared and how he felt. She'd watched the steamer pause and pass again, seen the pale yellow lantern flicker and fade as the dinghy came in across the bar. She ached for him, this man she'd grown so close to. They'd grown up together, slowly and carefully replacing childhood friendship with adult love, and he would always be her dear boy.

Upstairs at the big house William Welby Hadfield sat motionless at the window, watching the dark sea and the steady flashing of the lighthouse beam as the long night passed towards dawn. Now a gull cried harshly, then a morepork called from the bushes and a weka shrilled an answer.

The old man lifted the candlestick from the dresser beside him and went to stand once more beside the rough cot at the foot of his bed, to watch the child who slept there. Her cheeks were like magnolia petals, velvet to his touch as he bent to take the tiny thumb from her mouth and smooth the bedclothes at her neck.

So like her mother, and so dear...

FAREWELL SPIT

NEW ZEALAND

GOLDEN
BAY

NORTH IS.

COLLINGWOOD

TAKAKA

ABEL
TASMAN
NATIONAL
PARK

SOUTH IS.

TASMAN
BAY

KAITERITERI

MOTUEKA

LOWER
MOUTERE

MAPUA

WOOD-
STOCK

UPPER
MOUTERE

NELSON

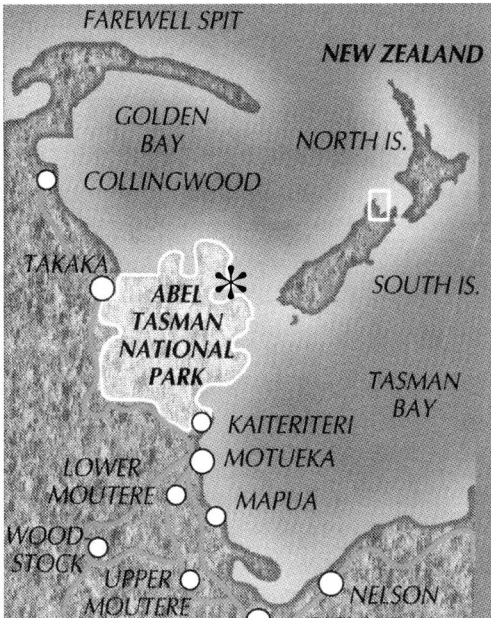

*Awaroa Bay, where
Hadfields have lived and
farmed since 1863

Awaroa Inlet, now part of the Abel Tasman National Park

Tasman Aerial Photography, Richmond

THE FAMILY OF FREDERICK AND ANN HADFIELD

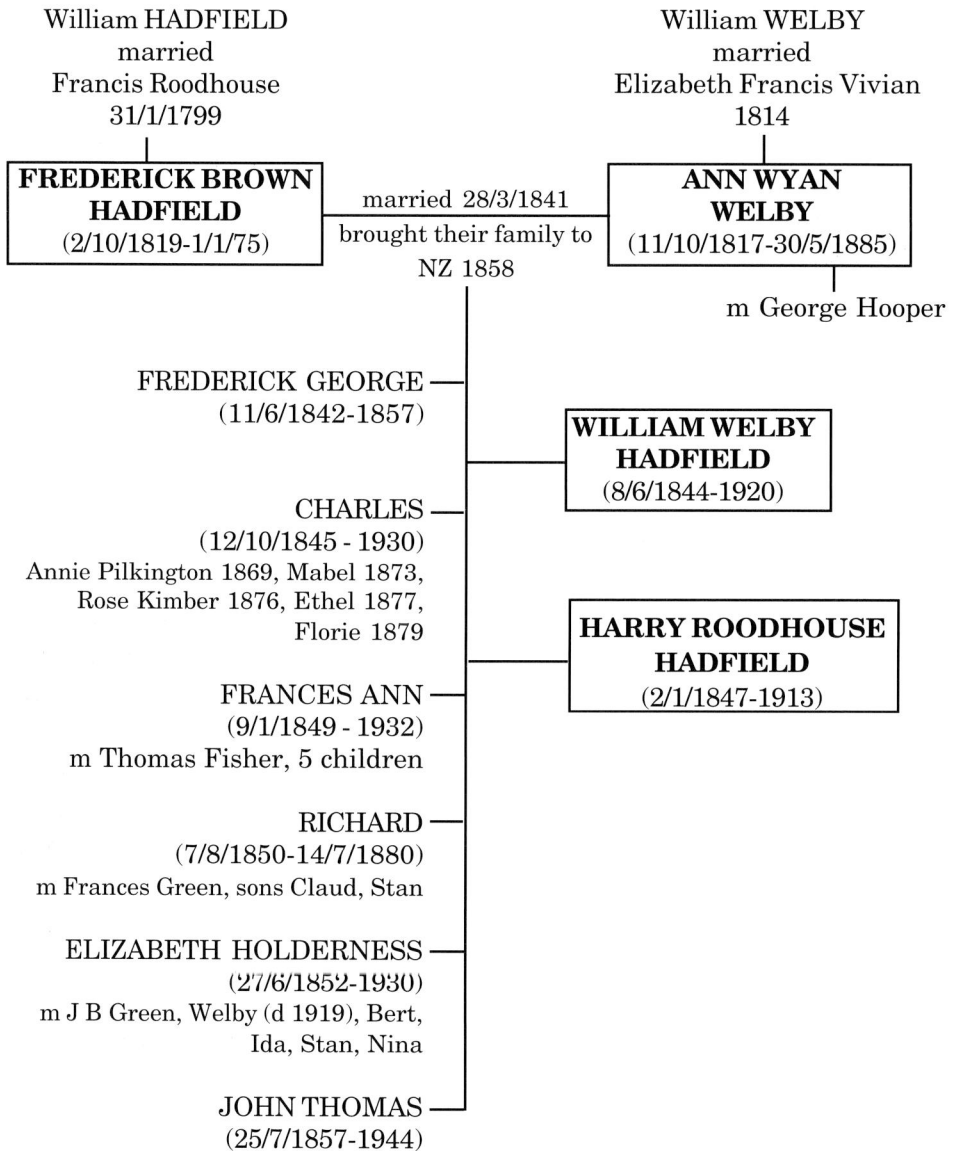

William HADFIELD
married
Francis Roodhouse
31/1/1799

William WELBY
married
Elizabeth Francis Vivian
1814

FREDERICK BROWN HADFIELD
(2/10/1819-1/1/75)

married 28/3/1841
brought their family to
NZ 1858

ANN WYAN WELBY
(11/10/1817-30/5/1885)

m George Hooper

FREDERICK GEORGE
(11/6/1842-1857)

WILLIAM WELBY HADFIELD
(8/6/1844-1920)

CHARLES
(12/10/1845 - 1930)
Annie Pilkington 1869, Mabel 1873,
Rose Kimber 1876, Ethel 1877,
Florie 1879

HARRY ROODHOUSE HADFIELD
(2/1/1847-1913)

FRANCES ANN
(9/1/1849 - 1932)
m Thomas Fisher, 5 children

RICHARD
(7/8/1850-14/7/1880)
m Frances Green, sons Claud, Stan

ELIZABETH HOLDERNESS
(27/6/1852-1930)
m J B Green, Welby (d 1919), Bert,
Ida, Stan, Nina

JOHN THOMAS
(25/7/1857-1944)

CHAPTER ONE : ENGLAND TO AWAROA

1857

WILLIAM HADFIELD REMEMBERED back down sixty long years, to where it had all begun across the other side of the world. When he had been a little child he had slept in a cot like this one, but there had been no waves lapping softly in the night there, no deep stillness like the stillness of Awaroa. He had shared a room with his brothers, the cobbled street below their window ringing with the clopping of hooves, the creaking of the night wagons waking them and soothing them to sleep again.

The Hadfields' house at Bury St Edmund in England was substantial. William's father was a chemist and a man of importance, his grandfather the doctor even more so. His boyhood days were filled with fishing in the local streams, wandering over the meadows, playing in the yard behind his father's shop and running errands to the infirmary where the nurses all spoke respectfully and called his grandfather Dr Welby.

The Welbys were his mother's family. She had been Ann Wyan Welby, brought up living next to the post office at Newark where her father was a surgeon at the hospital. Will loved hearing her tell of how she had fallen in love with his father when they were youngsters living across the road from each. The Hadfields had been carriers at Wakefield, but by the time Will's father Frederick Brown Hadfield was born, the youngest of thirteen, they had moved to Newark where they were hay merchants. Frederick Hadfield qualified as a chemist, as his older brother had already done, and he and the doctor's daughter were married at the Academy Chapel in Hoxton, London.

William was born at Bury St Edmund in 1844. His brother Fred was two years older, and after William came Charles and then Harry, born in 1847.

The family seemed to divide itself then, when the first girl came along. That was their sister Frances, then came Richard and Elizabeth, all three of them babies together while the elder boys were a close-knit gang of four.

In 1853 William's father stood for election as a town councillor. William was impressed by the engraved cards he helped to deliver around the town. "Mr F B Hadfield, Candidate, East Ward, respectfully solicits your vote and interest," they said. His Hadfield uncles and cousins might still sit outside the tavern, red-faced and smelling of beer and hay as they smoked their pipes, but his father was a gentleman, and a man of importance.

William enjoyed his own schooling, especially Greek and the Classics, but he never wanted to be a chemist or a doctor. When he left school at twelve he went to live with his father's older sister Emma and her husband Charles Bloodworth on their farm in Empingham. They called him Will, and soon everyone else in the family did too.

He was glad when he was sent to work for Aunt Emma and Uncle Charles. They were kind and he enjoyed the early mornings in the milking shed, up in the dark to light the lanterns and work in the warm cowdung of the yards. He loved the smell of the animals, the big, gentle horses, the soft flanks of cows and the cats insinuating themselves around the warm pails steaming with creamy milk. There were no sheep at the Bloodworths' farm, just cows and chickens, rich green pasture, wooden railings, sturdy oaks and meadow flowers. There was a sense of richness, of joining in a pattern set years earlier. The houses and farm buildings were old and weathered, the land had been cultivated for generations and he felt at home.

The day his brother died started like any other. He woke in the dark, his uncle's hand on his shoulder, and tumbled out of bed to pull his breeches and socks on. His boots were at the back door and he fumbled with the laces, shivering with the cold, then ran across to the cowshed where the other men were already at work by the light of the kerosene lanterns. They each had their own cows to milk, and Daisy was already in the stall waiting for him to fetch his stool and begin the gentle, rhythmic tug on her udders, his numbed fingers quickly warming as the milk squirted into the first bucket.

When they came out of the shed it was daylight, and Will's turn to take the last of the cows down to their day pasture, closing the gates behind them while his cousins sluiced out the cowshed and yard. He was cold again when he got back to the waterpump in the yard, and he pumped the handle and splashed his face and arms clean for breakfast. He was still at his porridge with the other men, Aunt Emma busy with the loaf of crusty bread, when the news came.

"Here's Jem the carrier," Uncle Charles said in surprise, as the dogs barked and yapped around the front yard. He went to the door cheerfully, but when he came back his face was grim. He nodded curtly to the men, who one by one finished up their meals and slipped out.

"Not you Will, you stay," he said, and he slipped his arm around Aunt Emma. "There's news from your mother, and it's bad."

They broke it to him as gently as they could. His brother Fred was dead, and he must go home at once.

Will felt his heart leap, and he couldn't take it in at first. Fred was two years older, a hero who had led the games and adventures, climbed the highest, run the fastest.

"But how? How could he be dead?" he cried in bewilderment. "Our Fred's not even sick."

"Aye, he was sick all right," Uncle Charles said grimly. "Diphtheria, Jem says. It gets you suddenlike, does that foul plague. Your father told Jem the boy was ill for three days, mebbe four, that's all. It's the fever, you see, and it rages and there's no dealing to it, and it just takes you."

"My poor Will," Aunt Emma cried, running to him to cradle his head in her bosom. "My poor poor boy."

Her poor sister-in-law too. Ann Welby, gentlewoman, doctor's daughter was shattered to lose her firstborn. She was in charge of a household of sixteen people including servants and apprentices, and her life was busy enough even without illness and tragedy.

William arrived home to hear that the house at Bury St Edmund had been turned into an infirmary and his mother, still weak from bearing her eighth child, had stayed up night after night putting cool cloths on her eldest son's fevered forehead, trying everything she could to nurse him through and praying for him to live. She had moved wearily between her eldest and youngest sons until her father forbade her the sickroom for the sake of her own health. Then while the new baby, John Thomas, had lain crying in the nursery fifteen-year-old Fred had died in his bed, his parents and grandparents gathered round him.

William found his parents distraught with grief, his brothers and sisters shaken by the suddenness of Fred's death.

"You should have sent for me sooner, Mother," he told her. "I would have helped. I would have done anything."

"I know, Will, and the others did everything they could, but there was nothing more any of us could do, believe me," she said. "Our Fred's gone now, and we must all accept God's will."

She looked at him through her tears. This gentle, strong fourteen year old William had never been any trouble as a child, the way the other boys had been. It was Fred who led them into scrapes, Harry who always ended up with mud all over his breeches or with his knees scraped and his clothes torn, Charles who so often came home with a bloodied nose after a fight or a rough and tumble. Will was a sturdy and sensible lad, the reliable one of the four.

He was also the one who took after her side of the family most, she thought. Perhaps that was just wishful thinking because he was the one they'd named Welby after her own dear father and mother, or perhaps it was because of the name that he was already like her father, with intelligent, gentle eyes that seemed to see and understand other people more clearly. It was William who had brought home an abandoned puppy when he was only four and begged to be allowed to keep it, William who always picked her the best flowers in the garden for her birthdays, and who was, according to Charles Bloodworth, a natural farmer.

There had never been any doubts that young Fred would find a career in the military, perhaps the navy, and that Will's future would lie on the land. About Charles, Harry and the two younger boys the future was less certain. They were still so young, and there had always seemed plenty of time.

Now Fred junior was gone, dead at fifteen, and it was time for his parents to take stock of their lives. Frederick Brown Hadfield had lost eight of his own twelve brothers and sisters, six of them while they were still young children. His parents were both dead and now his eldest son was gone too. He was an astute man and as he and his father-in-law Dr Welby worked every day with illness and disease, doling out the mixtures and potions, they knew they could ease pains but not always cure the diseases brought on by poverty and poor living conditions.

They decided to emigrate to New Zealand, where there might be a better future for their children. Encouraged by his father-in-law, Frederick Hadfield settled his affairs and booked a passage for his family.

"We're doing the right thing, Ann," William heard his father tell his mother at Fred's graveside. "I only wish we'd done it sooner."

William was not so sure. When his father had first talked of emigration he'd been thrilled at the prospect, reading all he could about the new colony across the other side of the world. Other people in the village had gone to Australia and New Zealand and sent home tales of gold to be picked like buttercups and wild savages peering out from forests.

Now he found himself at fourteen the eldest son, no longer able to tag behind Fred, and he found the idea of sailing to a new country a bit frightening.

His brothers and sisters looked to him for leadership and he wasn't sure how well he could lead them through a long and strange sea voyage.

He went back to Empingham on the carrier, quiet and thoughtful, to help with the haymaking. It was hard, hot work but at least it was familiar, as were the people around him.

"Won't be doing this in New Zealand, young Will," one of the men called. "They say there's no grass there at all yet, just jungle, and wild animals everywhere."

"Don't you listen to them," his uncle told him with a twinkle in his eye. "I've heard there's good land aplenty, and that the grass grows so fast you don't even need to cut hay, there's plenty of good fresh fodder all year round."

"Aye, and so much gold there's no need to fork hay at all," a lad called wryly. "You'll be wearing gold buttons on your waistcoat soon, our Will."

"And you'll have nowt to buy buttons with at all, Clem Johnson, if you don't work faster than that," Uncle Charles rejoined, and they set to again in the watery English sunshine.

Before he left the farm for the last time William walked around the garden with Aunt Emma, and she helped him cut healthy slips from his favourite shrubs and pack them carefully in moistened hay and heavy paper. She gave him a bundle of young rose bushes, their roots packed and bound in clay and linen to let them breathe.

"I've done you up a basket of flower bulbs too," she told him fondly. "Ann always loves the spring flowers, and I know she won't have time to take anything from her garden up there. You take care of these for her, and plant them in New Zealand."

"I will," he said gratefully. "And I'll write and tell you how they grow."

It was summer in England, the air rich with pollen and drowsy with bees and everywhere he looked there were flowers. He drank them in, wondering if he'd ever see their like again. How could there be fruits and flowers like these in the jungles of New Zealand?

His last days at the Bloodworths' farm went swiftly, then he was home to help his parents pack their furniture and sea chests and tick off the lists of new clothes, boots, tools and provisions they would need to take with them. There was a lot of advice to be had about emigrating, and the message was clear. Nothing was yet manufactured or produced in New Zealand, and everything that could not be quickly grown on the land had to be taken from the old world to the new.

There was land, timber and gold to be found in abundance, and it was known that there were seals and wild fowl and seabirds, but boots and shoes, needles and thread, pots and pans and books and axes and shovels were all best carried on the voyage or the new settlers would find them priced out of reach when they landed ashore.

The Hadfields left England 30 June 1858 on the ship *Robert Small,* bound with more than 80 others for a new life in a new colony. They were among the more well-to-do passengers and they travelled first class, not steerage, but even so their family cabin opening off the saloon seemed very crowded and uncomfortable. William, Charles and Harry, the three eldest children, ran loose on the deck every chance they got. They all enjoyed talking to the sailors and watching the sea under the bow.

For William it was the first taste of boating and he learned everything he could, not knowing that one day he would be turning the experience to good use in his own boatyard. He spent hours watching the men at their work, and he soon managed to persuade one of the older sailors to find him an end of rope to learn his knots and splices with. He watched them mend sail and his hands itched to try the heavy palm and needle for himself. Passengers weren't allowed to mix with the crew or visit them in their quarters, but Will watched and learned, and the older men saw his interest and were kind to him.

He and his brothers learned to study the sky and sniff the wind on that long three month passage, revelling in the sunshine and giddy with the movement of the clouds racing above their full sails. At first they were alarmed and queasy when the wind grew stronger and they had to stay below and watch their lantern sway on its hook in the tiny stuffy cabin, but after the first few weeks they got used to the groaning and creaking of the timbers. The days passed in a routine of eating and sleeping, playing and helping with the few chores their parents could find for them. William read and studied, took part in concerts and musical evenings and watched the sailors at their duties. He read to the younger children, Frances, Richard and Elizabeth and taught them their letters while their mother looked after them and baby John.

They arrived in Wellington on October 12 and after a couple of days of bustle and strangeness were back at sea again, this time on the steamer *Tasmanian Maid* for the short voyage to Nelson.

That last leg of the voyage was wilder than anything they'd experienced on the ship from England. Without the steadying mast and sails above them the little boat pitched and rolled across Cook Strait, meeting the waves quarter-on rather than running with them. The ship seemed crowded with passengers, mostly rough-looking men, and their talk was all of gold, of hidden creeks and riffle-boxes and nuggets. There were Irish, Scots, English and Welshmen, some with brogues so thick Will could scarcely understand them.

Ann was ill and stayed below, leaving her husband and eldest son to take care of the children, and William found he had his hands full trying to keep Frances, Richard and Elizabeth from falling overboard as they watched the land come closer.

"We're here," Frances would shriek, and they'd watch eagerly for a sign of smoke or settlement on the hills, but then the ship would rumble on and the headland they hoped was their destination would slide away behind them.

"We'll be catching French Pass on the tide before nightfall," Charles told his brothers importantly. "I heard one of the men tell Father."

William caught his breath as they came closer and closer to the grey smoky hills. There were other boats around them now, little scows with heavy brown sails loaded with timber until they seemed nearly awash. Once, thrillingly, there was a Maori canoe filled with brown men dipping their paddles to a strange musical chanting the watchers could barely hear over their own engines.

There were little blue penguins in the water now, and white-faced shags that dived under the water and disappeared for ages before emerging again wet and sleek like water-rats. Then the ship turned, and there was a murmur from the passengers lining the rails. Will looked ahead and suddenly felt alarmed. The hills were all around them now, on both sides and ahead of them, and a thick belch of smoke came from the funnel as they seemed to increase speed rather than decrease it.

"Are we going aground, Will?" Harry asked.

Will grabbed the girls and struggled to keep his feet as the current began to race around them. He looked around to make sure the boys were all close by, and then watched fearfully, sure they would all be dashed against the sharp-edged black rocks that seemed close enough to touch as the foam swirled between them.

"Don't fret, lad," an amused voice said softly at his elbow. "It's French Pass, and the captain knows just what he's doing."

The steamer seemed to lift on the waves as they sped through the tiny gap, then the ominous black teeth on either side of them widened again and they turned and ran out into a widening bay, the hills on their port side rising high and substantial while the landscape to starboard changed from hill to rocky crag, and then to lower rocks over which the sea crashed and thundered.

"There. Like a cork from a bottle, and just as satisfying," the tall man beside William said cheerfully, as the steamer turned and ran out into open sea again. Now they were meeting the waves head on, the bow rising and falling with a thump over each one, and a new and more distant landscape began to unfold to the left.

Ahead of them mountains rose blue and smoky, and away to their left there were lower, greener hills. A thick pall of smoke rose from one distant hillside.

"Clearing the land," the tall gentleman told William. "Best way to deal with the undergrowth."

"Does the fire not get out of control?" Will asked. He had seen no cleared paddocks anywhere in this strange new landscape, no fences, nothing to indicate this could possibly be farmland.

"Burns itself out, sooner or later. Course you need to get the timber out first. There's good timber here, hundreds of acres of it." He looked curiously at the lad beside him.

"Here for the gold like all the others, are you, boy? Take my advice, go in for farm work instead. There's more future in it."

"I'm with my parents, sir," Will replied. "My father is a pharmacist and will set up in business in Nelson."

"A chemist? Nelson's sorely in need of more good businessmen," the man said with quickened interest, and his shrewd eyes took in the tribe of younger brothers and sisters. "I'd like to meet your father, lad. I'm William Lightband. Perhaps you will introduce us?"

Before long the two men were deep in conversation, talk that lasted until the *Tasmanian Maid* began to draw closer to her destination. William and Charles helped their mother feed the younger children and put them to bed, as they were to stay on board until first light.

The older boys were allowed out on deck with their father as they docked, and Will thrilled at the sight of the horses and men below them on the wharf. At Wellington they had been overwhelmed by the sights and sounds after three months at sea, but now after this much shorter voyage he was ready to observe and learn again.

"Well, young Will Hadfield?" Mr Lightband was beside him again briefly. "Your father's told me you're keen to work on the land, not spend your life in a shop. What do you say? Will you be off up the riverbeds digging for gold like the rest of them, to live in a tent and take your chances?"

"I'll work where my father thinks best sir," William replied, and Lightband clapped him on the back.

"You'll do, my boy, you'll do. We'll meet again, I'll be bound."

There was little sleep for Will the rest of that night. For the first time since he'd left the Bloodworth's farm all those long months ago, he thought about working among men again, about feeling the haft of an axe or a shovel in his hands, the warmth and smell of farm animals around him, the mud of a farmyard on his boots and the weariness that comes after a hard day's work.

Suddenly he was impatient with his mother's skirts, his father's dry, scholarly talk and the childish prattle of the children, and he longed to get on with his new life. When dawn came he was eager and ready to shoulder his share of the load. He and his father went ashore to secure a horse-drawn cab, then he waited with it while the boys came carrying the lighter boxes and bags.

Ann carried John, only just over a year old, while six-year old Elizabeth clung to her skirts in wide-eyed awe. Frances was nine and Richard eight, and Will helped them into the high seats and gestured to Harry to hand the luggage in. There was not room for all of them and the boarding house where they were to stay was not far away, their father told them as he swung himself up onto the box with the driver. The cab rattled off, leaving the boys to follow on foot.

Will, Charles and Harry Hadfield walked along Haven Road for the first time, part of a steady parade of men, horses and wagons. On their left the shallow waters of the bay stretched out, hemmed from the open sea by a natural bank of boulders which formed a perfect harbour. To their right were wooden houses and taverns, wedged under a hill which rose abruptly from the road edge. Ahead was Nelson, the town that had been planned and established 17 years before by Colonel Wakefield and his New Zealand Company, the town that would be their new home

It was October 16, 1858.

The first boatloads of carefully-chosen English immigrants had divided up the land between them, purchasing town sections of one acre and country sections of a hundred acres or more. That the subdivision had been done in England seemed irrelevant now, and those who had drawn good viable farmland had stayed and prospered while those whose sections had turned out to be raupo swamp or rugged hillside had soon sold them and moved on to settle other parts of this huge empty land.

The first payable goldfield in the colony had been discovered the year before at Aorere, a mere days' sea journey from Nelson or three days' hard and rugged ride, and gold fever had come and gone through the province. Now there were solid businesses, elaborate houses and well-trodden streets. A grand new government building was being planned, and small farmers were being encouraged. Frederick Hadfield set up his pharmacy business in the centre of town, and was soon busy selling his rat poisons, liver pills, potions for rheumatic fever and salves for cuts and bruises.

ANN WYAN HADFIELD
1817-1885

FREDERICK BROWN HADFIELD
1819-1875

Trafalgar Street, Nelson, as it was when the Hadfield family lived above their shop.
In the foreground is Miller's Acre.

Nelson Provincial Museum photo C3582

Trafalgar Street ran up towards the big wooden cathedral on the hill. All around were little farms and the streets were busy with horses and carts. The shopping centre served a big district now, and there was talk of Marlborough, across the mountains to the east coast, forming its own provincial government.

They lived above the shop, their back yard barely big enough to grow a few simple vegetables and store the boxes of goods they had brought with them on the voyage. Will helped at the shop while his younger brothers and sisters finished school. He delivered prescriptions around the town, as he had back home at Bury St Edmund, and helped his father mix and measure the potions they sold in glass jars. Will quickly got to know the other shopkeepers and the farmhouses that were closer at hand. He loved going into Victoria House, the big emporium owned by the Snows a few doors down, and soon became a favourite with Mr Snow who looked out for him and gave him sweets from the big glass jars behind the counter.

"Mr Snow's son discovered the gold at Aorere," Will told his brothers and sisters. "There's a river named after him, Snow's River."

"It was Mr Lightband's son who found the gold first," Charles argued. "I've seen the nugget they brought back. The place is called Lightband's Gully, near Gibbstown."

The argument raged until William Lightband, now a regular acquaintance of their father, was called on to settle it. His son George had indeed developed the first payable goldfield with the help of several Nelson backers, and it wasn't during the main gold rush, but later in 1857 that George and Tom Snow had been fossicking further up the Aorere Valley and found gold at Snow's River, a tributary of the Aorere. Their discovery sparked a big rush up into the hills.

The Hadfield boys were impressed by George Snow when they finally met him. He was only five years older than William but already a man of the world with an attractive young bride on his arm. The fact that he was a goldminer and had a river named after him was glamorous enough, but the Snow boys also had a reputation around Nelson as being rather wild, and three of them had even been in prison.

Edwin, Tom and George Snow had been charged with assaulting an old man at the Turf Hotel in 1854, after a ball at which everyone had become very drunk. *The Examiner* reported the case in great detail, and everyone had followed the testimony avidly, how the old man, William Harvey, had suffered serious injuries, corroborated by medical evidence, after being thrown violently from his bed at 5am and set upon by three young men, how it could not possibly have been the Snow boys because there were a dozen witnesses to say they had been in a dozen other places at the time, how there had been other persons in the room who had been seen to assault the old man, and how these other persons, whom no one knew by name, had mysteriously left the Turf Hotel within minutes of the alleged assault and had not been seen since. After a confused and at times hilarious trial at which the only undisputed claim was everyone had been intoxicated at the time, the three Snows were sentenced to a month in gaol. By the time the Hadfields arrived in Nelson the incident had been all but forgotten, but Will and Harry heard about it from the other boys around town.

The Snows were restored to society because of the respect commanded by Mary Snow and because her husband William was an important shopkeeper, even if he was known to drink a little more than was seemly, and to be less than frugal with the money in his pocket. He was a gambler and so were his sons, but his wife had no part in that and they were well-liked. Edwin, the eldest of the Snow boys, was a crack shot with a rifle, and finished near the top of the field of well-respected Nelson men in a government-sponsored championship shooting competition in 1861. Ann Hadfield, Will's mother, soon became firm friends with Mrs Snow and the two families met regularly at church.

Will and Harry were sent off to work on sheep stations in Marlborough, William for the Goulters and Harry for Brinsdens. Both were big stations, established by English settlers who had not long been in New Zealand themselves, and the boys were soon at home in their new environment. They worked long hard days out with the sheep, played music and read in the evenings, and joined the family and the other hands for church on Sundays.

They were happy days for Will, following the wide, braided shingle riverbeds that meandered down broad valleys towards the huge flat Wairau Plain. It was sheep country at its best, far different from the lush green pasturelands of England. Here there were acres and acres of low grey scrub and yellow tussock, and when they burned the scrub to sow English grasses the fires swept for miles, fanned by the winds which lifted whirling duststorms from the river flats.

Will had never ridden horses before, although he'd learned how to care for them and harness them at the Bloodworths. There they had been beasts of burden, sturdy engines to haul carts and hay wagons. Here the big stations used lighter, riding horses, loading them with food and blanket rolls and using them to travel the vast miles where there were no roads and seldom even tracks wide enough for wheels. Will learned to trust the horses he rode at Goulter's Station, letting them pick their own way up and down the hillsides as he concentrated on spotting the maverick sheep hiding in the scrub, or the ewe down in a gully while her lamb bleated plaintively above her, or worse, lay semiconscious like an old white garment dropped carelessly on the ground.

He learned to make camp away from home, to cook rudimentary meals for himself, make tea in a billycan and bake bread in a camp oven and to take care of himself and his clothes in the rough wooden huts the men used when they were working away from the homestead. It was the first time in young Will's life that he had seen men cook and clean for themselves, for though the women did all the baking and housework at the homestead and sent out plenty of provisions, there were many days out in the field when the shepherds had to make their own stew and damper, and a man's ability to handle a cooking fire was as well respected as his skill with hammer and nails.

Under the hot Marlborough sun Will's confidence blossomed as his body filled out. The Wairau Valley was good for both sheep and men, hard enough to keep them fit and active, but without any real hardships. Station life was civilised and comfortable, and there were plenty of new faces coming and going, and new social contacts to be made. It was twelve months before he was back in Nelson, fitter and leaner now, tanned by the sun and strong from the saddle.

"You look a real New Zealander," his mother told him admiringly. "How long are you home for?"

"Mr Goulter said I might have a fortnight," he said happily. "I think Harry might be home soon too, as the run is quiet at the moment. The sheep are all up in their winter pasture and it's too cold and wet to do any fencing."

His father was full of questions about the big sheep station, and William found himself drawing maps and explaining how they moved the mobs from one high valley to the next. His little sister Elizabeth was a fascinated listener, her eyes wide when William described the heat and dust of the high country and the mountain flowers that bloomed in spring. Although the run was not too far up the valley he had already been further afield, riding to meet a mob driven through from Molesworth.

Will came home each year to Nelson eager to see his family again and exchange news. Richard was at Nelson College now, Charles helping in the shop and the two girls already starting to teach little John his letters.

It was in 1862 that Will met his future wife, although neither of them knew it at the time. William was eighteen and impatient with his mother for dragging him along to visit the Snows in their new home in Waimea Street.

"They're calling it Snow's Hill," Ann told her son. "Mr Snow used to own all this area around here but I believe he's sold most of it now. They've just retired and Mrs Snow has invited us to see her new home. I hear she's already laid out a beautiful garden."

SNOWS' HILL, 1860s. The large house at centre right, with a long driveway up from the gate on the corner of Waimea Street and Waimea Road, was built by William and Mary Snow in 1862 and is still standing. The title was registered to Sarah Snow, their 22-year-old daughter who later married Nelson businessman Ambrose Moore. It was here that William Hadfield first saw his future wife.   *Misc collection, Nelson Provincial Museum*

There was a touch of envy in her voice, and as they drew nearer to Waimea Street William could see why. His own family were reasonably well-to-do merchants but they owned only the shop and the house above it, with a small garden out the back. Those who had arrived in the first ships and bought shares in the New Zealand Company had been allotted prime land and had prospered more and more as the colony grew to a provincial capital. The Snows newly-built home had a carriageway winding up to an imposing front entrance, and already there were flowerbeds laid out and new trees and shrubs planted down the slope.

William felt uncomfortable in his town clothes and was soon stifling hot and bored. To his relief, the younger Snows were home and he was able to escape to the garden. Sarah and John were older than he was, Ada was about the same age. They were fashionably dressed and in high spirits, and for the first few moments he thought he had escaped from the frying pan into the fire.

Then he found himself enjoying their company, and Ada asked him all sorts of questions about the sheep farm.

"My sister Emma is married to Mr Dodson, and they live in Spring Creek, near Beavertown. They are very grand. Mr Dodson is on the Roads Board and Father says he might even be elected to Parliament one day."

"I believe he may be right," William told her, glad to be on familiar ground. "Mr Goulter and the other big owners think highly of Mr Henry Dodson. I have heard he is a successful brewer, and very wealthy, and that he has a fine head for public affairs."

"Emma has the most wonderful dresses, and a carriage of her own," Ada said eagerly. "Will you buy a farm in Marlborough yourself?"

"Hardly. The runs are all very big and not likely to be divided, and we are not wealthy and important like Mr Dodson. Father hopes to buy land somewhere in the Nelson area, and when Harry and I have finished our cadetships we will set up in a much smaller way."

"Oh I do hope you can be by the sea, and not inland like poor Martha," Ada cried. "Her family are on the Waimea plain and it's so hot and dusty. She doesn't ever get to the beach, and now she and George are at Hope they are even further from the sea."

"Do you like the sea that much, Miss Snow?" he asked her curiously.

"I wish I were a man, and then I would sail the oceans and visit strange lands and have a tattoo on my arm."

Her sister was shocked but William laughed. Ada was a tomboy, he could tell, in spite of her demure Sunday dress and straw bonnet, and he warmed to her company at once. He was telling her about the snow and how it looked on the manuka and tussock when she broke away and rushed to the front path.

"Oh look, George and Martha have come, with their baby. You must come and see her quickly, she's so beautiful. Her name's Martha Adele Ann Snow, and I'm her aunt, did you know that? "

Will thought George Snow's young wife was very beautiful indeed. The couple were in their early twenties and Martha was pregnant with their second child. Her dark eyes lit up when William dutifully admired the little girl.

"Here's Mr Hadfield, Addie," she said softly. William bent down and held his hand out to the dark haired girl, whose grey eyes looked solemnly up at him. A chubby hand reached out to take his finger, and she lost her balance and sat down abruptly in the gravel. William waited for her to cry, but instead she laughed, a happy, gurgling laugh that everyone joined in, and he swept her up into the air and joggled her so she laughed again in delight.

"Isn't she lovely," Ada cried at his side, but it was Martha's eyes that held his as he set the little girl back on her feet and dusted her off with gentle hands. Mother and daughter made a charming picture, Martha in dark blue trimmed with darker velvet, the child in white lace with the same blue velvet ribbons. There was a quiet dignity about young Mrs Snow that William found strangely comforting, as if she was already familiar to him, and when their eyes met there was a grave intelligence that they seemed to share.

"Come on, Ada, you know chaps aren't usually very interested in babies," George Snow told his sister impatiently. "Will and John and I might retreat to the back porch and discuss more serious affairs, and you girls can take Adele to the parlour to see her grandmother."

The moment was gone. William smiled at the little girl once more and Martha turned away, handing the little girl over to her sisters-in-law as all three of them vanished into the wide hallway.

The more serious affairs turned out to be bottle-shaped, and William soon forgot the girls he'd been talking to before he was rescued. George Snow was a much more interesting companion. He had been goldmining in the Aorere Valley, over on the West Coast and at Wakamarina, and he had much to say about the prospects for work. He and his father already owned several hotels and George was a man of the world, full of good advice.

"Of course I have to settle down a bit now," he chuckled, nodding towards the house where his wife and daughter were the centre of attention. "I'm thinking of heading back over to Collingwood. There's good money to be made there still, and I know where to look for the gold. It's not all in the creeks and rivers, either, some of it's in the diggers' pockets and it's easier and drier work mining it from that source, I can tell you."

"So you don't recommend the goldminer's life?" Will asked him seriously.

"Oh, I recommend life on the goldfields, I assure you. I'll probably open a tavern in Collingwood, and do very well."

By the time they left Will was overwhelmed by the warm sun, the beer and the talk. He sat at a careful distance from his mother on the gig, but she didn't notice his slightly erratic driving.

"What do you think of Ada, my dear?" she asked carefully. "The Snows are a good family and she likes you, I could tell. Of course you're both far too young to even think of courting yet, but the Snows are good friends and she's a well-brought up young lady."

"Now don't you start matchmaking already, Mother," Will said. "I'll be thirty before I can support a wife, and I'm far too young to even think of it. Besides, I don't like girls like Ada. She's far too outspoken for my taste."

His mother sighed. "Oh William, perhaps you'd rather wait until little Adele is out of her cradle and a grown up miss? I'll be an old woman before I see my grandchildren, I can see that now. I'm going to have to start looking for a good wife for you."

He gave her a sidelong glance, and hoped she was joking.

It was 1863 when Will first saw Awarua. He was nineteen and Harry was sixteen, and the family had been in New Zealand for five years.

While the boys had been learning how to farm, their father had been searching for land. Most of the good flat land close to Nelson had already been taken, but there was still leasehold land in the outlying areas, and five years after the family settled in Nelson, Frederick Hadfield bought 1,000 acres of land at Awarua, a large inlet up the coastline towards Separation Point.

Collingwood and Nelson were the two major ports and the most important towns in the northwest of the South Island in those early days, and Awarua was between them. It was a large inlet with plenty of flat land and it was right on the main shipping route between Blind Bay and Golden Bay. There was timber to be cleared and the land was cheap. To the businessman from Nelson it looked like a place of promise and opportunity.

As well as the land he bought outright, Fred Hadfield and William Lightband with another man called Jackson had leased 2,000 acres the year before. The land ran from Abel Head to the north of where they were camped to Marahau away back down to the south. While the two boys were away learning their trade in the dry tussock lands of Marlborough, their father had been planning their next move. They were to become farmers in their own right, here among these steep ridges and golden beaches, and would work to pay a good return on the investment others were making in them.

Will and Harry sailed from Riwaka with their father and Lightband, a prominent Nelson goldminer and merchant. The younger Hadfields were not yet used to handling small sailing craft and they left the work to Mr Lightband and the old sailor whose boat it was. They were content to sit back and watch the bush-covered coastline slide by, seeing Maori canoes on the beach at Riwaka, a three-masted schooner in the distance, the split rock that looked curiously like an apple along the coast.

There were signs of activity at Kaiteriteri and smoke rose from a chimney at Sandy Bay, but after that the only living creatures they saw were two dolphins that met them and swam with them just before they landed at the north end of a long, golden beach.

"Onetahuti Bay," Frederick Hadfield told them as they leaped into the water and helped pull the boat closer. "That headland is Abel Head, named by the Dutchman Abel Tasman when he came here in 1642."

"More than 200 years ago, and it looks as if nothing's ever happened since," Harry commented, looking around the deserted sandy beach. There were no buildings, no footprints, no signs that any human being had been there ahead of them, but the old sailor whose boat they had arrived in picked up a piece of whitened driftwood at the high tide line.

"This must have been here a mighty long time then, if it's from a Dutchman's boat," he chuckled, and he showed the boys what he had found. It was about two feet long and a uniform four inches in diameter, rounded by craft and not nature, with a scrap of leather still clinging to one side.

William held the weatherbeaten scrap in his hands, his face alight with interest.

"Look Harry. Remember the ship we came out on? It's an oar just like the ones they used on the longboat. See, here's where it was leathered to slide easily in the rowlocks. What sort of wood do you think it is, ash?"

"Firewood," Harry snorted, and made to seize it, but William held the stick and shook his head.

"This one's not for burning."

He put it carefully aside and turned to help the others. When their few possessions were ashore and they had set up their rough camp for the night the younger men explored the long beach, looking curiously at the swampy stream feeding onto it and at tiny Tonga Island behind them. The dogs they had brought with them from Marlborough yelped excitedly, starting up weka from the bushes and crashing away into the bush after them until William and Harry called them back.

Their father and Lightband had a survey map with them and they pored over it late into the evening, sitting over the embers of their dying campfire. Harry was soon asleep but William sat up, listening to the waves slapping the sand and hissing back from the rocks as the tide rose. It had been a long time since he had heard the sea at night, and the harsh crying of the seagulls took him back to that long ocean passage, five years earlier.

In his hands he held the weatherbeaten scrap of oarshaft, fingering it in the darkness, and in his mind he heard the creak of the ship's timbers again and heard the crack of sails and rope in the wind. Was this to be his destiny after all?

The next day the party walked inland, looking for flat land they could run their stock on. They slowly made their way two miles over Abel Head to the next bay, Awarua.

They arrived as the tide was nearly out and looked down on a long golden paddock of sand, small channels meandering up through the middle and disappearing into blue shadows in the distance. There was smoke from a distant chimney, and a boat of some sort lay far up the inlet on the edge of the sand. A dog barked somewhere under the hills. Before them was a slightly raised plateau of flat land and another to their left, the stream they had followed feeding into a shallow estuary in the middle.

"This might be the place to look around for a house site," Lightband advised. "It's part of the leasehold, and clear enough to bring stock into almost straight away. There's fresh water here, and good shelter."

"Make a fire, William," his father told him, getting his survey map out again and a pencil and notebook. "We'll sup here and start making a list of what you'll be needing."

There was no grass on the flat, which was covered with a low, grey wiry shrub, here and there a taller tree reaching out to tangle them. The boys did not recognise any of the foliage around them, and William's heart sank as he tried to visualise what his father expected of him. It was all so alien, so different from anything he had been used to, and he wondered where he could even start to transform it into recognisable farmland.

At Goulters sheep station the mobs of sheep had scattered for miles on dry, open country. Harry had ridden the same long hours in the saddle tending his flocks at Brinsdens further south. They could see at a glance that this would be farming of a very different sort, hot work with axe and saw before any sheep could be safely tended. There were gullies and thickets of deep bush to lose young calves in or ewes at lambing time, and damp swampy ground to rot their feet. But as the men talked and planned around their meal the tide started moving back in and the clear water covered the sand. The spirits of the two young men lifted.

"Race you down to the water," Harry cried and the two young men shed their boots and sprinted for the sea, their dogs leaping around them and splashing into the shallows.

ADELE'S FAMILY - THE SNOWS AND THE NEWTHS

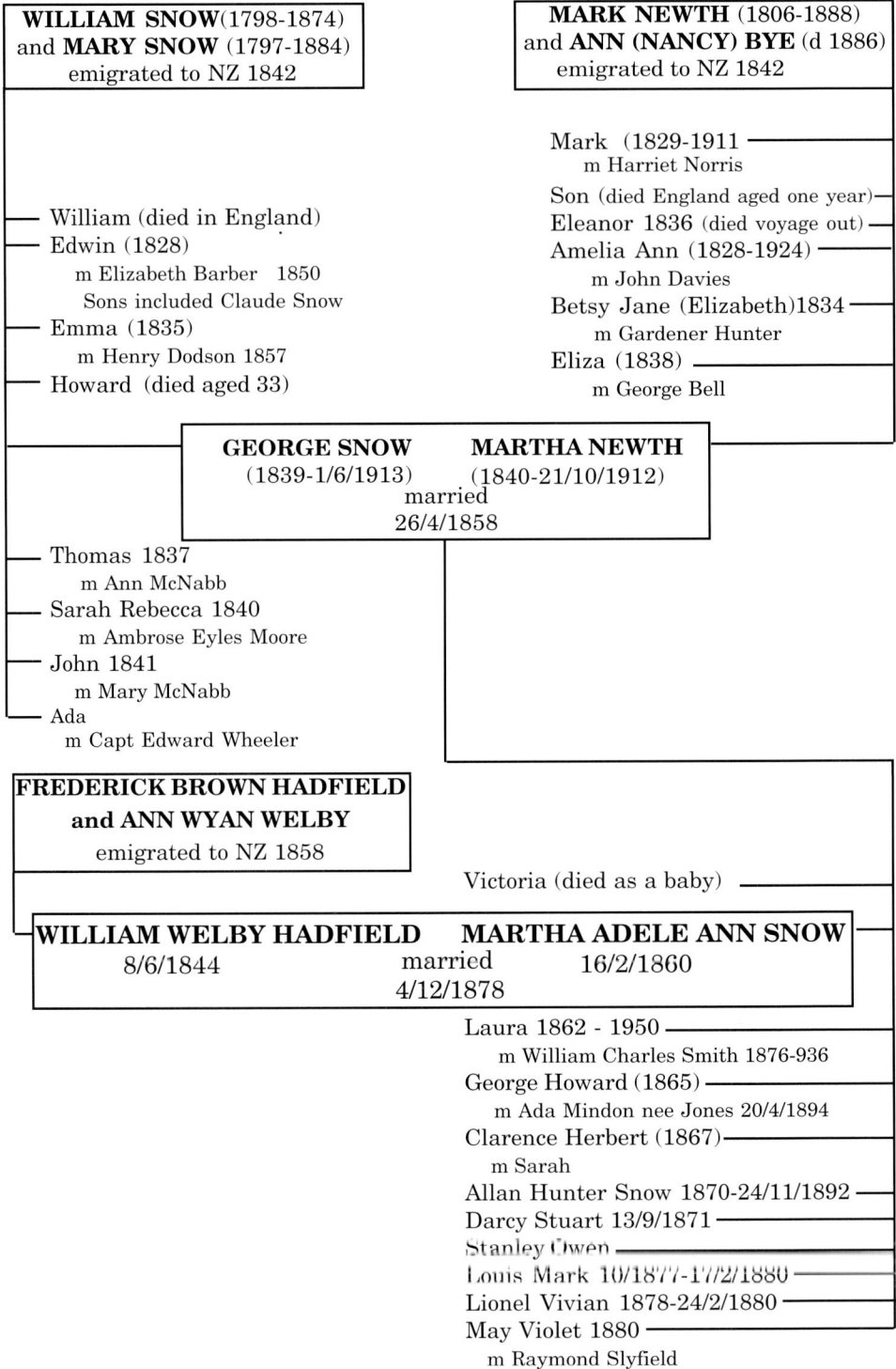

WILLIAM SNOW(1798-1874)
and **MARY SNOW** (1797-1884)
emigrated to NZ 1842

MARK NEWTH (1806-1888)
and **ANN (NANCY) BYE** (d 1886)
emigrated to NZ 1842

Mark (1829-1911 ————
    m Harriet Norris

— William (died in England)
— Edwin (1828)
    m Elizabeth Barber   1850
    Sons included Claude Snow
— Emma (1835)
    m Henry Dodson 1857
— Howard (died aged 33)

Son (died England aged one year)—
Eleanor 1836 (died voyage out) —
Amelia Ann (1828-1924) ————
    m John Davies
Betsy Jane (Elizabeth)1834 —
    m Gardener Hunter
Eliza (1838) ——————
    m George Bell

GEORGE SNOW   **MARTHA NEWTH**
(1839-1/6/1913)   (1840-21/10/1912)
            married
            26/4/1858

— Thomas 1837
    m Ann McNabb
— Sarah Rebecca 1840
    m Ambrose Eyles Moore
— John 1841
    m Mary McNabb
— Ada
    m Capt Edward Wheeler

FREDERICK BROWN HADFIELD
and ANN WYAN WELBY
emigrated to NZ 1858

Victoria (died as a baby) ————

WILLIAM WELBY HADFIELD   **MARTHA ADELE ANN SNOW**
8/6/1844   married   16/2/1860
            4/12/1878

Laura 1862 - 1950 ————
    m William Charles Smith 1876-936
George Howard (1865) ————
    m Ada Mindon nee Jones 20/4/1894
Clarence Herbert (1867)————
    m Sarah
Allan Hunter Snow 1870-24/11/1892 —
Darcy Stuart 13/9/1871 ————
Stanley Owen ——————
Louis Mark 10/1877-17/2/1880 ————
Lionel Vivian 1878-24/2/1880 ————
May Violet 1880 ————
    m Raymond Slyfield

CHAPTER TWO : WILLIAM AND HARRY

1863

THE OLD MAN CHUCKLED as he sat at the window remembering. Meadowbank stood on the edge of the inlet, quite close to the beach where he and Harry had first raced into the water shouting and splashing their breeches while their father and William Lightband sat and watched from the shore. Since that day in 1863 there'd been many dunkings, some by choice and others by necessity, and he'd learned to govern his life by the Awarua tides.

After that first visit with their father William and Harry Hadfield came back with stock and possessions, camping in a tent at first until they had built a more permanent home. Their mother admonished them to read their Bibles, keep good health and send word home to Nelson whenever they could. Their father, more practical, packed a medicine chest and new axes and reminded them that they would need to work fast to have the land ready for sowing spring grass. They went ashore with their clothes and boots in chests, nails and timbers, a crate of chickens, their dogs and a milking cow.

Two trips to shore in their heavy workboat, which had been towed behind the scow which brought them up the coastline from Riwaka, landed everything except the cow. Then she was tipped unceremoniously from the scow's deck into the sea, a sailor sending her on her way with a cunning push to her hind quarters after he made sure the boys, down in their rowing boat, had their end of her rope tied firmly to its bow ring. The cow made out to sea until the boys, rowing with all their strength, hauled her around and got her heading inshore to where she could find her feet. When the boat grounded William leapt out and headed up the beach, gathering the slack in as he ran so she had less rope to dance on, talking gently as he tried to calm her down.

"You've got your work cut out for you, lads, and that's for sure," a cheery voice called from the bush behind them, and William spun around so hastily he tripped on the chickens, fell heavily and dropped the rope. There was a shout of laughter as the cow, wild-eyed and indignant, surged up from the surf and set off for the bush at a gallop.

"I'll get her," a boy called, but the newcomer shook his head. "Nay lad, she'll not go far. Let her settle, and trail her rope, and you'll catch her more easily in hour, I'll warrant."

"There's nowhere to put her anyway," Harry said despondently, but William was already greeting the older man with a courteous smile, taking his outstretched hand and shaking it heartily.

"Mr Ricketts. Delighted to meet you again sir. As you can see, we're here to stay this time."

"Aye, I can see all right," Ricketts said wryly. "And you'll not be staying here long, any road. We saw yon mast, and thought you'd need a help."

The tide was on the turn, which was why the scow hadn't come into the inlet across the bar. The wind had been against them from Riwaka and forced them to make slower time than planned. Mailbags and provisions for the other settlers had all been dropped in the Hadfields' boat, and now there was a huge mound of boxes and goods on the gritty golden sand.

Will was pleased to see their Awarua neighbours. He'd already been wondering how and when he was to deliver their goods to them. But the first priority was to move their great jumble of possessions into some semblance of order before nightfall, and that seemed problem enough.

Ambrose Ricketts was a wheelwright by trade, now turned boatbuilder, and he and his family were the first of more than a dozen landowners to settle at Awarua. They lived back up the inlet where one of the two contributing rivers flowed down into it. He was a big, heavy man in his forties, his eldest son Bill a year older than William Hadfield, and they'd brought 12-year old Tom down with them in their heavy rowing dinghy.

"We'll not be staying long," he said now, glancing at the water level dropping. "So let's make shift to help you with this, shall we?"

They set to with a will, and between them managed to manhandle the supplies up through the soft, dry sand and onto firmer ground. It was hard, sweaty work, and more than an hour had passed before the last of the boxes had been piled on a bed of dry branches to keep the damp out. The dogs had settled down now, and although the hens still squawked indignantly in their crates the scene was peaceful, the spring sun turning the hillsides golden.

"You'll need to make haste, will you not sir?" William asked anxiously as he saw how far the tide had receded from the Rickett's boat.

"Yes, or we'll be walking home with the mail. But will you not come up and stay with us tonight? There's always plenty of food for an extra mouth or two, and you won't have much organised here yet."

But William and Harry shook their heads. They did not mean to ask favours so soon of their neighbours, and there was a lot to do. And besides, they wanted to begin this new life of theirs as a landowners, not as another family's guests.

"You'll come up Sunday then? Mrs Ricketts will look to see you at dinner, and you haven't met us all yet. We're quite a tribe, you know."

"Father, you'll put them off from coming altogether if you make us sound so forbidding," Bill protested. "We'll see you Sunday. Do come."

William and Harry waded willingly into the shallow water to push the heavy boat off, and as they watched it receding up the estuary again William lifted his hand in salute, and Bill Ricketts shipped an oar to return the wave.

"Father said they were nice people," Harry said warmly when they were alone again. "I can't wait to meet all the other families up there."

"Aye, but we'll do well to remember what we're here for, and it's not visiting," William answered him, and they turned to face the pile of freight in the scrub. "Let's find our old campsite and make it a permanent one. And then we'll find the cow."

Over the next few days they walked the land, trying to see where the best grazing could be found between the ridges and swamps. They were responsible for 3,000 acres altogether, but much of it was impossible to reach, and for the first few years their father had suggested they concentrate on clearing land around the inlet, learning as much as they could from their neighbours and their own experience.

Awarua had been intermittently occupied by Maori for many years before it was first surveyed by the English in 1843. The first land sales were in 1855, when absentee owners like Dr Ralph Richardson, a wealthy Nelson immigrant, invested in large blocks they divided up for resale. By the time the Ricketts family arrived in 1861 there were sawyers already working in the area, floating their logs down the rivers and out into the estuary at high tide to store them behind a boom in Pound Gully, across from the Hadfields' farm.

Jim Spanton was one sawyer who became a permanent resident, planting an orchard of peaches and summer pearmain apples to feed the growing settlement. There were several families clearing and developing farms, as the Hadfields planned to do, and others who were squatting while they worked the timber out.

The Hadfields had already made the acquaintance of entrepreneur Thomas Askew, a storekeeper, boatbuilder and hotelier who had made his money in the early days of the Collingwood goldrush. He bought land at Awarua in 1857. Askew was a friend of Lightband's, but more interesting to William was the fact that he had built the sixteen-ton schooner *Necromancer* in Nelson ten years before. The Hadfields had passed her along the coast on their first trip to the inlet, and he thought her a fine ship.

William still had the weathered ash stick they had found at Onetahuti Bay when they first arrived. He'd held on to it because it was good English wood and nicely shaped, he told himself, and would be useful for something sooner or later. He knew without consciously planning it that he would use it on a boat, when he learned more about this craft, and he looked forward to talking more with Ambrose Ricketts who with Askew and others was heavily involved in the coastal shipping trade.

That first Sunday the Hadfield brothers learned more about the tide, and it was very nearly a disaster. William had been up to the house on the right bank of the Awaroa River once, with his father and William Lightband on that first trip, and it had taken them several hours to work their way up. The tide had been falling, and they'd waded a couple of swampy creeks and skirted the bushline, following a rudimentary track that led them to the river mouth. Then they'd found a canoe dragged up under the bushes, and crossed the river easily to the rough-sawn cottage that was home to Ricketts and his family.

"Are you sure you know how to find your way?" Bill had asked them that first day they'd arrived. "It's mid-day tides, so you'd best come up earlier and that way you can bring your boat up to the river mouth."

The boys dressed with anticipation after their morning chores, washing and changing into their one set of Sunday clothes. William fretted about his footwear, having nothing but heavy boots to wear.

"We'll clean the mud off, and then carry them with us and roll the legs of our breeches up," suggested Harry. "That way we can arrive dry-shod."

"And empty handed," William said wryly, looking around their barren campsite. They'd moved their goods into a tent and used the still-filled boxes for furniture, but there were few luxuries. "We can't even take flowers for Mrs Ricketts, for we have none here."

"Flower bulbs, though," Harry said, and his brother's brow cleared.

"Of course. The autumn crocuses from Empingham." He took a few minutes to separate half a dozen of the tiny bulbs and rewrap them in a torn piece of the paper they were stored in, then slipped them in his pocket.

"Right, Harry. We're off for a holiday."

"And a good dinner, I hope. That's something I really miss."

It was after ten when they finally left their camp and made their way down to the heavy rowing boat. As Bill had predicted, the tide was flowing in but it was slow work rowing up the shallow estuary. They grounded every now and then, misjudging the channels and currents until they managed to make their way out to deeper water.

"You're heading miles away," Harry said plaintively at one stage. William looked around to see and snagged them on an upturned log.

"Swap places then. You row. I'll be the helmsman and steer our course."

It was hot, heavy work, and more than once they had to pole with their oars to get themselves back into the channel. It was nearly mid-day before they reached the top of the estuary, and then they dragged the boat across to the right bank of the river and tied it to a tree.

"We'll walk up from here," Will said confidently. "There's a track."

Boots on and breeches rolled down, they set off, but soon found themselves hopelessly lost in a forest of beech.

"We've lost the river, haven't we?" Harry asked at last.

"Aye, and lost our dinner too," Will confessed. "I've led us up a false path, I'm afraid."

"Best head back to the boat and start again then."

It took the best part of an hour before they found the river again, and not before Will had slipped into a swamp up to his knees and Harry had torn his good Sunday shirt on a sharp kanuka.

"Cooeee!"

The call came from downstream, and Will answered with a glad shout. "Over here!"

"You got lost, didn't you?" Bill was grinning from ear to ear when he came up to them, and their rueful expressions sent him into open laughter. "You look a proper sight, the pair of you. How could you end up here? And where's your boat?"

Will had to confess he wasn't sure, although he'd tied it firmly wherever it was, and his new friend found that even funnier.

"You'll not be sitting down to dinner in those breeches, any road. It's a good thing you're about my size, and you too, Harry. Mother will have that shirt off your back and mended even if it is the Sabbath, I'll be bound."

To their embarrassment, the family was still waiting for them, the dinner still ready in the stove although it was two o'clock. Mrs Ricketts clucked at the sight of them and sent them off to change and wash, bustling away their awkwardness in a way that reminded Will of the women at Goulters' Station.

He was starting to relax and feel at home when he became aware of another woman in the room, younger, slimmer, altogether prettier and more interesting.

"I don't think you've met our Emma, Mr Hadfield? She was away visiting when you came before. Mr William Hadfield, Mr Harry, may I present my daughter Miss Emma Jane Ricketts?"

Her hair was red-gold, her mouth a perfect rosebud and her eyes were china blue, and laughing at him.

"Mr Hadfield," she murmured.

"Miss Ricketts. Please, call me Will," he stammered.

"And Harry," his brother said, not to be left out.

"Will, Harry. And how are you enjoying Awarua? I hear that you're both fond of nature walks? Pray tell me, was it an instructive walk you had this morning?"

"Emma," her mother remonstrated, but not before a ripple of suppressed laughter had swept the table where the younger boys were standing behind their seats.

"Lord, for what we are about to receive...." Ambrose Ricketts began the grace, and the Hadfields bowed their heads with the others. Before the amen William dared to raise his, and found himself meeting six pairs of eyes. Five boys, from fourteen to four, and one young woman watched him, frankly curious, and there was fresh laughter in Emma's eyes as they demurely dropped to her plate again.

Dinner was a lively meal, and it was nearly four before Will found himself back in his own breeches again, now dry from the sun, with a fresh-baked loaf tucked under his arm and Harry in his neatly-mended shirt clutching a basket of fresh-dug carrots and cabbage.

"The boys will help you back to your boat. I fear it will be a long haul if you don't hurry," Ambrose warned, but Will suddenly remembered his gift.

"Here's something for your garden," he told Mrs Ricketts, but it was Emma's eyes he met as he displayed the handful of bulbs, their paper wrapping disintegrated around them. "They're autumn crocuses, purple and gold. I brought them from England."

"Then they're too precious to be planted here," his hostess demurred, but he smiled as he explained.

"Five years ago I brought a parcel of bulbs from my Aunt Emma's garden, for my mother. We planted them in Nelson and they've bloomed and multiplied, so now they can bloom at Awarua."

"We've been here so long now it seems, I've almost forgotten crocuses," Mrs Ricketts said in wonder. Emma said nothing, but smiled her thanks.

By the time they found the boat, tied up the blind channel William had mistaken for the river mouth, the tide was dropping fast and the two young men found it quicker and easier to wade and haul it, the empty vessel riding just lightly enough for them to drag it over most of the sandbars in their path. It was a losing battle though, and halfway down the estuary they realised they must abandon it and walk. They dragged it as far up the drying sand as they could and marked the site with a leafy branch broken from a nearby tree and speared into the sand to make a flag. Harry tied the painter around the stick as a precaution and they set off walking, knowing they'd have to come back in the darkness to retrieve it as the tide rose again.

"At least there's a moon," Harry said cheerfully. "Miss Ricketts was nice, wasn't she?"

William didn't answer. He was thinking of purple crocuses, and it wasn't Emma Rickett's laughing blue eyes they reminded him of, but quieter, steadier grey ones. There were many more Sundays at the Ricketts house, and William soon realised that Emma Ricketts singled him out for special attention. He did nothing to encourage her but he was aware of Harry watching him curiously from time to time, and if Mr and Mrs Ricketts realised there was more attraction at their house than a good dinner and lively conversation, they never indicated the fact.

William was more interested in Bill and his father, and in learning all they had to teach him about trees and timber. He found himself looking forward to their conversations, eager with questions, and he longed to have leisure to watch Ambrose Ricketts at work with his boatbuilding tools.

The Ricketts-built cutter *Moonraker* and schooner *Triumph* were among the visitors, and there were larger ships dumping their limestone rock ballast off the entrance and taking on logs instead. Sawyers dragged white pine logs into the inlet and floated them to where they were wanted, often keeping them stored in the little inlet still called Pound Gully on the northwest side of the inlet. The green timber was shipped to Australia as ballast, but loading was tidal and very difficult, the largest vessels to come across the bar around 30 tons. Ships under ten tons needed no licence and there were many smaller craft in and out. The Hadfields soon learned to write their letters and have mail and orders ready for the next opportunity to send them out.

It took a long time to get the measure of the inlet. A sandbar formed across the entrance, changing shape over the years as it responded to wind and the tide, and to the north the channel was deep and guarded with rocks. At high tide the harbour behind the sandbar was wide and long, deep enough to get boats right up into the river mouths. When the tide was out the inlet was an expanse of clean golden sand with only the main channels still flowing.

Awarua had been intermittently occupied by Maori for many years before it was first surveyed by the English. There were shell middens at Sawpit Point, where the Hadfields and others later worked pit saws to cut timber for their homes. Stone artefacts indicated Maori used Awarua from the sixteenth century although there was no one living there when the first Europeans came. Awaroa was a winter camp, a safe harbour and a source of easy food for the Ngati Rarua, Ngati Tama and Te Ati Awa. They gathered flax and pingaio from the swamps and ate pipi, red cod and barracouta and tarakihi from the inlet.

"Our inlet is called Awarua, a Maori name which means two rivers," William wrote to Aunt Emma and Uncle Charles. "It is long and shallow with a narrow entrance, and is fed by two rivers, the Awaroa and the Awapoto, whose names translate as Big River and Little River.

"I find it interesting that the Maori names are all physical descriptions, and that we English simply copy them. This is a raw, new land with no history, no ancient names or great deeds to be commemorated as they are at home. It is like writing on a blank sheet of paper."

He wrote his letters at night, bent over the crate that still served as their table, and rationed himself to a single candle a week. Strange, he thought, that after five years in this new colony he still could not call it home, even though he would never return to England. Outside a weka called, and he dipped his pen into the inkpot again.

"We have built a house for the hens and cleared and fenced a field, and now we are working hard to get in a garden before the winter. The soil is light and sandy, and we bury fish and seaweed in it to build up its goodness, but it will be some time before we have leisure to think about flowers. We have yet to build ourselves a house, but do very well under canvas, and we keep our earth floor well swept..."

Soon there were sheep and cattle on their land and they were working from dawn until dusk, cutting fence palings, tending their stock and taking care of their daily needs. There was the cow to milk and eggs to gather, and vegetables to be grown in the garden.

They ate little meat, mostly mutton, and found the skills they'd learned on the Marlborough sheep stations stood them in good stead when it came to baking bread or golden syrup puddings. Fishing was a new skill, and they soon learned where to set their nets and when to clear them, and both became adept at handling the heavy sixteen-foot boat.

They lived and worked on what was to be Harry's farm, the low plain near the entrance to the inlet where they had camped from the beginning. A large flat area by the Awapoto River at the head of inlet was William's but that first winter they managed little more than a few expeditions to plan where they should sow grass.

They got to know the other Awarua families and managed to find their way back to the Ricketts' house at Big River quite often through the winter months. It was warm and lively there. Emma always found something from the kitchen to send home with them when they left, but no matter how hard Harry tried to impress her it was William's hand she usually managed to tuck it into, William's eyes she sought when she and her mother waved goodbye to them.

"She really likes you, you know," Harry said one Sunday as they rowed home. "I wish she could be my sweetheart."

"Time enough for that another day," was William's only reply. "There's work to do here for years before there's any talk of sweethearts, and Miss Ricketts will be long married before you or I can look at courting any lass."

Fate intervened, however. They had been there barely 18 months when there was tragedy up the river. The boys first heard about it from Bill Ricketts, who rowed down to them on the tide that night.

"Our Tom's dead," he said bluntly. "The poor blighter hooked Father's gun on a log and it went off."

William poked the fire up and made a pot of strong tea, wishing he had something stronger to offer his friend. He stirred sugar in, knowing it was what his mother always did when there was an upset in the house. Harry was silent, shocked by the news. They'd both liked young Tom, a lad only just 13.

"Silly young fool was out working with Father and John, and he grabbed hold of the gun. We always take it out when there's a chance of a pigeon or a kaka for dinner, and they had left it leaning against a log ready loaded. Father was working a bit further along, and he heard the gun go off so he came running back, and ..." His voice broke, and the Hadfields stared tactfully at the fire until he recovered.

"Father thinks Tom leaned over and grabbed the gun by the muzzle to try to lift it up, and the hammer must have caught in the bark and fired it. Poor Tom just looked at Father and sighed, and the next thing he was dead."

"Your poor parents," William said softly. "Is there anything we can do, Bill?"

"We're burying him tomorrow. Father's making a coffin now. He said to ask you, William, if you would read some words over him. He says you're the one with book learning, and perhaps you could read the Bible. Mr Frazer's going to say a piece over Tom, and lead the hymn, but he's not much for reading and Mother wants Tom to have The Lord's My Shepherd."

William and Harry were among the mourners at the little service behind the Ricketts house, along with everyone else who lived at Awarua. Thomas Ricketts was buried in a simple grave, marked with a wooden cross recording his death, on 24 February 1865.

Emma's china blue eyes were filled with tears as she supported her mother at the grave side, and soon afterwards, with heavy hearts, the Ricketts family left the inlet to re-establish their boatbuilding activities closer to civilisation.

Will and Harry were down to help the men load the scow with the Ricketts' furniture and possessions, and when they parted there were fond handshakes all around.

"Let's meet again one day soon," Bill Ricketts told William.

"Aye, when you've built something big enough to sail to Nelson in," his father added with a twinkle in his eye. "And you'll not forget what I showed you about the rata and matai woods, and how to check for knots?"

"I'll not forget sir, and I thank you heartily," Will told him. "I'll look to see your boats along the coast and in here at the inlet."

For Mrs Ricketts he had an equally warm farewell, and if he noticed Emma's disappointment at his quick and formal parting he said nothing. He liked her as a sister, but her clear blue eyes were not for him to lose his soul in.

That first flurry of settlement and activity was nearly over by the mid 1860s, and many of the sawyers moved away, leaving the inlet to those who were prepared to face the hard work of clearing and farming. The old name of Awarua, meaning two rivers, was gradually forgotten and the inlet came to be called Awaroa, or big river. Shipping was still very active, and the Ricketts brothers were to be constant visitors to the inlet as they skippered their various trading vessels up and down the coast.

David Gilbertson arrived at Awaroa in 1865, and set up a boatyard towards the head of the inlet on what later became known as Samuels Point. Gilbertson had brought the 42-foot schooner *Australian Maid* from Sydney to Nelson eleven years earlier, and he built *City of Nelson*, a vessel of 29 tons, and the smaller *Bonnie Lass* before moving to the inlet. He had a large family too, but they were younger, and by now William and Harry had their hands full with their own farm work.

After the first few years the two Hadfield farms began to take shape, Harry's on leasehold land and William's freehold. They grazed some of their animals further down the coast but the 2000 acres their father leased in 1862 proved impossible to farm productively and they soon confined their stock to the area around the Awaroa river and Abel Head. They ran sheep and a few cattle, never more than they could manage, gradually building the numbers up as they cleared and burned their farms.

They seldom saw their father but were in constant commerce with him as he handled their affairs in Nelson, sending supplies up the coast and selling their small wool clip and surplus stock for them. William wrote him long reports about the land, records of lambing rates and wethers killed, and his father managed the accounts and sent instructions back.

To the Hadfields, such vast acreages seemed like the realisation of an impossible dream after their experience of English farms. Back home every inch of land had been worked for generations, whether it was ploughed for crops, planted as meadow or forested as woodland. Trees grew slowly in England, hedgerows stayed neat and tidy and the rolling hills were covered with a good rich topsoil. It was to be many years before the new settlers came to realise the vast differences between the old land and the new.

Like the other settlers along the rugged coast, the Hadfields lived in comparative isolation with the sea their only access. They sold wool and stock when they could, but their land was only marginal, the topsoil thin, and their farms did not really prosper. They gradually realised they were never going to have the grand sheep stations they and their father had dreamed about, and they learned to make do with what they had. They worked hard and the days merged into one another, marked only by the changes in the tides and the seasons and by a few rare highlights and adventures..

There was a wonderful day in late October 1869, when a sailing ship was cast up on the outside beach, fully rigged and totally unmanned. William was 25 then, strong, fit and ready for anything.

It was Harry who spotted the sails first, and as soon as they'd finished milking the two men rushed down to the beach to look.

It was a schooner, about 70 feet long they judged, with a crude wooden figurehead painted in bright colours and her decks high with timber.

"She's no beauty," William snorted, looking at the modestly-shaped and covered carving and the name painted along the bow. " *Elizabeth and Ulvaria Cameron.* I wonder which the figurehead represents?" But Harry's eyes were on the deck, where there was no sign of movement.

"She's well aground," he said excitedly. "Look how far she's leaning over. They must have gone off to seek help."

The ship sat calmly a few yards from the shore and sideways on, her sails banging and slatting in the wind. A rope had flicked loose and trailed down the side of the hull and the anchor was still catted.

"Look at the sand," William said slowly. "There are no footprints. No one's come ashore from her."

They looked back at their big sailing dinghy, beached well clear of the high tide mark. The tide was out and it would take time and effort to drag it all the way to where there was enough water to float it.

"If I could catch that rope..." Harry said speculatively. He stripped his jacket off and waded into the water, heedless of the cold. About halfway to the ship he began to dogpaddle with his hands, his bare feet kicking behind him and William held his breath until he saw his brother touch the wooden hull and move along the side towards the rope. A quick tug to ensure the end was fast and then he was up, climbing the side like a monkey, his back arched out as he braced himself and pulled on the rope, hauling himself hand over hand while he walked up the side.

Then he was on board and he disappeared for a long few moments before running back to the bow and calling excitedly.

"William! There's no one here. No one at all!"

William thought fast, aware that the dry sand at his feet was dampening with each new wave.

"Is she floating at all?"

"No, she's stuck fast."

"Then we've got an hour or two before the tide lifts her. She must have gone aground at low tide. We might get her off at midnight, or perhaps sooner. The tides are falling away again so she'll be well ashore if we can't do something pretty quickly."

They looked anxiously at the sky but the big sails filled only lazily, the breeze slight. Dave Gilbertson was away from the inlet, and the only other settler was James Spanton who would be away in the bush working. There was no one else there to turn to for advice.

"The wind will come up again early in the morning when the tide turns, won't it?" Harry called. "Should we anchor her?"

"That might drive her further ashore in a blow, then she'll batter on the beach."

"Shall we sail her to Nelson and claim salvage?"

It was a wild idea, but the more the boys thought about it the more it seemed the right thing to do. The big schooner was 41 tons, a wide, beamy shallow-drafted vessel but not too big for them to handle if the wind was right. She was too vulnerable where she was, and if they tried to take her through the channel into the inlet they could cause even more trouble for her owners by running her onto the rocks and damaging her keel. Besides, the idea of sailing her into Nelson and being rewarded by her owners, even claiming ownership themselves under the laws of salvage, had a lot of appeal.

They decided to anchor the ship, hoping the rising tide would float her free as the rope tightened and kept her from floating any further up the beach. Harry threw the big anchor as far clear on the seaward side as he could, and secured the rope to a stout bollard. It would do for an hour or two and that was all they needed. They planned to sleep aboard that night.

Harry went back into the water a lot faster than he'd gone up, and splashed his way back to his brother, shivering with the cold. They ran back to the farm and while Harry rubbed himself dry and gathered clothes and food William looked to the animals, tying the dogs where they would be safe for a day or two, turning the calves back out to their mothers so they would manage without the morning milking. He checked the lambs, collected the eggs and went back inside where Harry had made a rough meal of bread and cold meat.

It was dusk when they'd finished eating, and they stuffed their pockets with food and matches. William made sure he had a stout knife and Harry took up the hurricane lamp and they were off.

They dragged their dinghy down to the rising tide and rowed out to the schooner, now bobbing as the stern floated freely. This time William climbed aboard first and Harry rowed around to the seaward side of the schooner, tying his rope to the stern, taking the anchor rope out further and using his weight on the oars to pull it back. William hauled in the sheets and felt the hull shudder as she tried to free herself from the sand. An hour later they were afloat.

There was a shout in the darkness, and Harry raced to the bow, straining his eyes to see. A splash of oars told him to look north, and he waved the lantern.

"What ship?" came the call.

"*Elizabeth and Ulvaria Cameron*," he replied nervously, and took the rope that was tossed to him. It was the captain of another schooner from Totaranui and he was amazed to hear their story. He and his crew had sailed along within sight of the *Elizabeth and Ulvaria Cameron* for a couple of hours, little dreaming there was no one at the helm. They'd been puzzled and concerned when they'd seen her sail into Awaroa rather than following them in to Totaranui to the north, and they feared she might have struck the bar and run aground. They'd come down to offer assistance.

"I've never heard of such a thing," the captain said, scratching his head in wonderment. At first he seemed suspicious of William and Harry, as if he thought they had done away with the original crew, but after they had searched the ship together they concluded she had been abandoned for some reason.

"Well, she'll have to be sailed to Nelson, and her owners telegraphed," the captain said. "She can't stay here, she'll be blown onto the bar and wrecked."

"That's why we got her off," Harry said pertly. "We thought of sailing her to Nelson ourselves, and claiming salvage."

That earned him a sharp look, but William and Harry both knew the law was on their side. The ship had been abandoned and they had possession. She was fully laden with fresh produce and tugging gently at her anchor as the tide rose, and the captain had his own ship waiting at Totaranui to worry about. They accepted his offer to telegraph ahead to the port, but shook their heads when he offered to put one of his own sailors on board.

"I dinna think the pair of ye have enough experience to handle her if things go wrong," he said worriedly. "I cannae force ye, but I'm thinking the owner could be ready to sue you in the courts if ye damage her, and I'm a witness that she's ashore here in sound condition."

William paused, remembering Thomas Askew's schooner *Necromancer* which had been wrecked a bare few months before. She'd stranded on Farewell Spit and broken up, and Askew had been bitter about his loss and blamed the skipper and crew for their handling of her. There was a lot of money involved in coastal shipping, and a wreck could bankrupt people. William knew he could not take that on his conscience, opportunity or not.

The problem was solved when James Spanton hailed them from his dinghy. A seaman turned sawyer, he'd seen the masts from his cottage further up the inlet and come down to find out what was happening, and he readily agreed to come with them for a share of the salvage money. Both William and Harry were secretly relieved at the idea. They didn't intend to drive a hard bargain with the owners at all, simply to take the chance of an adventure.

Dawn saw them sailing briskly, Harry at the helm, their heavy dinghy towing behind them. They kept well out to sea, thrilled and not a little frightened by what they had done, and headed for Nelson.

"The compass does not seem to be working at all," William told his brother. "Do you think we'll make Nelson by the tide?"

"By moonlight, if we have to," Harry shouted back. "I think father will be very surprised to see us."

"I just hope he approves," William replied sombrely.

The Hadfield brothers and James Spanton sailed into Nelson harbour that afternoon and anchored the *Elizabeth and Ulvaria Cameron*. William and Harry rowed ashore and told their story to the harbour master, who made sure their actions in saving the ship were duly noted. He had alerted the owners the previous evening by telegraph, as soon as they heard the story from Totaranui, and had been authorised to pay whatever was necessary.

While the Hadfields were ashore there was drama on the deck of the schooner. Eager eyes had watched them leave the boat, and as soon as they were safely away a dinghy had been commandeered from along the waterfront and a determined little group of men had rowed out to her. They'd crept quietly alongside, seized hold of the ladder and prepared to board.

"Not so fast, matey," a gruff voice had muttered as the first man swung his leg over the ladder onto the deck, and to his horror he'd looked straight down the muzzle of a loaded gun. James Spanton was on guard, and he stayed on guard until the men from Awaroa had been paid for recovering the *Elizabeth and Ulvaria Cameron* and delivering her safely to Nelson.

When the schooner was officially handed over to the agent the Hadfields made their way home to Trafalgar Street for a hot meal and a comfortable bed, while Spanton, still chuckling, headed for a hotel with money in his pocket and a good story to tell. All three of them were delighted with their adventure and the unexpected holiday in town, and even the prospect of a long row back home in their dinghy didn't damp their spirits. It was days before the full story came out.

The *Elizabeth and Ulvaria Cameron* was one of the first of the Lyttelton traders, built two years earlier at Heathcote Valley in Canterbury by the Cameron brothers whose wives she was named after. She was 68ft 6ins with a beam of 17ft 3ins and she drew six feet in the water. She normally worked the timber trade between Heathcote, Lyttelton and the Banks Peninsula bays but occasionally made longer trips and it was on one of these she had run aground on Farewell Spit on 30 September 1869.

Her compass had been faulty, causing her master, George Donnelly to run her too close to the low-lying sand bar and when she'd grounded he and her three crew had gone ashore and set off back to Puponga where there were settlers who could help raise the alarm. Captain Donnelly was later reprimanded for acting with want of judgement in leaving his vessel deserted on the shore with all sails set.

The schooner had slewed around in the sand, making a pool of water and when the tide rose she also rose, drifting gently free and sailing herself off along the spit and around into open water off Golden Bay. The winds and sea currents had been generous and she'd moved quietly along, clear of all the rocks and obstacles closer to shore, and around Separation Point. With the change in wind direction the ship had gybed gently and run towards the land, nosing herself safely into the beach at Awaroa.

Captain Donnelly and his men had returned to find their ship gone. Ruefully they'd made their way by road to Collingwood and boarded the steamer for Nelson, not dreaming as they passed down the dark coastline that night that they had actually passed their own ship riding safely off the Awaroa beach.

When a crew member saw her anchor in the Nelson basin he could hardly believe his eyes and called the others together to board her. They hoped to reclaim her without any fuss but Spanton's muzzle loader had forestalled that and the irate owners had already telegraphed their instructions. Captain and crew were paid off, leaving the *Elizabeth and Ulvaria Cameron* at the wharf until minor repairs could be carried out and her owners arrived from Lyttelton to pay their dues and take her home.

The story was reported in the shipping columns of the *Nelson Evening Mail* November 4, under the heading "A letter from Totaranui.

"There have been no fewer than eight crafts into Totaranui within the last few days and, singular to say, amongst them a derelict schooner of 60 tons, which, with all sail set and not a soul on board, sailed in company with four others, they not knowing but what she was manned. The four came to anchor and she went on to Awaroa Roads then turned in towards the river and got aground in its mouth. The captain of one of the vessels lying here went down to see what was the matter....."

There was no mention of the Hadfield brothers and the crew's abortive attempts to reboard her, and on November 12 she was listed once more in shipping news, cleared for Dunedin in ballast. By then William and Harry were back with their stock, fattening the young lambs on fresh new grass and planning how many they could sell that season.

As the seasons passed at Awaroa, there were very few such excitements. Moments of drama perhaps, when stock were caught by the tide or when a storm brought down trees and damaged fencelines, and many times of quiet joy as the brothers stopped on a hilltop to look down over the picture-postcard magic of the coastline, or stripped their sweaty clothes off to swim in the clear waters of the inlet.

There were times when one or other of them helped a ewe birth her lamb, or played with a litter of young puppies or was woken by a chorus of bellbirds, and felt in their hearts a deep sense of happiness. But they were Yorkshiremen and seldom said anything about such moments, even to each other

By 1870 their brother Charles had married and moved to Christchurch, and the elder Hadfields already had their first granddaughter. Frances was married too and in Dunedin, and young Richard had taken on the running of Hadfields the Chemists.

Frederick Hadfield came to Awaroa on the new paddle steamer, *Lady Barkly*, now running a regular service between the ports of Nelson, Waitapu and Collingwood. *Lady Barkly* was built of gum hardwood in Australia in 1861 as the private yacht of the Governor of Victoria, whose wife she was named after. She was sailed to New Zealand and used as a gunboat on the Waikato River before Nelson's first pilot Captain Cross brought her south in 1868 to run her regular trading route between Tasman and Golden Bays. She operated according to the tides and soon became a familiar sight as she carried mail, stores and passengers up and down the coast. William, Harry or one of the other Awaroa settlers would row out to meet her when there were stores to send or supplies to be collected from her.

Their father arrived with stores, books and newspapers, and with gifts of preserves and fresh-baked cakes from town. He looked over the farm, the gardens and the livestock with approval, but pulled a face at the dark newspaper-lined and smoke-stained walls of their little home.

"I think it's time you lived a little better, boys," he commented. "This hut's still not a proper house, is it?"

"We need a better dwelling at Awapoto too," William told him. "I'm spending much of my time up there now, and have my eye on timber to build with this winter. We've made a hut there, but we need a house."

"Aye, you cannot bring a bride to a hut like this," his father agreed. "Your mother is worried about finding wives for each of you. She wants more grandchildren."

"No bride would want to come here," Harry said despondently, but William disagreed.

"There's good land enough for milking cows and fruit trees and a garden, and timber enough to build with. It will just take time."

"And here's something to save time," their father told them, and he began to spread papers out on the rough table. "I've brought these from a Nelson merchant for you. Timber that's ready cut, and plans to build to."

The houses were kitset wooden cottages, pre-cut rimu, totara and matai with white pine floors. They were chosen from the immigrants' handbook of the day, *Brett's Colonists' Guide* which was first published for British settlers in Canada and then released in a New Zealand edition. Brett's Guide covered everything from

Huffams' farm at Bark Bay. Timothy Huffam and his four sons were the closest neighbours to the Hadfields in the 1870s and both were bachelor households.

Courtesy Newton Nalder

Harry Hadfield's house and land, near the mouth of Awaroa Inlet where William and Harry first camped and began to establish their farm. The building on the left may have been Cunliffe's house, built in the 1880s.

Courtesy Gibbs family

medical emergencies, seafaring and farming instruction to the preserving of wild game and building of brick ovens, and included plans and instructions for four standard houses. Entrepreneurs in Nelson had taken each plan and worked out the timbers needed for it, and it was, the boys agreed, a convenient way for busy farmers to house themselves.

The timber was ordered and landed by sea, and that winter when the animals were all turned out to pasture Harry and William set to and built their new homes. Harry's house, built where they had both lived those first years, was plan number three, later built up with a second storey. It was set back against the hill and faced the afternoon sun with a fine view out over the inlet.

"Well Harry, here's a home fit for a wife," William told his brother the day they nailed the last sheet of heavy zinc on to the roof.

"And now to find a wife fit for the home," the younger man replied. "I don't see a bride out there, do you William?"

They both chuckled, gazing with a familiar fondness across the farm. So much had changed in the ten years they had been there. There was English grass where once had been nothing but wiry scrub, and poplars and willow trees shooting their fresh green against the darker native foliage. The dogs that sniffed their way along the paling fence were a new generation, whelped at Awaroa and trained to their work there while their parents lay in peaceful graves under the sand.

Awaroa was still accessible only by sea, but with the regular passage of the *Lady Barkly* there were more visitors now. Stock was landed and loaded from Harry's farm, and William's land three kilometres away at the head of the inlet was used to winter the ewes and hoggets.

He had been spending more and more time up there, planting trees and building a paling fence around the site he'd chosen for his house. Behind his rough hut the hills rose steeply as the valley narrowed, and in front of him a broad grassy plain was laid out, bounded by the river which swept across in front of him. It was a pleasant aspect, warm and sheltered in the summer sun, but William's favourite time was spring at Awapoto. Then the rains came warm and heavy, and sometimes when he woke the whole valley was wreathed in mist. He liked to walk up on the hills then, and look down to see his land covered like a blanket, a still, quiet world apart from any other.

William's house was to be plan number one, with four rooms. The timber came in on *Old Jack*, one of the few vessels small enough to come right up the inlet on the tide and offload at the mouth of the Awapoto river. Dave Gilbertson came over to help and so did Jim Perrott, an Englishman of about Will's own age who was felling timber for Gilbertson.

"You'll be wanting an extra hand I'm thinking," Perrott suggested quietly when the last of the load was safely ashore and the men sat with their bread and pound cake and mugs of tea.

"We'll build it between us," Harry said cheerfully. "Will helped with mine, and now it's my turn to work up here."

William poked at the fire, thoughtful. Unloading the building materials had been hard work, the little group of men driven by the urgency of the tide, and they'd thought no further than getting *Old Jack* on her way again. Now the little eight-ton schooner was safely back down in the deep pool near the entrance, and at midnight she'd be on her way out across the bar, her skipper skilled enough to sail her out by moonlight as soon as the tide was full and turned again.

It had taken them about three months to build Harry's house, but that had been in the winter when the days were shorter. True, there had been less farm work to do, but there had also been days when they could not work because of high winds and driving rain. Now it was September, and in a few weeks they would both be busy with lambs and young calves. The house could be built between them, but not as quickly as the last one, because their farm work must take precedence.

Already Will had planted rhododendrons and other trees and planned a sweeping avenue up to his chosen house site. Now he wanted nothing more than to live and work on the farm that was to be his own.

"We may need some help this summer," he conceded. "We'll look out for you if we do, Jim. There's a lot of work to be done, but we're not yet ready to pay wages, so we'll wait and see."

There were a few days of work for Jim Perrott, but not many, as Harry set to with a will to help his brother. By the end of that summer William's house was finished too, at least to the stage where it was weatherproof, and he settled down to live on his own land. He and Harry still spent much of their time together, working on chores that were easier with two, and they ran their farms as one business but gradually each man developed his own land in his own way.

Their neighbours to the south were the Huffams, also young men in their late teens and early twenties. They lived at Bark Bay further down the coast, and theirs was a bachelor existence too. The Huffam brothers, Blake, Fred, Richard and Gerald, were younger than the Hadfields but they became firm friends, drawn together by their common lifestyle. They met infrequently, usually when William or Harry walked the track over Abel Head to deal with stock or when the Huffams sailed into Awaroa in their boat *The Modest Boy.*

Like William and Harry, their diet was bread, fish, potatoes and garden produce, with the occasional pig. When the Hadfields killed a sheep for mutton it was often traded for Bark Bay produce as it would not keep long enough for the two of them to eat. Like other coastal pioneers, the Huffams and Hadfields learned to catch sharks which they hauled up to the gunwales of their boats and bashed with a tomahawk. The livers were the prize, boiled to extract the oil which filled their lamps at night. The carcases were discarded or buried in the garden.

Their drink was water, tea when they had some sent from Nelson, and the Huffams made a coffee with mashed maize which they grew. Lemon trees were soon established and provided refreshing summer drinks. Tobacco was home-grown, but the Hadfields had the advantage of a business base in Nelson where their father kept the farm accounts for them, sold their produce and sent back supplies regularly.

There were a few fishermen scattered along the coast, and each of the Hadfields had their own visitors. Harry's farm had the advantage of being near the entrance, and thus he always knew when boats came in and out of the bay. Will was closer to the few other settlers, the sawyers who came for timber and the few who visited the head of the inlet for raupo or other materials. News and newspapers were always shared, and visitors invited to stay for a meal.

William was a quiet, reserved young man who reflected his mother's values and enjoyed books. He treasured a volume of Tennyson's poetry and annotated it with allusions to the Greek classics as he read. He also read the Bible and kept a daily diary of his activities. Like Harry he loved gardening, and as the mail systems became more regular the mailbags were often filled with catalogues, seeds and orders. The Hadfields grew vegetables as well as raising livestock, and sold their surplus off whenever they could.

William met Adele Snow again in 1873. He was 29 and she was thirteen, and it was her grandparents' 48th wedding anniversary. The Hadfields had been invited, and since William was in Nelson for a stock sale his mother had pressed him to drive them out to Waimea and join the party.

As usual he was relieved when the bowing and courtesies were over and he could escape to join the other men and talk farming and politics. George Snow clapped him on the back and led him aside to talk about the Aorere Valley and the sluicing projects that were being developed. The Snows were now living at Rockville, supplying produce to the goldminers from their small farm they'd called Glen Howard on the banks of the Aorere River, and George was doing contract work on the roads.

was now in her thirties. Her waist had thickened and her dark hair was tinged with grey, yet she was still, Will thought, the most beautiful woman in the room. She was dressed quietly in a dove grey dress trimmed with lace, which enhanced the steady grey eyes.

Young Adele had the same striking features as her mother, and with her youngest brother in her arms to quiet him she looked much older than her thirteen years. William found his eyes straying back to her more than once that day. He noticed her straight back and strong arms, her rich blue-black hair and her intelligent eyes, the traits he had always most admired in her mother, and he wished that Martha's daughter was older, or that he was younger.

Despite the differences in their ages and upbringing it was inevitable that William and Adele would keep meeting over the next few years. In Nelson his mother and her grandmother moved in the same circles. William and George found they had common ground too. George and Tom Snow had run stores at the Mangles, the Grip and later at Maruia, and knew Awaroa landholder Thomas Askew well. Another common acquaintance was William Lightband, still a partner with the Hadfields in their grazing lease at Abel Head.

On New Years Day 1875 Frederick Brown Hadfield died from a heart attack. He was only 56 and his death was a shock to the whole family. He had brought them from their native Yorkshire and seen each of them started in their new lives, backing them up with sound advice, business skills and contacts. He was a strong leader and a good father, and none of them was prepared to lose him quite so soon.

Richard and Elizabeth were married now, both into the same family. The Greens were Marlborough runholders, and the Hadfields had met them while Will and Harry worked in Marlborough. Richard married Frances Green, and the two had set up house in Nelson where Richard now took over the chemist shop completely. Elizabeth married John Green, and before her father died he had seen her settled on their Marlborough farm. William was especially delighted by his younger sister's choice, as she had always been interested in station life and he counted John as a good farmer and a steady husband.

Now Charles, who was between William and Harry in age, was living and working in Christchurch. All the family were settled except Frances, the elder daughter who at 26 was able to support and help her mother through the shock of Frederick Hadfield's sudden death. John, eighteen, still lived at home and had work with the railways.

William and Harry were left each with their own house and farm at Awaroa. Harry's land around Abel Head and Tonga were now freeholded, and the less practical leasehold areas had been abandoned. One year William was forced to supplement his farming income with work on the Wakamarina goldfields, leaving Harry to manage at Awaroa, and they both went to Collingwood and Nelson on business and to attend the stock sales.

By now the Hadfield brothers were in their 30s, grown men and eligible husbands. They were also men of considerable strength, skill and resourcefulness, well used to both land and sea and familiar with their coastline.

When William had business in Collingwood he made a point of seeking out the Snows. and soon he was a regular visitor at George and Martha's home at Glen Howard in Rockville.

Dave Gilbertson built and launched the 71ft, 59-ton vessel *Awaroa* in 1875. Her launching was a grand day for the inlet, a day when everyone stopped work to join the celebration and vessels came in across the bar from all over Blind Bay. *Awaroa* was the largest boat ever built in the inlet, and the only one to bear the name of the long river which flowed down into it. She went into service for Captain James Cross and his sons, plying her trade between Nelson and Collingwood.

Settlers rowed or sailed their own smaller craft too, and by the 1870s communications were easier, the mails regular and farms becoming more established up and down the coast. Adele Island rock was used for building the new sea wall and breakwater in Nelson and the vessels *Welcome, Wanderer,* and *Advance* worked up and down the coastline during 1876 to carry it. Roads were being opened up, the population was increasing and a new generation of New Zealanders was born.

In 1877 another boat landed unexpectedly on the beach, this time a ship's lifeboat with exhausted survivors from the immigrant ship *Queen Bee* which ran aground on the tip of Farewell Spit just after midnight on 7 August.

Queen Bee was a fine, roomy vessel of 726 tons, built at Sunderland in 1859. She had first landed immigrants in Dunedin in 1866 and since then had made ten successful trips, stranding just hours from the end of a 102 day passage from England. The passage had already been a troubled one, with a fire breaking out in the galley above the gunpowder hold causing them to jettison cargo off the coast of Spain. When they had first sighted the South Island of New Zealand there had been relief and excitement on board, and a grand dinner was held to celebrate their successful voyage.

When she ran aground and began breaking up, passengers and crew took to lifeboats and headed for Nelson, and one of the boats, with the second mate, four sailors and eight passengers on board, made a landfall at Awaroa.

After providing them with a hearty meal William Hadfield and Richard Huffam, then 22, boarded the lifeboat and helped the weary crew members navigate their way down the coast to Riwaka.

They pulled the boat up the beach at Riwaka and walked from there to the Motueka river which ran in three separate streams and which they had to cross in three different punts. By this time it was pitch dark and it took them some time to find the road. The shipwreck survivors were still wet through and suffering exhaustion and exposure, the two Awaroa men in better shape in spite of the long haul down the coastline. They had brought lantern and matches from Awaroa and with the aid of these faint lights they managed to reach the Post Office Hotel where the exhausted men could be looked after and found beds and dry clothes.

The Motueka Postmaster, Mr Gilbert, was roused out of bed to open up the telegraph office and send a message to Nelson. Steamers were despatched to look for the survivors, and the next morning the Awaroa men set off for home in the *Queen Bee*'s lifeboat, stopping on the way to transfer the sailors to the paddle steamer *Lady Barkly* which had already rescued passengers from a second lifeboat.

Among the passengers were the Cheel family, later to keep a boarding house in Nelson, and the Gibbs family. Mary Elizabeth Gibbs was a widow who had sailed from England with nine children aged between seventeen and one. She had been on deck when the ship grounded, straining to see the first lights of their new country, and she and her two youngest daughters were in the liferaft that beached at Awaroa. It was to be days before she was reunited with her other children, separated in the confusion and taken onto another lifeboat under the care of their eldest brother.

William and Harry Hadfield heard the fate of the rest of the passengers and crew a few days later when a small trading boat, *The Bruiser,* called in to Awaroa with the news that the naval vessel *Aurora* had found the survivors from the third lifeboat, the captain's gig, on d'Urville Island.

Although the *Queen Bee*'s shipwrecked passengers and crew suffered physical hardship and exhaustion and only some of their possessions were salvaged, only one life was lost. The ship's carpenter drowned while trying to struggle ashore from the capsized boat at d'Urville Island. Those who did make it ashore were welcomed and helped by Maori living on the island. The immigrants were at first terrified when they were met by half-naked brown-skinned people who spoke no English, but they soon realised they were being offered food and shelter and they accepted it gladly until they were rescued a few days later.

The wreck of the *Queen Bee* was the talk of Nelson for the rest of that year. Some of her cargo was lost, some plundered and some salvaged to go under the hammer at auction or to be sold in Nelson stores. Many said there was more water-damaged stock from the *Queen Bee* sold in Nelson that year than the ship could ever have carried from England.

There were women and children among the survivors and Nelson rallied to their support. Those who helped in the rescue were heroes, and among them William Hadfield and Richard Huffam had their share of the credit. They also had the ship's lifeboat which stayed up a creek at Awaroa for years and finally fell to bits. It was not well built, the Awaroa men discovered. For flotation there were hollow zinc tubes six inches in diameter lashed under the thwarts and benches, but they were badly corroded and when they were thrown overboard only two of them floated.

The passengers and sailors in that first lifeboat had sung Moody and Sankey hymns to keep their spirits up, and on the long haul down to Riwaka with William Hadfield and Richard Huffam on the oars had sung *Pull for the Shore* and *The Bareboat Sailor*. For William who had sailed from England 19 years earlier it was a strange experience to be the first to greet the weary new immigrants and to play a part as rescuer and guide. He was reminded just how much he had learned about living in the New World.

William had learned a lot about building boats too. First Ambrose Ricketts and then Dave Gilbertson had given him advice and encouragement, and by the 1870s he and Harry were sailing their own sturdy Awaroa-built workboat. Will was encouraged to build rowing dinghies for others, including his sister Bessie Green. After she and her husband and children came to visit Awaroa, she commissioned him to build her a rowing boat. She paid him £10 for it and another fifteen shillings for a pair of oars.

Will iam still had the broken ash stick he'd picked up from the golden sands all those years before on his first trip to Awaroa. He'd kept it by him for a long time, intending to use it in the first boat he made for himself, but when the time had come he was reluctant to place it in the construction. Now he decided to use it on Bessie's boat, a symbol of the long journey they'd travelled. The little girl who'd looked to him for leadership on the ship from England all those years before was now Mrs John Green, a fine land-owner's wife, and their father was gone.

"I know it didn't come from our ship, Bessie, but it came from England," he wrote. "I've carved a little figurehead from it, to remind you that we are New Zealanders with a little of England still in our hearts."

For himself, William no longer needed the ash stick. The living shrubs and trees he'd planted at Awapoto were all the reminders he needed of his family's origins. Like them, he'd sent his roots down into New Zealand soil now, and he called it home.

After his father's death William took over the farm accounts and found himself travelling to Collingwood or Nelson regularly. Harry grew potatoes with exotic names like Brown River, Lapstone Kidney, Albany River, Pattersons Victoria, Coldstream and King of Carlies. By January 1875 William was running 160 ewes, seven rams, 68 wethers and 94 lambs, and buying more stock to put up the river. He subscribed to *The Colonist*, shipped pumpkins, mutton, hides and sheepskins out to Nelson, and sent accounts out to Messrs Huffam, Hargreaves, Franzen, Ricketts, Lightband and Webster who were all regular customers for his goods. He cut hop poles for Mrs Barford, and he could afford to spend £2 on a new set of sails, and to order books, copper nails, socks and new boots when he needed them.

After fifteen years of living in isolation both William and Harry were keen to marry. They were now well into their thirties and their farms were established to the stage where they could raise families of their own. Their mother, who soon remarried and became Mrs George Hooper, encouraged them to look for suitable wives and talked longingly of more grandchildren.

Harry began courting Mary Anna Reynolds, a recent immigrant from Penrith in Cornwall, whose father had come to Nelson in 1872 on the *Schiehallion* and sent back to England for his wife and children two years later.

Mary Anna, known always to the Hadfields as Annie, arrived on the *Forfarshire* on 6 March 1874 as a girl of eighteen. She was ten years younger than Harry but by 1878 they had an understanding, and when there were stock sales to attend or goods to buy in Nelson it was Harry who travelled from Awaroa on the *Lady Barkly*, or sailed the heavy old workboat down the coast and into Port Nelson. Harry and Annie were married in Nelson on 28 August 1878, two days before her 22nd birthday.

While Harry was courting Annie Reynolds, William found more and more reason to go to Collingwood. In February 1878 he sold twenty fat sheep to Martha Snow for twelve shillings each, and found it necessary to escort them on the scow himself and make sure they were delivered safely. He was invited to stay at Glen Howard, where he spent much of his time admiring young Adele's handling of the stock on their small farm. His mother and her grandmother encouraged the match, and so did her mother Martha, although of course nothing was said. Such matters were for Mr Hadfield to sort out with Adele's father when the time was right.

William Hadfield was a gentleman and a landowner, acknowledged by the Snows as a very suitable husband for either of their daughters. The difference in their ages, which had made such a union unthinkable when Adele was still a child, no longer seemed important.

It was a distant courtship. Martha Snow always called him Mr Hadfield, and so did Adele, and he spent more time talking to her father and uncles than to her, but slowly the relationship grew. Harry's marriage was the final spur, and one cold wet evening in 1878 William called formally on George Snow at Glen Howard and was taken into the parlour. Adele and her younger sister Laura were sent upstairs where they knelt on the floor in their room and pulled a plug of wood from one of the floorboards, as they had done for years when they wanted to overhear private talk from the room below. Adele had her ear to the knothole and heard William ask for her hand, and in December that same year William Hadfield and Adele Snow were married by Reverend White at St Cuthbert's Church in Collingwood.

He was 34 and she was 18 when he took her home to Awaroa.

The paddle steamer *Lady Barkly* at Collingwood wharf. *Lady Barkly* went into service between Collingwood and Nelson in 1868. Her paddle wheels were replaced with a propellor in 1883. William Hadfield and Adele Snow were married at St Cuthbert's Church, on the hill to the right, in 1878.

Courtesy Gibbs family

WILLIAM WELBY HADFIELD
1844-1920

MARTHA ADELE ANN SNOW
1860-1906

AWAROA INLET, originally known as Awarua, looking out towards the sea from Mt Alma. Awapoto (Little River) is to the left, Awaroa (Big River) to the right.

CHAPTER THREE : ADELE

1878

ADELE caught her breath in excitement when the *Lady Barkly* pulled away from Totaranui. Harry and Annie were down below, but Adele stood out on deck as she had done almost all the way from Waitapu, holding on to the railing and staring at the lush green hills and sparkling water. A little blue penguin surfaced a few yards away and stared up at her as if it was irritated by the noise of the steamer.

"The next bay's ours, Mrs Hadfield," her new husband said at her elbow. "Are you ready to get in the dinghy? Don't be nervous, you'll get used to it."

Adele was determined she would. She was unused to boats. She'd spent her eighteen years up river valleys, first at Hope inland from Nelson, and then at Rockville up the river from Collingwood in Golden Bay. She'd done an occasional trip before on this rolling paddle steamer but it had always been to Collingwood or Nelson, embarking from one solid wooden wharf, disembarking onto another. There'd always been someone there to grab hold of her if she slipped, and she never had done.

The Hadfields had just watched Mrs Betsy Gibbs manage her plump body and full skirt with dignity and elegance as she'd been helped down the side ladder and into the ship's dinghy to be rowed ashore. The Gibbs family were the main landowners to the north of Awaroa, and they had owned their 272 acres at Totaranui since 1856. William Gibbs also owned 1,000 acres of land between Wainui and Totaranui, including Separation Point, and had a grazing licence for a further 600 acres down to Awaroa River. He was the Collingwood MP and gold warden, a successful landowner who had made a great deal of money by owning the Aorere peninsula, formerly Gibbstown and now renamed Collingwood, when the gold rush began.

In 1878 William and Betsy Gibbs finished the main building of their showpiece home at Totaranui. They were a cheerful and fun-loving family with eight children, open-hearted in their hospitality and known to entertain the gentry. Their house was double-storeyed with gabled ends, set in elaborate gardens with a carriageway and a fountain. There were porcelain basins in the bedrooms, running water, hand-painted wallpapers and paintings by William Gibbs himself on the walls. There was to be a conservatory, a glasshouse and a model dairy. Everyone in Collingwood knew about the house and read the descriptions in *The Colonist,* although few had seen it.

Adele had gazed with fascination at the big house, which they could see from the water, and at the people hurrying down to the beach to meet the boat. Now she was the wife of a landowner in the next bay, she looked forward to a similar lifestyle and she wondered just what her new home would look like.

"You must come and visit us, Mrs Hadfield, now that we are neighbours," the great lady had said with a warm, cheery smile and Adele had responded with a quiet thank you. It was strange to be a married woman, and she was determined to learn the part and meet each new challenge graciously.

As she had already done, she thought with a blush. Her new husband had always been courteous and gentle with her, but he was so much older than she was, and she had been anxious about their wedding night. Like most girls of her generation she knew very little about what would happen. Her mother had hinted at something frightening, even violent, but William could not have been kinder.

Upstairs in the hotel in Collingwood Adele had been nervous when she put her new cotton nightdress on and waited. There'd been kisses from Laura and her mother, and jokes and raucous laughter from the bar below. The men's voices had been loud and harsh, her father's among them, and for a moment she had fought the urge to run from the strange bedroom with its brown wallpaper and huge double bed. She was unsure which side of the bed she should get in, or even if she should get in it all, and so she sat stiffly on the edge of it, straight-backed and anxious, her hands clasped in her lap. Her mother had told her to let her hair down and brush it smooth, and even that felt strange. She usually plaited it into a long braid that hung down one side while she slept.

"Work hard and remember your manners," her mother had told her. "Mr Hadfield is a gentleman, and he will expect you to keep his house up to a high standard, and to behave like a lady at all times."

"You've done well for yourself, Addie," her father had said proudly. "My daughter, a landowner's wife."

William Hadfield's wife. Mrs William Hadfield.

Outside on the mudflat an oystercatcher had called, its harsh cry reminding her of the sea and the boat journey that was still to come. Adele took a deep breath and slid between the sheets, feeling them cold on her calves and ankles below her new cotton underwear. Her nervousness gave way to a frisson of excitement as she arranged her thick black hair around her shoulders, and boldly loosened the ribbon at her neck. She had felt that same tingle in her spine a few days earlier, when he had taken her hand in his and kissed her on the cheek, his moustache tickling her skin.

She closed her eyes as the door opened, listening to him moving at the dresser. It seemed to take ages for him to take off his wedding suit and don his night clothes, and she hoped he would not use the flowered china chamber pot.

"Adele," he said gently. "You look beautiful. May I come to bed now?"

She'd opened her eyes and smiled at him, standing at the foot of the bed in his nightdress. His own eyes were kind, and she saw nothing in them to trouble her. Reassured, she nodded, and then her eyes widened in shock when he took off a hairpiece and hung it on the bedpost. She had never dreamed that men wore false wigs to thicken their fashionable full heads of hair.

Her new husband was half bald, his pate reflecting the candlelight through thinning strands of hair, and no one had prepared her for that.

Adele's wedding night taught her something that she had never imagined. Although she was but eighteen years old and her new husband was thirty-four, she learned that he was vulnerable too.

The knowledge sustained her through Will Hadfield's gentle and considerate possession of her body that night, and through the next morning's bustle of purchasing and packing and farewells. As they boarded the *Lady Barkly* and followed the coastline around from Golden Bay, Adele felt brave and strong again, ready to tackle whatever her new life held for her.

Now as they rounded the next headland her grey eyes sought her new sister-in-law, four years older, whose thick Cornish accent she was still learning to interpret. Annie had been shy at the wedding, blushing when Adele's uncles had danced her boisterously around the room. Harry had seemed to enjoy it more, and William had spent a lot of the time chatting with old men about business, only remembering to play the bridegroom when his new wife managed to catch his eye.

"Here we go," William said at her side, and Adele realised they were off a deep inlet which must be Awaroa. The steamer lay still and Harry was already down in the dinghy, her boxes and Annie's small suitcase passed down with a rope. She held her breath as a sack of flour wavered dangerously over the water, then sank safely onto the floor of the boat. Their wedding presents had been simple, but several were breakable and Annie had helped her pack them among her clothes and the precious new linens she was bringing.

Before she knew it Annie was gone from her side, then it was her turn and she forgot her determination to be graceful and swung her legs wildly towards the boat, aware of Annie's giggle and Harry's encouraging shout. Then she was down, sitting where she was told to, risking a cautious wave at the passengers on the deck. A sailor rowed them to a wide golden beach and the men, their boots already off and their best trousers rolled to their knees, leapt into the water and steadied the dinghy as they pulled it closer in.

Bewildered, Adele let them help her step ashore, misjudging her stride and plunging one new black button boot into deep water. She forgot to lift her skirts and the hems soaked up salt water like a blotter, wrapping her ankles in clammy cold. She stood and watched helplessly while the men unloaded the contents of the boat onto the gritty sand and pushed it off again.

Soon the *Lady Barkly* was disappearing around the headland and they were left there on the beach.

"Come on, let's get home and put the kettle on," Annie suggested with an encouraging smile. "The men can bring the horse and sledge back down for our gear and carry yours to the inside beach ready for the tide turn."

Adele didn't understand what she was talking about. She looked up expectantly as they trudged through the coarse golden sand. "Where is my husband's house?" she asked. "Is that it over there?"

"No, that's ours."

Annie stopped and turned to face her. "You do realise that we are not exactly close neighbours here at Awaroa?" she asked quietly. "We'll be able to visit now and again when the tides are right, of course."

Adele looked up at the hill, where a modest two-storeyed wooden house was planted neatly in the late afternoon sunlight, wisteria blooming along the verandah posts. She turned back to look out at the huge deserted inlet, channels of water trailing across a wide expanse of sun-drenched sand. The two men were striding towards them, their arms filled with luggage and she waited for her husband to reach her.

"Where is our home, William?" she asked.

He smiled fondly at her. "Down there behind that low point. You can't see our valley from here but there it is, Awapoto, nestled under the hills and blessed by the sun. When the tide's turned and half way in again we'll be able to row home, my dearest wife. We'll be there by nightfall."

Adele followed his pointing finger down the long, drained estuary and into the foot hills, where a low promontory crossed the sand like a blue smudge. Behind it were shadows, darkening into the distance. Her heart sank as she followed her sister-in-law indoors.

As they got to the head of the inlet that evening the boat seemed to Adele to cross into the shadows and she glanced back at the rising water still dappled by sunlight near the open sea. She felt as if the hills were closing around her like a prison.

Adele found the reality of life at Awapoto very different from her experience at Rockville. Her family home at Glen Howard was bulging with people, full of life and activity and she had been used to the bustle of the goldfields, to the passing of horses and wagons, to weekly mail and newspaper deliveries and to the proximity of Collingwood with its church, shops and hotels and regular steamer service. Here there were no other voices, no vehicles and no visitors, and her only companions were the birds and animals and a shelf of books.

William had been brought up a gentleman, his love of reading and gardening sustaining him in the years of isolation from other people. His fifteen years at Awaroa had matured him as a gentle, quiet man, old-fashioned in his habits and manners. Adele was barely more than half his age and at Awapoto she was alone with her new husband, her contact with other people limited by distance and the tides.

She had seen her gentle mother worn down by the hard life of the goldfields and the raw manners of the Snow men. All her life she had longed for something better, and now she had her chance she was determined to make the most of it. She was physically strong too, with a good figure, long dark brown hair and grey eyes that could be disconcertingly direct. She had been brought up to be capable in the kitchen and on the farm, and she was used to handling animals, firmly in charge of her younger brothers and sisters. Now she had her own home she made up her mind to be a good wife and play an active part in her future.

Her first few days passed in a blur of packing, cooking and cleaning. The little house was neat and tidy, as she had expected, but she set to with a will to make it hers.

"You've baked enough for an army," William chuckled on the third morning. It was nearly midday, and she had been busy since breakfast. The eggs had been gathered, the milk separated and loaves of fresh bread sat cooling on the wooden table, their crusts hard and golden. There were fresh scones and a fruit loaf, rich with golden syrup and raisins. Adele was red with exertion, her bare arms floury and her white apron stained with black soot from the pans and kettles she'd been lifting on and off the fire. She quickly set places for their meal and filled the teapot.

"I hope you like blackberry jam?"

"And I hope you brought plenty with you," he said. "There are no blackberries down here, so we'll have to rely on your mother for next year's batch."

"What can I use to make the jam this summer?" It was one of a million questions she still had to ask him. So far she'd scarcely had time to leave the house, and the garden and fruit trees were still unknown territory.

"Cherries. They're ready for picking now, and the plums will soon be ripe too. And peaches and raspberries." He looked fondly at her. "I've longed for jam, but never had the time to make it. Now the fruit won't be wasted."

"Do you like cherry pie?"

He looked at her strangely. She'd served him cherry pie before, she remembered, when he'd come for dinner at Glen Howard, and he'd complimented her mother and asked for seconds. But that was before she even dreamt of marriage, before she realised this would be her lot in life. It dawned on her that he'd been aware of her for a long time.

She wiped a strand of hair back from her face and poured the tea.

"About tomorrow, Will? "

"Yes?"

"It's Sunday. Will we visit Annie and Harry?"

Her heart sank when she saw his expression of surprise. "Surely we can observe the Sabbath, even here. Is there not a service, or a gathering in one of the houses? Surely there will be visitors, at least?"

"Adele, my dear wife." He reached for her hand. "I'm sorry, but the tides are wrong."

She stared helplessly, not understanding.

"We have to leave on a rising tide to row down to the inlet, then return before the water drops too low again. We get big midday tides once a fortnight, on the full moon and the new moon."

He might have been talking Greek to her, so little did she understand it. Inland at Rockville where she'd been brought up there was a road past the house, and although she'd always known that vessels like the *Lady Barkly* came and went on the tide she'd never really thought about the cycles of the sea. Now she learned that she was imprisoned by the moon. From that night on she watched it, always knowing when it waxed plump and full and when it waned down to a tiny sliver, because those were the times the tides would let her out.

As the reality of her isolation sank in, Adele tried to lose herself in work. There was plenty of it. The house was small and simple and there were only the two of them to feed, but it was December, with food to harvest and process for the coming winter. While William was busy with the animals and the garden, Adele's days passed in a blur of washing and cooking, churning butter and stirring jam, setting her bread to rise by the open fire and dealing with meat kept in a safe under the trees. She and William settled into a routine, each adjusting to the other, and more than once she blessed her mother for teaching her the household skills she'd sometimes hated back at Rockville.

The first mail came ten days after her marriage. She was as excited as a schoolgirl as William emptied it onto the table, so excited that she forgot to wonder how it had come. There were letters from Laura and her mother, one from her new sister-in-law Mrs Green, and one from Mrs Hadfield in Nelson with a gift of soap. There were newspapers and letters from shopkeepers, and she was thrilled to find a note from Grandma Snow.

"Look Will, there's an enclosure addressed to you." She watched him as he opened it, already knowing what would be inside. This was her secret, hers and Grandma Snow's, and she couldn't wait to see his face.

"Do you like it?" Excited, she left her chair and went to stand behind him so she could look over his shoulder. It was her wedding photograph, the only one she would ever have. Grandma Snow had helped her arrange it in Nelson, when she went to choose her bridal outfit the week before their wedding. A studio portrait, her hair done with care, her new gloves and boots worn with pride and her umbrella held with a jaunty air.

"Quite the young lady of fashion, Mrs Hadfield," William smiled fondly.

"I paid for it myself," Adele told him. "I wanted you to have a lasting picture of your bride."

"I have a picture of my wife right here every time I look at you," he said simply. She stared back at him in the flickering candlelight. Here at Awapoto he no longer wore his hairpiece every day, and his clothes were rough and stained from work. She wondered for the first time what she really felt for him, and whether there would ever be anything more. Suddenly she felt close to tears.

"I have to visit Annie," she blurted out. "I haven't spoken to a soul except you since we came here."

"But now you have your mail to read. Surely you can't feel lonely with all these letters from your family?"

"Please, Will?"

He nodded. "All right. We have a wool cheque, and there's money for some lambs I sold last month. Why don't you make up a shopping list and we'll

His strong arm pulled her upright at the top and held her for a moment, his brown eyes searching her laughing grey ones.

"Adele," he murmured.

"Yes William?"

"I'm so glad to have you for my wife."

She stared back at him, teasing. "Am I a good wife, William?"

"You fulfil your role very well, and make me proud to play the husband."

"You make it sound like a duty," she complained. She took his hands and slid them around her waist, leaning in to him. "Is there no pleasure in it?"

He kissed her forehead tenderly, his face flushed, and she fought the urge to wind her arms about his neck and pull him closer. She knew he would be shocked by her boldness even though there could be no one to see them, and so she dropped her eyes as well as her arms, her lips unkissed, and busied herself with the baskets.

That night in bed he turned to her, as she had known he would, but afterwards she lay awake, watching the moonlight in the trees outside their window and wondering. Was she truly wicked to feel such tingling in her body, such urges to caress and kiss rather than clench her hands and take the passive role? Her husband's lips had touched hers, had nuzzled at her neck and slid towards her cotton-covered breasts and she had wanted more than anything to respond, but had felt helpless, shamed by her own arousal. She was a respectable married woman, she told herself, and must behave like one. Her mother had not brought her up to play the harlot, and Will did not expect it of her either.

As the summer went on Adele met the other settlers around the inlet. There were Maori families at Waiharakeke from time to time and other white woman at Awaroa, but the farm at Awapoto was very isolated from any of them. Even Annie was a long way away at the other end of the inlet, their time together limited by the urgent need to watch the tides to make sure there was enough water in the estuary for the long sail or row back home.

Annie visited her, handling the boat with strength and practiced ease, and it was she who taught Adele to row. Soon she was confident enough to go down the inlet on her own, and she was much more independent of her husband.

She needed to be. They were both busy enough, Will with the animals and the farm he was still developing, Adele with the daily chores. She was thankful for the long hours of daylight as she laboured through her daily routines, tending the poultry and the household animals, keeping the fire burning so there would be hot water for the weekly washing which she did in a big galvanised bucket on the lawn under the trees, wringing the heavy clothes as best she could and pegging them on a line propped with a manuka pole.

There was the bread to bake and the meals to prepare, and in the evening there was always sewing and mending to do by candlelight while William read or did his accounts at the table. There were letters to write too, and she learned always to have the mail ready in case there was a chance to send it out to Totaranui or to a passing ship. William was frequently down at the inlet where there were other settlers coming and going, although Adele herself seldom saw anyone. She would sometimes climb the hillside to get a view of the sea.

While there were still just the two of them she found herself working frequently alongside her husband as they moved sheep or cattle, or tended the garden. Water was a problem through the long hot days of summer, and there were weary trips from the river to the vegetable patch with a full bucket in each hand. The sandy soil drained easily and even the fruit trees suffered if there were too many weeks without rain.

Adele was a good housekeeper and she soon learned to market her surplus produce, sending butter, eggs and fruit out to the *Lady Barkly* to trade in Nelson. Learning not to run out of supplies was more of a problem, and in that first summer of their marriage there were a few embarrassing days when she had to ration their flour or sugar, and once even the tea that was their staple drink. She made yeast from potatoes and kept it working in a big jar near the fire, and through the long hot summer mornings she made jam, storing it in precious glass bottles with their tops cut off and sealed with wax. Soap was made with lye and mutton fat, and there was always meat or chicken stock for soups and stews.

"I miss pigeon pie," she wrote to her mother in January. "We eat a great deal of fish here, and Annie has shown me how to make a dish of smoked fish and potatoes which father would love. William is smoking some snapper fillets and I will send you some so you might try the recipe."

To her delight a parcel of plump woodpigeons arrived from Rockville for her birthday, along with cards and greetings from her family. There was a letter from Ann Hadfield too, with a pretty embroidered handkerchief tucked inside.

"Well, this is certainly a birthday mailbag," William laughed as he sorted the letters and circulars. "Your pile is bigger than mine, and I have all the business letters."

Although her birthday was still three days away, Adele felt festive that Saturday night, and when she saw William tuck a small package away without comment she knew he had already remembered and planned a surprise for her. She got up early the next morning and baked pigeon pies for both Hadfield households, thankful that the tides were right for a visit to Annie. The baking made her queasy, even though she looked forward to the taste of the pies, and for a moment when she pulled the steaming golden pastries out to cool she

Trafalgar Street as it was when Richard Hadfield was the chemist.
Nelson Provincial Museum (Tyree 182194/3)

wondered if she was unwell. It was mid-February, hot and dry, and the proximity of the river meant the sandflies and other insects were out in force. She had to keep everything covered from the flies, and even though she kept her buckets in the shade the water was lukewarm and unrefreshing. She made a pot of tea and sat down to drink it, feeling the need to rest, but by the time William came back from his chores she was fine again.

"You look a bit peaky," Annie said quietly that afternoon. "Are you feeling the heat too?"

"I hope that's all it is," Adele replied. "There's so much to do in the garden, and the hot nights make me so restless."

"And your husband too?" the older woman chuckled, and then she looked at Adele more closely. "Are you sure it's just the heat?"

"No." Adele blushed. "I thought there might be another answer, although I confess I didn't expect it to happen quite so soon."

Her sister-in-law grinned with delight. "You've beaten me to it, you lucky girl. There's your birthday present, tucked under your apron already, and me still waiting to make my Harry a father."

Adele's head was still whirling when they left, and through the trip home, faster this time because the wind was with them and William hoisted a small sail. She felt ill again, and opened her mouth several times to tell him, then closed it. She knew how pleased he would be and wanted to tell him properly, with dignity.

She waited until after her birthday tea the next night. He had gravely picked the best rose in the garden for her and tucked it into the little glass vase he'd bought as a gift, and she reached out and toyed with it, loving the perfection of the flower.

"William," she began, then stopped, wishing not for the first time that she had flowery words and fine speech at her command.

Her mind raced as she tried to frame the sentence, conscious of his expectant gaze, but it was hopeless. She blushed red with embarrassment.

"There'll be more than lambs to raise next spring," she blurted out. "I think I'm carrying your child."

Their son was born 9 October 1879, nearly a year after their marriage, and Adele spent the last few weeks of winter waiting eagerly for the day she could take the boat to Nelson for her confinement. Annie's first child was due a few months later and would be born at home but Adele, whose home at Awapoto was much more isolated, left for the comforts of town where a midwife would be there to help her, a doctor on call if necessary. She left the inlet in their small sailing boat, unable to face the difficult climb up the ladder and onto the steamer in the darkness, and William fussed over her all the way to Nelson, tucking her shawl around her shoulders and trimming the sails to make sure their passage was smooth and easy. When they reached Nelson he handed her over to the care of her aunt Sarah Moore, her mother's younger sister who was married to a Nelson businessman.

Adele was nineteen years old when she gave birth to her first child in a cottage nursing home. The midwife comforted her through her labours and she wept with relief and joy when it was over.

It was the first time she had been in Nelson since her marriage and she drank in the sights and sounds eagerly, enjoying her rest from the heavy housework. She was bright and happy as she talked and laughed with the other women. She called her son Frederick George, after William's father and hers, and sent long letters home to her husband by steamer. She imagined him checking the new lambs, bringing the orphaned ones to warm by the fire as she had been doing, sitting in his chair on the hearth until he fell asleep. She bought him a new velvet smoking cap, the first gift she had ever chosen from a shop for him.

It was several weeks before she was ready to go back to Awapoto and when William came to fetch her she took him visiting to her grandmother Snow, now an old lady, and to her Newth grandparents who were also in their 80s. They also saw her aunt Ada, who had achieved her heart's desire and married a sea captain. She often went with her husband, Captain Edward Wheeler, on his voyages. They had brought the *SS Hawea* out from Scotland three years earlier, and as William talked shipping with her and her husband he marvelled at the handsome and assured woman who had once been a tomboy teenager.

William's younger brother Richard was unwell and his wife Frances was worried about him. So was his mother Ann, now Mrs George Hooper, because Richard had never been strong. He had rheumatic fever as a child, and his heart was weak. Frances had borne him two sons but had lost a third child, and now she was carrying out most of the work in the shop, her husband too ill to do more than supervise. Her own family, the Greens, were supportive and so were the Hadfields, but there was little anyone could do to help. Hadfields the Chemists in Trafalgar Street was doing well, and they could only hope the remedies sold over the counter might help its proprietor.

William and Adele took their son home to Awapoto late in October, and began adjusting to parenthood. Adele was well used to looking after baby brothers and sisters, but that summer her workload seemed heavier than ever and sometimes she longed for the days when she had only two to wash and sew for. But little Fred delighted her, and as he grew old enough to make his first sounds and play with his toys she found him company through the long summer days. Sometimes she would sit outside to nurse him, watching the lambs at play or the ducks by the river, one of the farm dogs protectively sitting by to warn her if anyone was coming.

Their home was in an open river valley, sunny and attractive, the land around the house planted with English oaks, apples, plums and grapes. But it was still lonely and inaccessible and Adele found it a depressing place, surrounded by lowering hills and encroaching bush, cut off from even a glimpse of the sparkling waters of the bay or of the tall masts of passing ships.

At night and in bad weather particularly the loneliness got on her nerves, and when William was away for long hours she found her utter isolation difficult to bear. She did not have the musical background that he did, nor his love for books and poetry, and she went about her chores in the house and garden mechanically, unable to lose herself in them. She wrote long letters to her mother and her sister Laura and to Grandma Snow in Nelson, and fretted if the replies were slow in coming.

Early in 1880 a diphtheria epidemic swept the Aorere Valley where Adele's family lived. Her two baby brothers Louis, two and a half, and Lionel, one and a half, died within a week of each other. Adele's own baby was only four months old, and she could not possibly take him to Aorere and expose him to the dangers of the epidemic, so she had to stay helplessly at Awapoto, unable to comfort her bereaved family except on paper.

Her mother was pregnant again and distraught with grief, and Adele wept when she had a letter saying her parents were to move to Wanganui in the North Island. She put little Fred in the bow of the dinghy and rowed all the way down the inlet to Annie's house so they could wave a pillowslip from the beach when the *Lady Barkly* passed with the her family on board.

Adele was the eldest of the ten Snow children, and her brothers and sisters were all close to her. George Howard, five years younger, went to Westport to work on a farm and the other two older boys, Clarence and Allan, stayed on at Glen Howard and worked in the bush. Adele and William lived too far from Collingwood to see them very often, but when her parents and the younger children moved right away from the district Adele felt more lonely than ever.

She was unhappy at Awapoto. She grew quick tempered, almost violent at times, and became upset at the smallest things, although her moods passed as quickly as they had come. She hated William to leave her and was happiest when he worked close to the house and could share her delight in little Fred's first steps and smiles.

But William was forced to work further from home. The going rate for a farm labourer was nine pence an hour, and he took the work where he could find it. Their farm was not doing enough to support them all year round, and he and Harry helped each other on bigger jobs like droving the cattle. Sometimes Adele went with him and helped, but as Fred grew bigger and needed a closer eye kept on him that became too difficult to manage. When the weather and tides permitted she would go to Annie and the two women would sew and chat together. She could not leave the farm often, though, because there were never-ending chores, the cow to milk twice a day, the milk to skim and the butter to churn, the hens to feed and the eggs to gather, lambs to be nursed or a sick calf to mother, the fruit and vegetables to tend and store. At night there were clothes to be aired by the fire, or mended by candlelight,

Soon after their marriage William began working with Mr Gillstrom who had bought a property at Awaroa, often called Big River. It was familiar land to William and Harry who had visited the Ricketts family there nearly twenty years earlier. He was away from home for long hours, clearing the bush and fencing on the far side of the inlet. He could get there more quickly and easily by boat than on foot and sometimes he stayed overnight there, making the most of the light and the fine weather, although Adele always preferred him home. If the tides were wrong but the weather fine he could walk as far as the opposite bank of the Awapoto River and cross it on a primitive raft or wade it near the mouth at low tide, but if the river was up he could not make it easily.

Adele found his absences distressing. There were days when she saw no one at all, days when she chattered to the dogs, the sheep and the hens as well as to little Fred, simply to keep from weeping at the silence. On those days she often found herself hurrying faster and faster, pushing herself until she stumbled, or spilled the water or burned the bread, and although she was never unkind to the child he learned to play quietly lest he distress her more. Sometimes when she put him down to sleep in the afternoon she would lie down too, but more often she would set to and turn out a cupboard, scrub the floors or take to the garden vigorously with a hoe. On those days she would feel the valley closing in one her, the brooding hills towering all around like prison walls and the silence overwhelming her. On those days it took all her willpower not to snatch the boy up and run towards the sea.

William came back just on dark one night and saw no smoke rising from the chimney and no light in the window. He hurried his footsteps, alerted by the barking dogs, and found her semi-conscious on the ground near the landing, the little boy crying beside her. He knelt beside her and chafed her hands until she came around, and took her carefully indoors to sit still by the hearth while he lit the fire and the candles and set water to boil.

"I can't bear you to leave me so alone," she wept when he asked her what had happened. "The hills crowd me and oppress me until I can no longer bear it."

That winter their brother Richard Hadfield died in Nelson, and there were black-bordered letters in the mailbag once more. Neither Harry nor William went to the funeral, and their mother was upset and reproachful. She could not possibly understand, William decided as he looked around his little kitchen after reading her latest letter. Annie was pregnant again, unable to do any heavy lifting and little Bert was just learning to crawl so Harry could not leave his farm. William was in the same predicament as his brother. There was simply not enough money to pay for both his fare and Adele's, and there was no one to manage the animals while they were away. And how could he possible leave his wife on her own, when her nerves were in such a state? Regretfully he wrote sincere condolences to everyone, wishing he could at least see Bessie Green again, and catch up with his nephews and nieces.

Adele went to Collingwood on the steamer for her next two confinements, taking her growing family with her each time. Welby Vivian, born in May 1881, was named after his maternal great grandparents from England, William Welby and Elizabeth Vivian. Her next child, born in Collingwood in January 1883, was a daughter and they called her Ivy Adele.

Now there were three children at Awapoto and Adele had her hands full managing the house and garden, washing, mending and sewing for them all. She baked her own bread and made her own butter, and every season there were different fruits to gather and preserve into jam, different vegetables to harvest and store. Her family grew healthy, but she felt the isolation more keenly than ever and seldom even saw the sea.

Some Sundays she and William would take the children down to Harry and Annie's house, but it was a long journey and they could only go when the tides were right for the return trip.

A post office was opened at Totaranui in 1883, and the steamer

Adele with her first daughter Ivy Adele Hadfield, who was born in Collingwood 22 January1883.
Photo W E Brown, Nelson.

Lady Barkly began calling there three times a week. Sometimes Harry or William would take one of their workboats up to the post office, or one of the other settlers would call with the mail. There were picnics and parties at Totaranui. The Gibbs family had lived there five years now and their grand home was the centre of social activity. Adele's isolation was the harder for her to bear, knowing her neighbours along the coast entertained so lavishly while she seldom left Awapoto. When Mary Anne Gibbs married William's old friend Frederick Huffam from Bark Bay, the Hadfields were among the guests at the wedding. For Adele it was a glittering occasion and only served to fuel her longing for company.

She took her children to stay with the Cedermans at their Riwaka home. It was a long journey by sea and then by horse and buggy but Adele loved visiting friends, attending church and joining in social life and conversation. She looked forward to such excursions for months, sewing long into the evenings so she and the children would be dressed in their best, and when she went home to the lonely house at Awapoto again it felt more like a prison than ever.

She began to look at it with fresh eyes. Their home was a simple cottage, comfortable but unpretentious in its sunny little river valley. Adele longed for a

Adele heaved a sigh of relief the day school started in 1895. Fred was old enough to put away his books and work, William had said, and the two of them had long gone out to the paddocks. Now the house was full of scuffling and laughter as six young Hadfields were called to order at the back door, shoes polished, hair brushed and lunches neatly packed up in their bags.

"You're to mind Welby and Ivy," Adele told young Darcy sternly. "And sit up straight and mind your manners for Miss Winter."

"I wish Edith was here," Ivy sniffed. "I always sit next to Edith, and now there's no one my age."

"You can sit by Laura," her sister Olive said, and there were giggles and nudges as the younger children looked at Welby. His hair was slicked down suspiciously, his face and hands scrubbed cleaner than they'd been all summer. He'd been rebellious when he'd learned he couldn't leave school like Fred, but William wanted him to have a last year of learning, and Adele was glad. No matter that her boys were destined to be farmers, she wanted them to read and write well, and to keep up a conversation with anyone. As for the girls - she swept little Roy up into her arms as they waved their family off towards the schoolhouse.

"Your sisters will marry rich society men, politicians or lawyers," she told him. "They'll wear the latest fashions and keep fine houses, and no one will ever say they are ignorant country girls, because they're not and never will be."

"I want to go to school too," the little boy said wistfully, and she laughed at him.

"Soon enough, Roy, soon enough. And then you won't be able to sit on the step with a glass of milk and a biscuit, will you?"

She sat beside him, knowing there was work piled up for her to do but savouring the moment. Cicadas thrummed, and bees were busy in the lavender beside the step. She could still hear the children's' voices faintly, as they'd rung all summer long. It was still strange that Annie was gone, and Harry and the children, and sometimes she could almost hear her sister-in-law's thick Cornish accent beside her in the kitchen as they had talked so many times together over a cup of tea. But in her heart she knew that the Winters and the Cunliffes had already been good for her children, who had known too few other youngsters besides family. There had been the Campbells, and others who'd visited, but the children were shy of strangers and kept to themselves.

This summer had been different, with Frank and Willie Cunliffe and red-haired Laura, high-spirited young people in love with life to tease her oldest children out of themselves and make them laugh, and Adele had revelled in the noise and fun and conversation as much as anyone. They had made her feel young again too.

Mrs Cunliffe was pleasant, and so was Mrs Winter but they were old friends, close to each other and older in years than Adele. So far they had seen no more of each other than ladies in town who were acquainted, and who met at church on Sundays or took afternoon tea now and again.

William had made firmer friends with Joseph Winter, and for that Adele was glad. The families had already spent a few evenings together and while the young people sang or played games the men had smoked their pipes companionably and liking what they saw in each other. Joseph was a few years younger than William, but he had worked in tanneries all his life, and his lungs were weakened by the chemicals he'd breathed in.

Joseph Winter was a good entertainer and knew lots of indoor games. He had been a lay preacher at the Wesleyan Church in Johnsonville, and he preached every Sunday at Awaroa. Once their new house was built there were frequent parties. Like the Winters, the Cunliffes were fond of music and art, and the two families brought a breath of fresh city air to Awaroa.

If Adele had a favourite among the newcomers it was Jessie Winter, Fred's age and named after her mother. She was a bright, well-read girl whose father, brother and older sister encouraged her studies and shared her love of books, and she could draw botanical specimens as well as any scientist. Jessie had done very well at Johnsonville School, passing the seventh standard when she was fourteen, and she had School of Design certificates for first grade freehand, model and scale drawing and practical geometry. She was not formally in school, because she was needed to help her mother run the house, but she had shyly confided to Adele that she wanted to pursue her studies and hoped to help her sister in the schoolroom when she could.

The Winters were interesting people and good neighbours, but rather poor farmers, it soon turned out. Their health was not good. Mr Winter and Christiana both had bad legs and weak ankles, and George had a shortened leg and a bad limp. They all went about their tasks willingly, however, and if it fell to Will Winter and the Cunliffe boys to do the heavier work, the others tried their hardest to help where they could.

After the Winters and Cunliffes came there were more visitors, and as the children grew older there were picnics, fishing, pighunting, shooting and boat trips. The women would supply cherry pie, Irish stew and boiled puddings, and when the families went out picnicking on the beach they would take a kerosene tin, fresh bread and vinegar and catch fish to cook up for lunch.

There were school picnics and sports, and although William seldom joined in Adele was always at the fore, organising the children and taking part in everything that happened. William was reserved about his religious observances too, and although he believed in God, led the family in grace at meal times and read his Bible, he would stay at home while his wife and children went to church services on their own.

He was a quiet and serious man, and his children only once managed to persuade him to take part in their fun. It was at a school picnic down by the sawpit. There were the usual races, for adults as well as children, and Jim Perrott challenged his friend to a running race.

"Come on, Father," the children urged, tugging him by the hands, and in the end he had no option but to take his hat and jacket off, roll his sleeves up and join Jim at the starting line. Amid the cheers of the families the two older men ran neck and neck, but William lost by a few inches, and after that, honour satisfied by having done it once, he never did it again.

Boats were of paramount importance, and William used frequently to have to cry "Hurry up girls, the tide is going". The whole family learned to handle boats and the children had at least one trip a day across the tidal creek to school. Their father built a flat-bottomed punt for them to use when the tide was in and they walked across the sand when it was out. Old Prince the draft horse would be called into service when the punt was on the wrong side of the creek, five young Hadfields on his long broad back, and would frequently walk straight up the steep bank and tip them off rather than using the path.

Awaroa at the turn of the century. This photograph taken from the Winters'cowshed looks down across the present airstrip towards Awaroa school, at the foot of the hill to the left, and Meadowbank behind the trees at the water's edge. The Winters' house was to the left.
Courtesy Tui Winter

On Boxing Day the Hadfields all went to the Winters haymaking, and with the Cunliffes and Jim Perrott there to help there would be about twenty people at work. Adele stayed behind to roast sucking pig and bake cherry pies for one of the boys to take over to the hay paddock on horseback. Mrs Winter would provide the vegetables and a large dish of junket covered with cream.

Harry Hadfield had run 190 sheep in his last year on the farm, but when the Winters took over their sheep the numbers dropped. In 1896 they ran 180 sheep, the following year only 121. William ran a small flock of between 60 and 70 sheep, and looked after around 150 for Gillstroms at Big River, and Richard Anslow had another 137 at Awapoto. There were small mobs of cattle on various properties, and every householder had a few pigs and milking cows. From an early age the children learned to handle animals and everyone helped when there was a big job on the farm.

Adele was a firm mother, determined about her own needs and expecting a lot from her children. They were all brought up to be capable and competent inside and outside the house, and she led by example.

Once when the men were driving cattle through the bush from Wainui a steer went wild and got away from them. It jumped over a bluff to land on the sand and dash out into the high tide. Adele and the smaller boys were watching from the beach, ready to help when the mob arrived, and when she saw the steer swimming out towards the entrance she acted very quickly.

"Help me with the boat, boys," she called as she snatched up a stout piece of rope and ran to the heavy seventeen-foot workboat. She hitched up her skirts and dragged the heavy dinghy down into the water.

"Stay right where you are and don't move an inch until I get back," she told them over her shoulder and she rowed down the inlet as fast as she could after the panicked steer. When she caught up with it she reached out and slipped a loop of rope over its horns, tying it firmly, then she turned the boat and started the long haul back to where she had left the boys.

At first the steer tried to jerk free but it was out of its depth and had no leverage against the rope. Snorting and thrashing in the water it allowed itself to be towed along and by the time Adele got back near the beach it was exhausted with the effort. She couldn't risk letting it near the boys and she had to keep out of its way herself so she solved the problem by anchoring the boat in waist deep water. She slipped over the gunwale on the side away from the enraged steer and waded ashore, leaving it standing in the sea, firmly anchored and bellowing. By the time the men arrived the steer was completely subdued and Adele laughed off the discomfort of her sodden skirts. William told the story with pride and the point where the steer jumped was always called Bullock's Bluff after that.

The Awaroa families were as self-sufficient as they could possibly be, and the Hadfields always produced a surplus of fruit, vegetables and butter which they traded around the bays. They kept nice flower gardens too. William grew oranges, lemons, apricots, peaches, water and rock melons, passion fruit, walnuts and hazel nuts, and much of the fruit was shipped to Kirkpatricks jam factory in Nelson. People would call and get fruit, vegetables, meat and home-baked bread. There was a detached bakehouse with a clay brick oven Adele had built from Brett's *Colonist's Guide.* Cream was churned to butter, apples and mushrooms were dried and preserved for winter, and the women found time to make clothes for the family and keep themselves neat and clean in white aprons.

The boys and their father set herring nets and smoked the catch, and when there were snapper or other fish in the bay they would all set to work to supplement their meat with fresh fish. Once a school of snapper was left stranded in the inlet, caught in a large crater by the outgoing tide, and on that occasion they fed the compost as well as the families.

Another time one of the boys set a net outside the entrance and caught a nine-foot shark. He had to row back into the inlet towing it to shallow water so he could untangle it and salvage the net.

Laura was the first to spot the blackfish which stranded in the bay one Sunday afternoon, just as a church service was finishing in the little schoolhouse.

"What is it?" she whispered to Olive, and they screwed their eyes up against the sun and stared at the two large objects bobbing about in the water and being quickly washed towards the entrance to the harbour by the swift flowing tide. One seemed to be more active than the other and they could see that it seemed to be steering the other one as it dived from side to side. By now the boys had noticed too, and their unusual stillness attracted the attention of their father.

"I believe they're pilot whales," he said slowly. "I hope they won't come in over the bar."

"Why not?" Darcy asked, but they soon found out. When the two huge fish arrived at the entrance the incoming tide quickly washed the slow one into the channel and the next minute it was inside the harbour. The children raced for home, the girls with one hand on their hats, another lifting their skirts out of the mud. William and Adele walked more slowly and by the time they reached Meadowbank the fish was aground on the beach, only a few feet from the gate. Then started a great fight to shift it out to sea again.

The dead blackfish, which seemed to have been steered in by its mate, weighed about two tons and the race was on to get it away from the house before it started to decompose. The tides were small so the boys had to dig a trench deep enough to float it again, and with the help of the horses they dragged it over to the other side of the harbour. It took two days to dispose of it but it made good compost, and the ugly teeth and jaw were kept as a souvenir.

As summer turned to autumn and winter, the upheavals of the previous year faded, and it was as if the Winters and Cunliffes had always been there. At Meadowbank Adele did the washing, baking, preserving and household chores, helped by the girls before and after school. The boys kept the supply of firewood up, tended the animals and worked in the garden, while William and Fred went further afield to earn cash.

The usual rate of pay in 1895 was six shillings a day, but one night William and Fred came home in particularly good spirits. They'd been working at Little River, and the news had come that the pay for agricultural labouring was going up to eight shillings.

"Father says we'll be able to buy new rams next season," Fred said importantly.

"And tools and nails to start on the new boat."

"And new dresses?" Laura asked, ducking her head to avoid her mother's eyes. "Laura Cunliffe's got the new catalogues from Kirkcaldies in Wellington."

Her father laughed fondly, but he didn't answer, and after tea was cleared away and the girls were busy with the dishes he and Fred got their account books out and sharpened their pencils to work out how best to use the increase. Adele sat by her husband's side quietly listening as she darned socks from her big workbasket. She knew more than any of the children how slender their resources were, and if she hankered for a visit to Nelson and a few yards of fine material and lace to make a Sunday dress with, she kept her dreams to herself. More money coming in might help the farm along by replacing worn out tools and buying seed and kerosene and nails and all the other necessaries, but little if any would trickle into her household budget.

They were never short of food, but only because they all worked long hours in the garden and the orchard. There were days when there was no meat because no one had time to kill and butcher another animal. Sometimes bad weather delayed the arrival of fresh supplies, and there were times when the children had only bread and dripping for their lunches.

One cold winter afternoon the children came in from school to find their mother had been baking and the tins were full of fresh cakes and fruit loaves. The rich smell of crisp sultana biscuits hung heavily in the air, and Laura simply couldn't resist taking two biscuits from the top of a well-filled jar and slipping them into her pocket.

Adele knew at once there were biscuits missing, and she lined her children up in the kitchen and asked them to turn out their pockets. Laura had already eaten the evidence, but she had forgotten the crumbs which her mother found caught in the pocket of her dress.

"If that's what you want to use your pocket for you're better off without one, Miss," Adele told her, and Laura was sent to the drawing room to unpick the pocket from her dress and hand it to her father with an explanation. Her blue serge pocket was then tacked neatly onto the wall above the fireplace where it shamed her for months afterwards.

"That's an unusual ornament, Mrs Hadfield," their visitors would say politely. "Is it a special piece of fabric?"

"We'll let Laura explain," Adele would say, and Laura would be sent for, to come into the parlour with her hair neat and her face clean. She'd have to stand in front of the pocket with her hands clasped together and explain how she'd taken the biscuits and slipped them into her pocket and hidden away to eat them when her brothers and sisters had none. It was the worst punishment she could ever remember, and she never stole food again in her life.

William and the boys cut fence posts and palings, tobacco stocks and hop poles. and did contract fencing for other landowners, but their 17 acres was not a viable farm and as the family grew William and Fred worked away from home more and more. One valuable contract was splitting totara shingles to re-roof the steeple of the first Nelson Cathedral.

Fred went to Westport in 1896 to work for his Uncle Howard and Aunt Ada Snow on their dairy farm, and his sister Ivy wrote to him with news from home. "Welby and Willie Cunliffe walked to Totaranui after dinner. There was lots of mail and there were letters from Grandma..." she wrote. Grandma Snow sent news from Wanganui of their young aunt May Violet's new job in Mr Craw's drapery shop. She had to walk two miles there and back, working until ten o'clock on Saturday nights, and she was to get no pay for three months. She was considered fortunate, as most shopgirls of the day worked for a probationary six months before their first pay.

Ivy's other news for her brother was more domestic. The wild sow Queenie they had tamed and built a sty for had seven little pigs, very strong, with silky hair.

His mother wrote as well, reporting on new puppies, the shearing and an unsuccessful pig hunt, telling him which boats had been into the bay, chiding him for spending money unwisely and being seen in Nelson in patched trousers.

"... I am glad the fare was so little, I wish I had the money to spare. I would be there for a trip too. What job have you got and how do you like it?

You must write a lot to me. Have you shaved yet and did Uncle Howard Snow know you? Does he think you are big enough for your age? Tell me what you think of everything if you can. Everyone will want to know. The boys heard we had a letter from you and Willie came over to hear what you said.

"I was there to Bible meeting last night and they all wanted to hear, so we will have to read bits of your letters; but I am going on ahead. Must go back to tell you that Miss Winter and Jessie came here the night you went to see if we were all right; they all came Wednesday night and Thursday night. We had such a gale I do not remember before...."

Fred was sweet on Jessie Winter and he used to walk long distances to get home and see her. He worked for a carrier at Denniston at one stage, and once he walked all the way up the notorious Denniston incline to see about a job in the coalmine. They were not taking men on and he came away without work, but as he walked down the line he was shocked to see discarded wire ropes lying unused beside the wagons and he talked for days about all the things they could have been used for back on the farm. A nikau still growing at Meadowbank was brought home to his mother from the Heaphy Track, the most direct route home to Awaroa from the West Coast.

By now there were many more boats in and out of the inlet. The *Lady Barkly*, now converted to a screw steamer, was joined on the regular bay trade by the *SS Wairoa* which the Ricketts family operated. The 22-ton ketch *Comet*, built by Jack Ricketts at Torrent Bay in 1883, and her sister ship *Transit* were trading up and down the coast, as were Burnard's *Felicity* and other vessels belonging to the Huffams, Westrupps and Nalders. Captain Kirk from Takaka owned *Morninglight*, Captain Westrupp had the *Planet*, and Dave Gilbertson's 49-foot *Pet* was another regular visitor. *Gannet*, *Coquette*, *Venetia* and *Minstrel* were also in and out of Awaroa, and the families looked out for the vessels and their crews, eager for news and always saddened when there were disasters and mishaps at sea.

In early November 1896 there were three vessels in at Totaranui at once, two big three-masters and one topsail schooner. A group from Awaroa set off to have a closer look, and to his delight Welby went aboard one, the *St Kilda*, with Willie Cunliffe, while William and the younger children were invited onto the *Rio*.

William Hadfield became more and more involved with boatbuilding. He found plenty of work but it became more difficult to get suitable timber and often it had to be brought in. William had an order to complete a boat for Mr Gillstrom before Christmas, and with Fred away it was left to Welby, finally out of school and not yet turned sixteen, to manage the farm.

JAMES PERROTT, who jumped ship in Nelson as a boy of fourteen and lived at Croisilles for some years. He spoke, read and wrote fluently in Maori as well as in English.

Perrott worked as an itinerant labourer from Totaranui to Riwaka, and was a skilled hop drier in Ngatimoti in the early 1980s. He went goldmining at Collingwood and the Mt Arthur Tablelands before settling at Awaroa, where he was a friend to three generations of Hadfields over more than 50 years.

The eight-ton schooner *Old Jack* high and dry on Bark Bay reef. Built by the Guards at Port Underwood and first registered in 1848, *Old Jack* traded regularly in Tasman Bay and was a frequent visitor to Awaroa. The vessel was rebuilt at Havelock in the 1950s.

He missed his brother, and wrote to tell him all the news from home, how they had been pighunting four times and come back with nothing but a kaka, how the Cunliffes and the Hadfields had gone up to Big River shag hunting and had got fourteen eggs and killed about two dozen young shags, how Snowdrop the cow had a calf, the old shed had nearly fallen down, and Mr Campbell had another one of his bad turns.

. "...Mr Perrott has gone to Wainui and on his way he nearly got wrecked in the *Kiwi*. I guess that will frighten him. Now I must say goodnight - Welby Hadfield."

Young Willie Hadfield, aged twelve, went off to Motueka for the first time with his father and the other boys.

"Willie thinks that's a fine place." Adele reported to Fred. "He went into the shop (Manoys) and bought a shilling's worth of lollies... he would have liked to have got an umbrella for me and a pair of boots for Laura..."

William was also away on the West Coast for a while the following year, and he and Fred also worked together in Collingwood on carpentering jobs, coming home on the steamer every few weeks or walking along the coastline to Takaka and then over the hill from Wainui to Awaroa.

Adele was pregnant again, and that summer she felt unwell, oppressed by the heat and by the weight of the child she was carrying. She relied heavily on Ivy, and was relieved when school was over for the year and the children could pitch in and help with the summer jobs. Welby and young Willie took care of the heavier work and milked the cows, Ivy ran the house under her mother's supervision and the younger children, Olive, Laura, Darcy and little Roy, spent long hours in the garden weeding, picking peas, beans and tomatoes and harvesting the fruit for preserving.

At Meadowbank there was a bank behind the house, the cowshed built into it with a haybarn on top. There were also ducks, geese, hens and turkeys. Looking after the domestic animals was as important as the gardening and housework and everyone in the family helped with the chores. Their cows used to wander up onto the hill behind house and sometimes one would go missing, fallen into a gully or hole. If there were broken bones the animal would have to be destroyed, a devastating blow if it was a house cow or a cow in calf. Hawks were a menace because they attacked the fowl house and preyed on the young birds. William would stake out raw meat on a fencepost then shoot the hawks with an old muzzle loader.

One of the legacies from William's father the chemist was a well-stocked first aid box, and both William and Adele were very competent in medical emergencies. When Mr and Mrs Alec Gilbertson were camped in Thompson's old orchard and their three-year-old daughter fell in the fire and was badly burned, it was the Hadfields who attended to her. Another time young Welby broke his leg and it was splinted and set at home and mended well.

There were few serious accidents. The children were taught to handle knives and axes with respect and to take care near the water, and no one ever made a fuss over small cuts and bruises. When the more urgent chores were done William would send the children out to pick up the cowpats, the lucky ones with garden forks, the others in their bare hands. Once Roy, who was the smallest, made a dive for a dry pat at the same time as one of his sisters stabbed it with a fork. He took one of the prongs fair between the third and little fingers of his left hand and bore the scar all his life. Another day one of his brothers took a fork through his foot, but their mother cleaned the wounds so well there were no infections.

As her time came near Adele began to drive herself and her children harder and harder, until by the new year William realised what was happening and made her rest. He finished the boat he was working on and divided his time between the farm and the homestead, worried about his wife's health.

She was 37, and although neither of them spoke of Annie that summer they were both aware of how important Adele's strength was to their way of life. She had born eight healthy children and neither she nor Will had expected another one. She fervently hoped this would be the last.

William sent Willie and Darcy down to Little River to get Mrs Campbell as soon as her labours started, and Laura was sent to the Winters' house to get Bessie. It was not going to be an easy birth, they could all see that at once, and as Adele lay upstairs sweating in the heat and Ivy stoked the stove up to boil kettles, William summoned the younger children to him.

"Ivy will give you dinner and a bottle of tea," he told them. "You're to go down to the meadow by the sawpit and pick the cowpats. Olive, you're in charge."

"Is mother going to die?" Roy whispered, white-faced.

"No, you goose, she's going to have a baby," Laura answered. "Then you won't be the youngest any more."

Roy was miserable all day wondering what he had done wrong. Picking up cowpats was an ongoing chore, often used as a punishment and as he laboured in the heat he agonised over why his mother was replacing him with another child. He had never seen a baby, and in his five year old mind he had a clear dreadful vision of some strange boy sleeping in his bed, sitting in his chair and cuddling his mother.

When Olive finally called a halt and served out their bread and jam and fruitcake under a shady tree, Roy was too upset to eat and sat alone, tears trickling down his face until Laura came to sit by him and comfort him.

Evered Rogers Hadfield was born on 4 March 1897, a small, fine-boned baby with a shock of dark hair. When Adele finally rested with her son cleaned and swaddled in the bed beside her she scarcely had the strength to look at him.

It was almost dark when the children were finally called home from the meadow and they were exhausted and sun-baked, the dry grass cleared of every speck of cow manure. After they had washed and eaten they were called upstairs to meet the baby but Roy had eyes only for his mother.

"See my darling, here's your new brother Evered," Adele told him, but he had no interest in the red wrinkled thing wrapped up beside her. He knew only a vast sense of relief. She hadn't died, and there were no strange boys in the house to take his place. Whatever he'd done wrong, she had forgiven him.

Fred came home at the end of summer, and later that year William went up the Aorere Valley to work at the Quartz Ranges. The Collingwood Goldfields Company, a London-based operation, set about an ambitious gold recovery operation which involved carrying water nearly four miles from Boulder Lake, a natural storage area which was to be dammed to double its capacity, to giant nozzles at the sluicing face. Step one of the project involved milling timber, carrying it across the Aorere River and up a tramline and constructing a wooden water race and fluming. Over 300 men were employed, and William earned good money although he was away from home for months at a time.

Fred was nearly eighteen now, and a conscientious and hard-working farmer. His father ruled with a firm hand, sending detailed instructions which Fred carried out to the letter, and although Adele was very much in charge it was Fred who organised his brothers in their daily workload, and whose approval they sought at the end of each task. He was as strict outdoors as Ivy was in the kitchen, and when one of the younger children behaved badly it was often Fred or Ivy who beat them.

Adele was slow to recover her health as she nursed Evered that winter, and the headaches she had suffered all those years ago at Awapoto now returned. She had recurring pains in her side and her nerves were bad, and although she worked just as hard as ever there were days when she confided to her diary that she found her life a struggle.

In 1898 William was still working at Quartz Ranges and Adele was lonely without him. She wrote letters to England and to her family in the North Island, supervised the children in their studies and spent long evenings reading or sewing alone by the fire after the rest of the family had gone to bed.

"All is well: I am in such a way. Will has not come yet. He sent letter and £5," she recorded in her diary in July. He had also sent a photograph taken by Mr Tyree. It was a black and white print showing the punt used to carry timber across the broad Aorere River from the sawmill to the tramline the men had set up. Fred, Welby and the other boys pored over it, eagerly discussing how the fluming was to be built and the machinery their father had described to them.

William arrived home at the end of July, after days of thunderstorms that had kept the family indoors and driven two large steamers into the shelter of the bay. Meadowbank was in an uproar, with visitors arriving all afternoon and evening, and Adele and the girls were kept busy in the kitchen. It was not until the next day that she had a chance to relax with her husband.

It was Arbour Day, August the first, and the little community kept the holiday by gathering at the school to plant trees and enjoy a picnic dinner. The sun shone down and it was as if the wild storms of the previous week had never happened.

"Fred should come to the Quartz Ranges with me after the haymaking," William told his wife as they watched the lively group around them. "Mace will take more men on next year and Welby is old enough to keep the farm work up. Young Willie is growing broad shoulders too, and Darcy will take over chopping the household kindling for you."

He laughed as the baby on Adele's lap reached a chubby fist into the air in his direction. "Pull my beard would you, young Evered? No work for you yet, but we'll have you pulling weeds before the century turns over, just you wait."

"And what of the girls, William?" Adele asked him gently. "Ivy will be fifteen this year, and what is she to do? Stay here and share the housework with me while all her brothers are away at work?"

"She can teach school perhaps, after Miss Winter's gone. And there is company enough for her here. She could do worse than marry our neighbour's son."

"Or fall for the first sailor who pays her any attention, and cause her parents grief?" Adele's eyes were sombre as she watched Ivy, Jessie and Christiana Winter. They made a pretty group as they sat with their sketchpads, big shady hats protecting them from the winter sun. The boys and the younger girls were playing cricket with a bat and ball from the schoolhouse, and Mr and Mrs Winter sat quietly chatting with Jim Perrott who seldom missed a picnic.

"There will be more people coming to Awaroa," William prophesied. "There's talk of cutting timber from all sorts of districts, and ours will be no exception. I heard there were to be surveyors at Anatimo, and with the money from Mace's project I think we will afford to buy more land at Little River for the boys to farm."

She looked at him, exasperated. "And then what? Awapoto is no place for a young woman, William, and nor is the rest of the inlet. There'll be few brides willing to follow our boys here and bear us grandchildren."

That night he gave her a pound note from his work at Mace's mill, but for the next few days he kept busy with the boys and the there was no more talk of the future.

The *SS Wairoa* stopped with mailbags and supplies a few nights later, and Fred and Will Winter who had rowed out to meet her came back with the news that William Gibbs was dead. Adele's mind was filled with memories of those early days, her first sight of Awaroa from the *Lady Barkly,* her hopes and dreams of married life and her admiration of Betsy Gibbs and her family. When her husband left again for the Quartz Ranges she felt depressed and listless, and when Fred took Welby and Willie off with him to sail to Riwaka with a load of fenceposts and firewood she felt Meadowbank grow strangely quiet and time hang heavily on her hands. She had pains in her side and took to her bed, leaving Ivy to look after Evered while the other four went off to school.

William wrote later that month asking for Fred, who caught the *Lady Barkly* for Collingwood the next day. Adele helped the boys finish off a new punt they had been working on, and when a fine sea breeze sprang up she willingly agreed to let them take William's boat, the *Mistral*, out for a sail. For the rest of the month the fine weather held and her health improved, allowing her to spend time down at the wharf oiling paddles, replacing rowlock leathers and enjoying the company of her sons. She helped them pack and sort skins for the Nelson sales, and sent them off to meet the steamer with a sack of tree fungus she had helped them gather.

Before the end of August there was a letter from William with £7 enclosed, wages from both him and Fred, and she realised that with the two men both earning good money there would be a chance for their lives to improve.

William had met Fred in Collingwood and walked back up to the Quartz Ranges with him. When they arrived at the camp above Bainham it was early evening and eighteen-year-old Fred was overawed by the air of activity. Trees had been felled and tents were scattered through the clearing. William strode confidently through the crowds of men, calling greetings and stopping to introduce his son and shake hands and they soon found themselves in front of a shingled hut where Fred Mace, the engineer in charge of the project, was taking names and allocating jobs to the newcomers.

William was sent back up to the top end of the water race to build the wooden fluming from the dam. It was work for the older and more experienced men, and young Fred was told to find a man called Richards who would give him work down by the mill at the bottom. The timber was milled down towards the settlement and punted across the broad Aorere River where it was loaded onto wagons and pulled by horses up a tramline to where the carpenters were waiting to take it on up the race.

Fred soon made himself useful on the tramline where his strong back and willing hands marked him out as a good worker. His manners marked him out too, and after a few days he was called aside. "Why do you call me Mr Richards, when the other men don't stand by such formality? Who told you to do that?" his boss asked him.

"I was brought up to call any man older than me Mister," he said simply. "My parents taught me to respect my elders."

The man looked at him keenly. "Where are you from, Fred?"

"Awaroa Inlet, sir, where my parents have a farm."

"And did your father also teach you to respect horses and work them properly?"

"Yes sir,"

"Then I'll give you the charge of them here."

Fred soon became a popular member of the loading gang, working as hard as any of the others and taking good care of the horses that hauled the timber up the tramline. He sat with his father and the older men most nights, listening to their yarns and learning what he could, and although he always sent part of his money home to his mother he put some of it aside towards the day when he could buy his own land at Awaroa.

The work was hard and heavy, and Fred developed strong muscles that saved his life when he was caught in the path of a runaway wagon. The heavy wagons were braked with a ratchet on the axle, and one day when Fred was near the bottom of the tramline the ratchet slipped on a wagon above him. He heard a warning shout and looked up but there was no time to get out of the way. He braced himself and took the initial brunt of the collision, then dropped down between the rails, flattening himself as best he could and protecting his arms, legs and head. The wagon ran right over him and cut deeply into his back, bruising his whole upper body, but by some miracle no bones were broken.

The accident was a result of carelessness by one of Fred's workmates and the men all agreed to hush up the incident for fear of repercussions. They covered up by doing his work as well as their own, letting him rest in the shelter of the wagons each day away from the sight of the boss until his wounds healed enough for him to get back to work. He carried the scars on his back for the rest of his life.

Once more the men were away from Meadowbank for weeks at a time and Adele and the younger children had to be very resourceful. She kept the farm dogs chained up at a big tree near the gate, an exotic pine still known as the dog tree, so they would bark and give her warning of approaching visitors. The children taught one dog, Joe, to bark at the names Mr Perrott or Mr Campbell. Provisions were more plentiful now and came several times a week on *Lady Barkly.* Towards the turn of the century there were lots of visitors, Maori and Pakeha, from Riwaka. The Parkes, Macleans, Cedermans and Whites sailed in to Awaroa. Many were church friends and there were meetings held in the living rooms on Sundays when the singing was outstanding.

Adele was always keen for her children to have an appreciation of music, but the only instrument at Meadowbank was her husband's violin. One summer she and the older children planted onions, which grew well at Meadowbank, and in due course the harvest was sold for £8. They bought a small piano from Albie Bolton's music shop in Hardy Street in Nelson, and had it shipped back to Meadowbank..

"It duly arrived at Awarua with a tutor as no one could play it," Laura recalled years afterwards. "But nothing daunted, she taught herself and in a short while we had music at our Sunday School meetings on Sunday mornings."

Above the piano there were strings of bird's eggs, part of another family ritual. The boys would go out and get a bird's egg on each birthday, and carefully prick the ends and blow the insides out. William would hang them on a string in the drawing room and that way each of the boys could mark their ages, an egg for each year.

On November 4, 1898 a meteor plunged towards the earth while Welby was walking home from the Winter's house, and he came back full of wonder and excitement, an excitement Adele and the rest of the family shared. A paragraph appeared in the *Nelson Evening Mail* reporting the meteor, and Adele wrote a letter to the editor describing it in detail.

"...As he walked he noticed the meteor appear in the sky, which was quite clear and starlight at the time. The meteor appeared quite red at first, but the colour became more pale as the meteor approached my son, and it reached within seventy yards of him - it being only some 20 or 30 feet above the ground - when it suddenly, and with the report as of a very large flame being extinguished, disappeared. The light it emitted was so powerful that my son felt for a moment or two that he must be blinded..."

Welby also felt the heat from the meteor, and when he had recovered his sight he ran the rest of the way home to Meadowbank, where he found his mother and sisters outside searching for the source of the strange noise that had interrupted their reading. They could find no trace of the meteor anywhere, and decided it must have exploded in a ball of fire in mid-air.

When Adele's letter appeared in the newspaper she carefully cut it out and kept it, and for months afterwards the whole family watched the sky whenever they were out after dark to see if such a strange phenomenon would recur.

The boys made good money ferrying people in and out to the steamer, and when Ethel Campbell left the inlet in September 1898 Adele spent £4 buying her hand-turned sewing machine, which Welby and Willie carefully brought down from Awapoto a few days later. It was the first machine Adele had ever owned and she and the girls were thrilled at how easy the mending now became. They still stitched hems and laces by hand, of course, and there were always buttons to sew on, buttonholes to make and socks to be darned, but now the hard work was gone from remaking hand-me-downs and there was much discussion about new styles and fabrics.

The family's two sailing boats, *Nipper* and *Mistral,* were painted and fettled ready for summer, Mrs Campbell's old stove was purchased and brought down to be installed at Meadowbank in place of the much older one Adele had cooked on for fifteen years. The final seal was put on their new spring mood when the school inspector came and passed everyone in the class that Bessie Winter had taught so well all year.

Adele and the boys determined to paint the house before Christmas, but Adele had worked herself too hard once again and the second coat of glossy white paint was hard work. William and Fred came home that December to find the house, boats and farm in much better shape than the mistress of them. Adele had been plagued with pain in her side since Evered's birth, and some days it was bad enough for her to record it tersely in her diary although she seldom complained to anyone in the family. An earthquake had rocked the bay a few weeks before, while the men were still away at Boulder Lake, and she felt lonely and isolated as she put on a brave face for the children and struggled to repair the dam which had been damaged.

She was worried about the isolated life her younger children were leading. Annie's death had unsettled her more than she had ever admitted to herself, and although the Winters were good people Awaroa had never felt the same since Harry had gone. The Breretons' tragedy had reminded her just how dangerous their lifestyle was, and the earthquake and even the meteor seemed like portents of doom. Money was still scarce in the household and she hated the thought of her daughters growing up without nice clothes or shoes or men to court them. She felt trapped and lonely and craved the social life of the town.

Most of all she felt that her marriage was breaking down, and as she and William grew older the gulf between them widened. She ran the household while he worked away, or ran the farm and built his boats with Fred and Welby, and they seemed to have little to talk about in the evenings any more. In two years he would be 56, the age at which his father had died, and the thought of living out her life as an impoverished and lonely widow at Meadowbank filled Adele with horror.

Her husband was with her one day at the wharf when two surveyors, members of a party camped in Winters' orchard, rowed past and doffed their hats. Adele knew she looked at her best, her black hair freshly washed and glossy in the sunlight and her feet bare as she unloaded a basket of smoked fish she'd been given by Jim Perrott over at Silver Point. William was further up the beach, his back to the men and Adele flushed when she heard their conversation carry clearly across the water.

"Now there's a lovely lady, Joe," the man in the bow commented with a low whistle. "I wonder who she is."

"I've seen the old man about," his companion replied. "I think he must be her father."

Adele's smile quickly faded and she stooped to the boat, horrified, but a glance at William reassured her he had not heard. She relived the snatch of conversation later, remembering particularly the handsome dark-haired young man who had paid her the compliment, and feeling more wretched than ever. Was she to spend the rest of her life keeping house for her family in that isolated inlet, turning more grim and grey as each day passed?

Awaroa was busier towards the turn of the century. They all went to Goat Bay for a New Year picnic to celebrate the start of 1899, and there was a bonfire and fireworks at night. There was a growing settlement up at Awapoto, and more and more boats headed up and down the inlet. The tide had turned since she had first come to Awaroa, Adele realised. Now she was lonely at Meadowbank while the main population was up at the head of the inlet.

Sunday services were still held at the little schoolhouse, the families dressed in their best. The Campbell girls and others from Little River came down if the tides were right. Bessie Winter resigned from her job at Awaroa School to take up a new teaching position on the West Coast, and Jessie went off to Nelson to buy new clothes. When school started again in 1899 it was Jessie who stood at the teacher's desk to hear a much reduced class of six pupils chorus "Good morning Miss Winter." She was to be the last teacher in the little school house for many years.

TRANSIT at the Awaroa wharf. Built at Marahau by J J Ricketts, the 49-foot *Transit* was launched on 30 October 1885, the same day there was a total eclipse of the sun.

Courtesy Glasgow family

A picnic party from the *Madge* (J Glasgow skipper, F Washbourn first mate) at Awaroa in 1901. Awaroa School (left) and Meadowbank can be seen in the background.

Courtesy Glasgow family

She and Laura Cunliffe, who was back in Wellington, corresponded often and exchanged news of their families, and Welby Hadfield also kept in touch with Laura. Jessie Winter and her brother Will were frequent visitors to Meadowbank, where they enjoyed Adele's straight-talking company and conversation as much as she enjoyed theirs in spite of the age difference.

Now only Olive, Laura, Darcy and Roy Hadfield were left at school with the two younger Winter boys each day, while little Evered kept his mother company at home. Adele's days were lonely again and she became more restless, feeling herself trapped at Awaroa while her husband and older children travelled further afield. Sawyers came back to the bay, and there were more settlers arriving. Survey parties came and went. Visitors came regularly and there was news of the wider world, talk of a war in South Africa.

Towards the autumn, made more restless than ever by her contact with the increasing numbers of strangers and itinerant workers passing through Awaroa, Adele made up her mind. She told William she wanted to move to Nelson. He could make better money building boats in Nelson than he could at Awaroa, she urged him, and they could find jobs for their sons and husbands for their daughters. Fred and Welby were old enough to stay and run Meadowbank between them until the family was resettled.

William was no match for his wife's arguments. He knew the boys could manage their farm just as well as he could. He also knew only too well that as his younger sons and daughters grew up they would have to leave home, and that he did not have the money to give them much of a start in life. Boatbuilding seemed more lucrative than farming, and he knew she was right in her suggestion that he would find more customers and cheaper materials at the port. He had good friends and good contacts there, and years of self-reliance had taught him skills he could put to better profit than farming.

"Would you not miss the sound of the sea?" he asked her. "What we have here is so peaceful, and the children have grown up happy and strong."

"But they have grown up, Will, and the eldest are no longer children. They deserve to go to dances and parties, without having to row or sail all day to get there and another day to get home again. And what of Evered's schooling? There are no other children his age and he will be left to learn his letters here at home when his brothers and sisters have gone."

For William there had always been a deep, quiet joy in walking through the orchard in the evening, examining a branchlet, a newly-set bud or a half-ripened plum and knowing it would grow to fullness in its allotted time. The changing seasons brought their own discoveries, each fitting to a larger pattern.

The songs of bellbirds or cicadas, the screeching cries of gulls in a winter sky and the busyness of oystercatchers after the tide had fallen were all part of the rich fabric of his life at Awaroa.

Adele had never really shared his closeness to the land. She'd worked it by his side, sharing the load and lending her strength and skill to tend the animals and the crops as well as she tended to the children, but she'd always craved social contacts much more than he had. Ironically, there'd been many times when he'd been away from home and longing to get back there, while for his wife the longing had been to leave the farm and go to town.

William had never understood, but he had always been in love with Adele and now that she had been his partner and helpmeet for so long he loved her more than ever. When he saw her old restlessness and anxiety returning he realised that after twenty years he still could not make her happy at Awaroa. Sadly, he let her persuade him to leave his beloved inlet.

He went ahead with young Will and Olive to keep house, and found work for a short time on the new Nelson railway wharf. Adele and the other younger children followed and they lived at a rented house at Stepneyville, in the valley behind the rowing sheds. When the wharf was finished William soon established a boatbuilding yard by the slipway opposite Russell Street.

William was not prepared to sell Meadowbank to buy a place in town, but Adele was determined not to go back to Awaroa. She liked the bustle of the port and decided to turn her housekeeping skills to use by opening a boarding house where they could all live and have an income. Although they still lived as man and wife, the strain between them widened when against William's wishes Adele took out a mortgage, bought a section of ground and planned an accommodation house. She talked her plans over with her Snow relatives and with her uncle Newth, who lived in Washington Valley, and reluctantly William agreed to build the house for her.

It was to be a new beginning for a new century. In late 1899 Adele Hadfield opened the doors of Haven House, just back from the corner of Russell Street and Haven Road, and prepared to welcome her first boarders.

CHAPTER FIVE : HAVEN HOUSE

1900

THAT FIRST YEAR of the new century was an unsettling time for every one of the Hadfields. Adele worked from dawn until late at night, washing, cooking and cleaning her boarding house, learning to buy food from the shops instead of taking it from the garden, watching over the children and anxiously counting her money as each boarder paid by the week. She had a big household to cook and care for but she also had modern facilities for the first time in her life, a gas stove and gas lights and even gas fireplaces, costly to run but much cleaner and easier to manage than the huge stacks of firewood her Meadowbank home had devoured all year round.

She learned to be firm with the men, remembering how her mother had coped with the goldminers her father brought home, and she forbade them to bring strong drink into her house. There were taverns along the road for that, she insisted, and if they went to the Albion or the Steamboat they should be sure they were quiet and mannerly enough to take their boots off at the porch when they came home again.

She kept her accounts for herself, determined to manage without asking William for help. The boys sent meat, eggs and fruit from Meadowbank when they could but without the rest of the family to help in the garden they were hard pressed to keep it up, and there was no time to grow vegetables at Haven House. Local fishermen and gardeners soon learned that if their produce was fresh and sound they'd get a fair price for it at Adele's kitchen door.

Her boarders were the labourers and itinerant seafarers around the port. Although the work was hard she thrived on it, enjoying the bustle and the lively talk around the table. Ships came and went, the shops were full of things from

England and the women talked of fashion. It was like the days of her childhood in Trafalgar Street, helping her grandparents at the Victoria Emporium, and she loved every minute of it. She was only just 40 and still an attractive woman. She laughed and joked with the men, who came to her table as much for her company as her cooking. Her father and brothers were still well-known in the district, and while she was Mrs Hadfield to the Awaroa community and the shipping folk from the port, she was equally one of the Snows of Nelson, hotelkeepers and business people.

The girls all helped with the housework, Ivy as a fulltime housemaid. She cleaned the rooms and made the beds, helped in the kitchen and did the laundry, and did her share of looking after Evered who turned three at the end of their first summer in Nelson. Olive, who was thirteen when they moved there, worked at Kirkpatricks jam factory for ten shillings a week. Laura May was only eleven and after a few weeks at Toi Toi Valley School she started the new year at Nelson Girls School.

Young Will's first job in Nelson was at Lukin's limeworks at the port, and it wasn't long before he had saved his wages enough to buy his first cycle from Moore's shop. Cycles were all the rage, and cyclists rode illegally along the asphalted footpath between the road and the railway lines outside Haven House until a cycle track was made for them. Will always enjoyed being out and about and he soon left the limeworks to work for the city council, riding his bicycle around the streets each evening to light up the gas lamps. When he came to each lamp post he leaned his bicycle against it, stood on the seat and lit the lamp, reversing the process in the early morning to turn them off. Later he worked at the auction rooms. His brother Darcy worked too, for Dr Barr who was the family's doctor. Darcy harnessed the horse, groomed and fed it, and accompanied the doctor around Nelson on his rounds, holding the horse outside each house while Dr Barr made his calls.

For young Roy, the port was a noisy and frightening place. He was only seven when he made his first trip to Nelson, sent on his own on the ketch *Pet*, owned by the Ricketts brothers. Old Captain Ted tried to comfort him but it seemed as if the lad was too frightened to breathe. He sat white faced and shivering on the deck, his brother's cast-off tweed jacket draping his skinny frame and hanging too long at the cuffs, gazing back at Abel Head as if he thought he'd never see it again.

The captain was a kindly man and when he saw tears trickle down the boy's cheeks he called to him and made him lie down in one of the crew's bunks with a warm rug around him. When the *Pet* docked and Roy saw his father and brother Will there on the dock to meet him he gulped and ran to them, forgetting his manners for a moment until his father reminded him to shake the captain's hand.

Roy stayed close to his father for most of that first visit, not really understanding what was going on around him and counting the days until he could go home, but there was even more upheaval to come. He returned to Meadowbank to find Adele surrounded by boxes and lists, and soon he found himself heading for Nelson once more, this time with Darcy and a cargo of familiar furniture in the ketch *Asa*. The unthinkable had happened. They had moved to town.

Roy went to school in Haven Road, where Mrs Scott was headmistress, but he had missed the end of year exams and spent two years in the first standard, where he said little and was too frightened to learn. The school and the town were busy, crowded places for the little boy used to the peace of Awaroa. He was nervous of the horses and wagons, intimidated by the rough men who frequented the waterfront and totally awed by the first contingents of troops marching to the port for their official send-off for South Africa.

The road from Nelson to the port was broad and busy, and on the seaward side a grassy strip divided it from the tramline. This was reclaimed land and a tidy seawall, built twenty years earlier, ran around the edge of the basin where coastal traders could anchor or tie up. William's boatyard was opposite the Russell Street intersection, across the road from Haven House and the Steamboat Tavern. It was in a good position, close to Franzen's Chandlery, and there was a slipway down into the water.

The Port was a busy place, with Burford's, Lukin's, Franzen's and Rickett's wharves each filled with trading scows or steamers, and more lying out in the harbour at anchor. The steamers *Wairoa* and *Lady Barkly* were both plying the coastal route to Waitapu and Collingwood, and Captain Scully was also operating a regular service in the little ketch *Lily*. The timber, flax milling and farming that was going on all around the coastline kept a number of smaller vessels busy. There was timber, coal, butter, wool and hides coming into the port all the time, and oats, flour, seed potatoes, kerosene and other household and farm supplies going out. Then there were the bigger ships, from Wellington, Lyttelton, Australia and even England.

Roy spent most of that first summer at his father's side, helping and watching as the businessmen of the town came to William with their projects. He was there the day Mr Moore from the cycle shop and Mr Healy from the shoe shop came to the boatyard, and that night he was bursting with the news.

"Father's to build a motor boat," he told Will and Ivy. "Imagine it. A boat that will be propelled along in the water without oars or sail. We could get right up to Awapoto and back in the same tide."

"I'd rather stay here and take the bus, thank you," Ivy said pertly. "At least now that we live here in town my feet stay dry."

Port Nelson at the turn of the century. Lukins' lime kiln can be seen opposite the shipping wharfs. Haven House is on the corner of Russell Street and William Hadfield's boatyard is across the road, with a pathway running between the road and the house. At the slipway are *Hera*, in the background, and the Huffams' boat *Modest Boy*.

Copy Collection, Nelson Provincial Museum

But Bill and Roy talked for hours about the new motorboat, the first in Nelson, and when the great day came that the hull was in the water and the motorcycle engine fitted into it was fired up, they made sure they were both around the yard, fetching and carrying and displaying their best manners until the men chuckled and took them for a ride around the harbour. From that day forward both were sure their futures would involve boats with engines.

William Hadfield stayed in Nelson through the turn of the century and the summer of 1900, leaving the lambing and calving to Fred and Welby but his thoughts turned more and more to Meadowbank and the inlet. He and Adele were distant, each involved with their own work, and the rift between them grew. He ate his breakfast with the other working men, and left the house early to spend his days at the boatyard. He became awkward with the children, who had long been used to his absence from the house and whose days were now full with new jobs, new schools and new experiences.

William tended a garden at Haven House but there was little room for more than a few shrubs and cuttings and the work didn't take him long. In the evenings there were always boarders sitting in the parlour or smoking on the verandah, and all too often they were much younger men who saw their landlady's husband as old and slightly odd for his old-fashioned courtesies and his country ways. Haven House was never home to William, and when it was time for his eldest son's 21st birthday he went home gladly to celebrate with him.

It was 14 October 1900, a calm Sunday night at Awaroa inlet, but anyone listening outside the Winters' farmhouse would have known at once a party was going on.

"Happy Birthday dear Fred, Happy Birthday to you..."

William Hadfield sang with the others, trying to make up for the absent members of his family. It felt strange to celebrate his eldest son's 21st birthday in another man's house, but Meadowbank was a lonely place now without women to warm it.

"How is the boarding house working out, Mr Hadfield?" his hostess asked. "It must be a lot of work for Mrs Hadfield and the girls. I feel so sorry they could not be here too. "

"No more than I," he said quietly. Fred wore a bright silk cravat from his brothers and sisters and a set of gold cuff links embossed with a gold oak leaf pattern that Adele and William had bought for him. The cuff links had been very expensive but Adele set her heart on them and William had given in. Secretly he had wanted to buy them for Fred as much as she had, even though he knew a farmer at Awaroa had little use for such ornaments. He was proud the boatyard was doing well enough to pay for them, and didn't mind doing without the new boots he and the boys sorely needed.

There was laughter from the group around the piano.

"I declare your son has no music in him at all, Mr Hadfield," Jessie Winter called over to him. "I begged him to join us in a song but he says he would sing so badly my mother would bid us all stop at once."

"I may not have a voice but I'm a good listener," Fred said hotly. "I wish you would sing for us again and not keep asking us to perform the impossible."

"How about a duet this time?" Welby suggested. "The one about the river is my favourite,"

"The one about the river?" Jessie giggled. "I think he means the Afton River, Laura, don't you?"

Their sweet voices rose over the piano, harmonising together as Jessie took the high notes and Laura the alto.

"Flow gently sweet Afton, among thy green braes..."

Their parents looked fondly across at them. There were Fred, Welby and Ivy Hadfield, Jessie, Christiana and the three Winter boys, Laura Cunliffe and her brothers.

"It's lovely to see them all together again," Mrs Winter said softly. "I've missed Ivy and the others, and of course I always enjoy Laura's visits."

"So does Welby, it seems," Mrs Cunliffe said meaningfully. "They write a good deal to each other you know, Mr Hadfield."

Joseph Winter caught William's eye and the two men rose to their feet.

"If you'll excuse us ladies, we might smoke a pipe on the verandah," Winters murmured and they made their escape.

Lilting voices followed them, faint and sweet in the night air. The song finished and was followed by a haunting lullaby. "Sleep little prince and be still..."

"...Soft are the sheep on the hill," Joseph Winter sang softly in the darkness. "Don't you miss the farm, William?"

"More than anything." He sighed. "The boatyard's busy enough, and I enjoy the work. Always did, you know that. But I miss the inlet, the moreporks and the bitterns booming down in the swamp."

"Mrs Hadfield's happy in Nelson?"

"Happy enough. She thrives on the bustle, and the girls seem to enjoy themselves well enough, although they work hard. I don't like to see Olive going off to work in the jam factory though. It's not what I would have wanted for her."

They were both silent with their own thoughts then, listening to the young people in the drawing room behind them.

"He's a good boy, young Fred," Joseph Winter said. "They both are. On Tuesday, when it was Fred's actual birthday I went down there to see him after milking, and your Welby had laid the table up properly and cooked a special dinner. There they were, just the two of them there in the parlour at Meadowbank with the best table linen out and roses in their buttonholes like gentlemen."

"Harry and I did that on our birthdays, when we were alone here," William said. "It was something to look forward to, you know, and we always made sure to cook a rolypoly pudding because that was our favourite."

He remembered back down through the years to other nights, when he and Harry had sat on boxes outside a rough tent and looked over this same starlit scene. What dreams they had dreamed then.

"It's good of you and Mrs Winter to put on a fuss for the boy," he said simply.

"It's not just for Fred, you know. Our Jessie's come of age too, and she and Laura put their heads together and planned this months ago. Jessie didn't want to celebrate her birthday in June but to wait and share it with Fred, and they made sure Laura would have a long visit and be here to wish both of them happy returns. That girl finds any excuse to persuade her mother to let her come down here from Wellington."

William sighed. "It's strange to think of all that's passed here, Joseph. A whole new century's beginning. Harry and I were only lads when we came, and here's young Fred and Welby, older than we were when we ran the farm together."

"Aye, and you've taught them well. Your land's in good hands until you come home again."

William looked out over the black water. There was no moon and the stars hung so low and heavy in the sky that it seemed they could fall. Out towards Silver Point a fish jumped, flashing silver phosphorescence. Over the scent of spring flowers was the raw, salty tang of the sea, and he filled his lungs with it thankfully.

"I'll be here for the shearing and haymaking, at any road," he said brusquely. "And now it's time we were all abed, or there'll be no work from any of us in the morning."

When he returned to Nelson, William finished off the work on hand at the boatyard and began turning down new jobs.

"I have to be back at the farm for the shearing," he told the men who offered him work. "I'll build your boats after the summer." As he wound down the boatyard he found his income dropping quickly and his decision was made almost by default. He went home with the problems of his marriage unresolved, knowing Adele had grown too far away from him to reach her.

Laura, Darcy and Roy came home to Meadowbank for their summer holidays, and the days passed quickly as they worked together to get the house and garden in order and get the fruit out to the market. It was the first Christmas the family had ever spent apart and William tried hard to make it festive for the boys and for Laura, who worked herself into exhaustion trying to bake the special treats they had always had. With the help of the Winter girls and her mother's careful training she did very well and it was a proud girl who served her first plum pudding at the Christmas table.

As William carved the leg of lamb he could not help remembering other years, when his wife had bustled back and forth with steaming dishes that smelled of butter and fresh mint. Now it was Welby who helped little Laura hand the plates, and the gravy lacked the richness of past Christmases. Not only did they miss Adele, but they were all conscious that Ivy, Will, Olive and Evered had stayed in Nelson with their mother, the older three because of work and Evered because he was still her baby and too young to be away from her. William was grateful he had invited Jim Perrott to share their table, otherwise he might have felt even more lonely with no wife and only five of his children home.

Back at Haven House there were plum puddings too, and every chair at the table was filled. Whether they had families of their own to go home to or not, every sailor longed to be in port for Christmas and Mrs Hadfield and her daughters were known to serve a good dinner. There were new potatoes, baby carrots and fresh peas and the honour of carving the turkey went to a boarder, Will Freeman.

William Knowles Freeman was a bus driver who came to board at Haven House late in 1900. He was twelve years younger than Adele, a tall, good-looking man with a smooth manner and a fund of stories. He had already met the Hadfields at Awaroa, where he had come with a survey party and camped on the Winters' farm. It had been he who made the remark that day at the wharf about the old man being her father, a mistake that had first hurt Adele, then confused and intrigued her. She had never let him know she had overheard him that day, but when he turned up again in her life she remembered him well. For his part he had long forgotten the incident but not the subject of it. Their attraction had been mutual, and it was no coincidence that he sought her out to be his landlady.

The South African war had been going on for more than a year and patriotic fervour was at its height that summer of 1901. There was a groundswell of prosperity and productivity, and a new optimism in the air. The city thrilled to the excitement of sending off more young troopers and there were subscription concerts and farewell parades. Ivy and Will went out dancing with their friends, and the port was lively with activity as the taverns spilled their customers out into the warm streets.

With her husband and younger children away and the older ones working Adele was restless and eager for company and she and Freeman would talk for hours into the long hot evenings. He made her feel young and alive again, and there was an energy and a recklessness about him she found exciting.

One night he told her he had enlisted in the army. Inevitably Adele was caught up in the emotion, and before long she found herself in Will Freeman's room and in his arms, swept away by a passion she had only dreamed about.

"You're a very beautiful woman," he whispered as she unloosed her jet black hair. "You deserve to be loved and adored and cherished."

"You're a wicked man," she teased him, but her heart as well as her body cried out for passion and abandonment, and she found herself responding to him in a way she had never imagined could happen.

William and the boys finished the haymaking early and he caught the steamer off Awaroa late one night, arriving at the port in the early hours of the morning. Too restless to stay on the boat that hot January night he walked the short distance up to Haven House before dawn and let himself in, eager to be with the family again.

But Adele was not in her room. The rest of the house was quiet and in darkness, the children all safely asleep, and reluctantly he faced up to the fact that his worst fears were finally realised. This was the confirmation he'd been dreading, and he sat in a chair by her window to wait for her, his heart heavy with sadness and loss.

The sky was streaked with grey when she came in, barefoot and dishevelled, her long hair loose and tousled around her head and her eyes still misty with lovemaking. Her robe was one he'd never seen before, sprigged with pink roses, and it clung to her body and made her look lovelier than ever.

He stood as she entered, as he always had, and she paled.

"William?"

"Did I frighten you, my dear?"

"How long have you been here?"

"Long enough. Who is he, Adele?"

"I'm sorry William," she said quietly. "That doesn't seem very adequate, does it?"

"It is I who should be sorry, for leaving you alone," he said, turning away to hide his anguish.

Adele stood very still, and when she spoke again her voice was soft. "I have tried so hard to be a good wife to you, you know that."

"I know."

"It wasn't his fault."

"Was it mine?"

They faced each other in the grey dawn light, finally separated by the gulf of their years. His beard was streaked with white, his face tanned and lined with years of work in the harsh Awaroa sunlight, and in his eyes for the first time Adele saw despair.

"I'm sorry it has happened this way, but you must have known sooner or later," she told him.

"Who is he?"

"No, this is between you and me," she said angrily. "I have betrayed your trust in me. I have given you grounds for divorce and I accept that."

"But I don't," he said tightly. "You are my wife and I won't shame you in public, not any more than you've shamed yourself and the children."

"The children don't know. At least I've not rubbed their noses in it, nor yours. I go out from my own room each morning."

"And am I supposed to be thankful for that?"

They glared at each other across the big bed, and William was suddenly aware of his own desire for Adele as she stood there flushed and lovely in her defiance. He passed a hand across his eyes and realised he was trembling.

"I'll leave you to dress. You'll have things to attend to. I'm sorry."

"So am I, William," she said softly, and tears glistened in her grey eyes. "I never meant to hurt you. I did my best, but in the end I could not stay."

He knew she was talking about the inlet as well as their marriage bed, and he left the room quickly, too upset to speak any further. He spent the day down at the boatyard, sorting out his business affairs and calming his soul among the familiar timbers, masts and rigging of trading vessels.

Will Freeman was not at breakfast that morning either, and Adele was pale and strained as she served porridge to her regular guests. By midday everyone knew that Mr Hadfield was at the port, and no one was surprised to learn that her favourite boarder had packed his bag and gone. For Adele it was a bittersweet parting, her relief at avoiding a scandal tinged with sadness at losing a love she had only just begun to enjoy. Freeman was more than ten years younger than she was, but their few stolen nights together had been more exciting than anything she could have imagined in all the lonely years at Awaroa.

She was not the kind of person to evade the issue, and while Freeman prepared for South Africa she prepared to face her future alone. She sent word to William that she wanted to talk to him, and asked for the sake of the children that he come back to Haven House as if nothing was amiss. It was early evening before he made his way from the wharf to the boarding house.

She was quiet and stern during dinner, bustling about the stove as she ladled stew for the people waiting at the long dining table. Ivy served the paying guests first and then her father, and it pained him to realise that she, like her mother, was avoiding his eye. The younger children were pleased to see him, and he talked to Roy and Laura and played with Evered until the boarders dispersed from the dining room and the girls were busy with the dishes.

William dreaded the interview to come, but Adele was resolute, and when the children were in bed and husband and wife were finally alone in the parlour with the door closed she squared her shoulders and met his eyes honestly.

"I'm very sorry for it, William, but I can no longer love you as my husband."

"For my part, I will always love you," he said gently. "You know that. I would still have you back at Meadowbank if you would come."

"I cannot," she said stiffly. "I have tried, but I cannot."

"What are we to do then?" he asked. "Are you asking me again to stay here, even now?"

She took a deep breath.

"I have given you grounds for divorce, William. You know I have been unfaithful to you."

William reached out and took her arms, looking down at her proud grey eyes. He could hardly trust himself to speak and his voice hardened.

"Adele, you are still my wife and I'm sorry indeed it has come to this. I'll not leave you alone and shamed. You must tell me the man's name."

"You have already found out, I don't doubt. He is Will Freeman and he has been a boarder here in my house."

"And where is this Freeman now?"

"Enlisted and bound for South Africa. He left this morning." She tossed her head. "He has that much honour at least, and so do I."

"He is going to fight the Boers?" William was horrified. "But Adele, he may not ever return."

"Then I shall support myself. Thanks to your kindness I have Haven House and the mortgage is in my name. I shall manage."

"I won't drag your name and mine through the mud of the divorce court," he warned her.

"Then what shall we tell people?"

"Only that we are living apart, and they know that already. The rest is between us."

"I want the children back here, William. They are settled at school, and you cannot care for them at Awaroa. They need their mother now more than ever."

"And what of this Freeman who has run off to war and left you to fight your battles for yourself. Will you swear to look after the children if he returns?"

"Of course I will. I've always been a good mother to them."

At last tears glinted in her grey eyes. "You don't understand, do you Will? You have always been so good to me and I've tried to be an honest woman and a faithful wife, but I can no longer call you husband when there is no love left in my heart for you. It's not your fault and it's not Will Freeman's fault, but whether he returns or not, our marriage is over.

"I was only eighteen when we married. I was just a girl, the same age as Ivy, and as Welby's Laura. I was too young to know. Next month I'll be 41 years old, and I feel I've only just begun living. I can't go back, can't you see that? Not to you, not to Awaroa, not to that old-fashioned life you love so much. Not now that I've found out what love can be really like."

She stood proud and defiant, a flushed and lovely woman. She'd taken her apron off when they entered the parlour and William saw with compassion that her dark blue dress was patched and worn, her hands were roughened with hot water. She no longer wore her wedding ring and that more than anything convinced him she meant what she was saying.

It was the last time he was ever alone with Adele. He left her house that night, and did not return until he'd sorted his business affairs at the boatyard and in the town. He left her what money he could, and when the *Lady Barkly* sailed for Awaroa again William was aboard her.

Will Freeman was still in camp in Wellington, training in mounted drill on the hard sands of Miramar and Lyell Bay. He left Nelson in haste and did not write to Adele, nor did he hear from her for some time. He had been captivated by Adele, but had no idea what would happen between her and her husband, and did not know whether or not he would ever return to Nelson and the little boarding house by the port. His one thought was to get away from an uncomfortable situation as soon as he possibly could, and he had done so.

He sailed as Trooper 3489 with company 18 of the Sixth Contingent on the ship Cornwall, leaving from Wellington on 26 January for Auckland and then South Africa. There were 560 men, 18 officers and 580 horses on Cornwall, the men in their different companies in hot and smelly accommodation below the stables. During the six week voyage the horses took a battering in heavy seas, and pickets were doubled to try to keep them on their feet. Many of the horses died and were hoisted up by cranc and dumped overboard.

The men had little to do except care for the animals, relax and learn their new battle cry, "Tutahi Hingatahi, Tutahi Hingatahi, Purutia te mana o te Kingi, Ake ake kia toa, ake ake kia kaha. Together we stand, together we fall and thus uphold the authority of the King. For ever and ever be brave, for ever and ever be strong."

During that hard, hot tour of duty the New Zealanders were to hear another battle cry, the constant call of "Hands up, Khaki!" from the Boer they were fighting.

Trooper Freeman sent a postcard to Adele from Table Bay when the ship first landed. By the time she got it she had already realised she was pregnant with his child and she knew William would have no option but to divorce her. She was still to discover that her lover had been using a false name and was already married.

By 1901 the tramlines which ran past their door between Nelson and the Port had outlived their usefulness. The horse-drawn City Bus was quaint and outdated and palace cars became the new mode of transport. They were a new sort of horse-drawn vehicle, open to the weather and with rows of seats aligned crossways. Most importantly, they didn't need to run on rails and so they were faster and more versatile than the bus.

The tramline was closed down, the rails alongside Haven Road pulled up and the horses and trams sold at auction. Fred came over to Nelson for the sale and stayed at Haven House, bringing fruit and vegetables from the farm for his mother. It was the first time they had seen each other for some time and was to be one of the last, although neither knew it.

Adele wore a concealing jacket over her skirt and brushed her hair with special care for her eldest son. Calmly she took him into the parlour the next morning after breakfast, and told him of the divorce, although not the reason for it. As she had guessed, William was too much of a gentleman to have told anyone about her adultery and the younger children still believed she was staying in Nelson to help them get their schooling and find jobs.

Adele kissed her son and told him to take good care of his father and his brothers and sisters, for her sake.

"And please give my regards to Mrs Winter and Mr Winter, and to the family. I suppose that Jessie will be leaving Awaroa soon, perhaps to live in Wellington?"

"She's needed at home still," he started, and stopped in confusion when he saw the twinkle in his mother's eye.

"And not just by her own brothers and sister, I'll warrant?" She stood eye to eye with him and her hand tightened on his arm.

"Oh Fred, how like your father you are. I warn you, if you want Jessie Winter you must learn to woo her and talk about more than timber and lambs and hay.".

"I cannot speak to her yet, mother," he said stiffly. "I have no farm of my own and will not have for many years."

"Then speak to her of love, not land." Adele said softly. "She's a good girl and she'll stand beside you through all the hardships in the world if you can only learn to listen to her dreams and share your own. Jessie's been brought up a lady and she will need your courting and your companionship long after the wedding day is over, Fred. If you win her you must never forget that."

Then she laughed, breaking the mood. "Oh how I wish I was 21 again, son. Don't grow old and serious too soon. And now you must go or you'll miss out on the big auction, and Roy will never forgive you for breaking your promise to take him with you."

Fred had arrived in the *Tauranga* with a load of sheep and pigs for the stock sales. He bought two mares, heavy, solid work horses still young enough to breed from, and he paid £5 for one and £15 for the other. He didn't own a saddle so he set off bareback for the long journey home, riding Dolly, the older of the two mares and leading the other. He couldn't afford to ship the horses from Nelson but he expected he would find some way to get them home. He had more than once walked home around the coastline from Motueka but there was no road, only a series of rough tracks through the bush between the beaches and river mouths.

When he got to Riwaka, he arranged grazing for the second mare and kept on riding around the coast, to Kaiteriteri and then to Marahau. The next day he arrived at the top of the headland above Winters' farm, his clothes sweatstained and salty and his boots waterlogged. The mare had carried him right up the coastline, across the sandy beaches and over the headlands, man and horse swimming around the rocky points when the tide was too high or they could find no other track. It was the first time anyone had ever ridden up the coast from Marahau to Awaroa, and a fortnight later he went back down and brought the other mare home.

Young Will was also proving his independence. He was a handsome boy, bolder than his brothers and there had been a succession of young women to attract his attention in Nelson. He signed on as a deckhand on a coastal scow, and sent his mother a postcard from Westport to say he'd arrived safely. Adele laughed when she looked at the card, a picture of a courting couple gazing flirtatiously at each other on a little bridge under a weeping willow tree. The caption read, "I've got a very steady job."

By July Adele's condition was obvious and so was Will Freeman's deception. His wife died at her home at St Kilda in Dunedin, and the police looking for her next of kin tracked him down to the Haven House boarding house. His real name was William Freeman Knowles, and with the news of his wife's death Adele decided to tell him about her pregnancy.

Reluctantly William Hadfield began divorce proceedings and Adele told the children she and Knowles would marry when he returned from the war.

To the younger ones the news meant little as it did not affect their daily lives. They'd quite liked William Knowles, who told them lively stories and taught them games and tricks, and they were accustomed to their father's long absences and rather distant presence. Ivy and Olive, however, felt their mother's shame deeply and were embarrassed and resentful about the pregnancy even though few people outside the family knew the child was not a Hadfield. Ivy shouldered as much of her mother's workload as she could, and quietly took over the shopping so Adele would not have to be seen in town.

On 8 October 1901 Dr Barr was called to Haven House, where Adele gave birth to a healthy son. She called him Reginald Knowles.

It was a hard time for Adele and the children, and the boarding house did not do very well. Nelson was prospering, looking forward to celebrating 60 years of settlement, but the construction work around the port was finished, the labourers moving away from town to work on the railways, and few men wanted to board in a house with small children and a baby.

Ivy was nearly twenty years old now and a hard-working and capable young woman. With her parents' separation she was ready to make her own way in the world. A man called William Roberts drove one of the palace cars and Ivy began to wear her best dress when she went to the shops, and to save her pennies for a ride home again. He always saved her a seat at the front, and before long they were courting.

Prince George came to New Zealand on a royal tour, soon before he became King of England, and once more flags were waved, bands played and the soldiers paraded in the streets. Roy and Laura along with all the other Nelson school children had a holiday and a bronze medal. At the end of that year Laura left school and started work with her sister at Kirkpatricks jam factory.

That Christmas of 1901 was one of the loneliest Adele had ever faced. The family was divided for the second Christmas in a row, but this time there was not as much food on the table, and very little laughter. William, Fred and Welby were at home at Meadowbank where they had no women to cook for them. Adele supposed that the Winters would invite her boys to their table, and she knew they would be glad to go.

There was very little produce sent from Awaroa that year, and she and Ivy did their best to spread a Christmas table at Haven House for their boarders. The family took smaller portions than their few paying guests, and there were only a few farthings in the plum pudding instead of threepenny pieces.

Will, Olive, Laura and Darcy all did their best, providing little gifts for Roy and Evered and for their mother who was still tired from feeding her baby.

Kirkpatricks' jam factory, where both Olive and Laura Hadfield worked
F N Jones Collection, Nelson Provincial Museum

For her own part she had sat up late mending and stitching so each of the girls could have a fresh lace collar or a new ribbon bow to wear to church at least, for there were no new hats or dresses that year.

"Not much of a Christmas for you," she said softly when she put Evered to bed that night. "I'll make it up to you on your birthday. You'll be five very soon, and I'm thinking of starting you at school early. Would you like that?"

"I'd like a hoop," he said wistfully. "A hoop, and a stick to bowl it with."

"And you shall have one," she promised.

When his birthday came early in March Evered got his hoop, bought with money Adele had saved penny by penny from her shopping trips, but it was nearly his undoing.

"Mama, come quick," Roy screamed a few days later, and she wrapped Reg in a shawl and ran out into the street, her heart filled with dread.

"What's happened?"

"Evie's drowned. He fell off the wharf and into the sea."

She flew down the road towards Franzen's wharf, where the scows and coastal traders tied up and where the children had been playing, but before she got half way she was met by a horse and dray with Evered on the back.

"He's alive, Missus," a gruff voice said and her heart lurched as she saw the little boy's sodden figure. Gus Mitchell, the skipper of the *Transit,* was on the dray too, and he was also dripping wet, but after he had carried the boy inside for her he disappeared. Dr Barr was sent for and Haven House was in an uproar as kettles were boiled, dry towels and blankets fetched and anxious questions asked. It wasn't until Evered was tucked safely into bed, warm and dry and out of danger, that Adele heard the full story.

Evered had been bowling his hoop along Franzen's wharf when a gust of wind had caught it and blown it over the edge. The little boy had rushed to catch it and lost his footing, falling down onto the railing of the *Transit* which was tied up at the wharf, and then into the sea. Luckily Gus Mitchell had seen the accident, dived in and pulled the unconscious boy out of the water. Evered had a mild concussion and a fright, nothing more serious.

Adele sat by her son until he fell asleep, then she took off her apron and smoothed her hair and walked down to the port. It was a place she'd avoided since the scandal, but she swallowed her pride and stood on the wharf above *Transit*'s deck until Gus Mitchell joined her.

"Thank you for saving my son," she said simply, and she held out her hand. He hesitated for a moment, and then shook it warmly. In spite of everything the gossips said about her, she was still Mrs Hadfield, and a woman of dignity.

In mid-May 1902 the 6th Contingent arrived back in New Zealand and was disbanded, their tour of duty over. Trooper Knowles had been in Transvaal, Orange Free State, and Cape Colony and he was awarded the Imperial South African War Medal with three clasps for the three battle zones. When he got back to Nelson he appeared before a medical board, claiming illness and disability as a result of his service in South Africa, and he was given a small pension.

He moved back in to Haven House where he found Adele and her family in a sorry state, the boarding house a failure. Adele was struggling to care for two children at school and an eight-month-old baby, and they were surviving on the wages of the two older girls and what little William could send for the care of the younger ones. She was behind in her mortgage payments and nearly destitute. Knowles had no money either, and after a few weeks they both realised the situation was hopeless. On 2 July 1902 her name was called in the Nelson District Court and she was declared bankrupt.

Haven House was sold up and Darcy went back to live with his father and older brothers at Awaroa. Ivy went into service as a housemaid and Adele and the younger children moved up into Washington Valley where they lived in a rented house.

Roy went to Central School then, and remembered being very poor.

"I can well remember my only suit of clothes being worn bare and holes in the behind of the pants, asking Mum if I could not have some new ones and she said she had no money but she would ask Olive and Laura who were working at Kirkpatricks at the time if they could let me have fifteen shillings between them to buy a suit. So Olive gave me one week's pay, ten shillings, and Laura gave me one week of five shillings for which I was very grateful."

Adele and Knowles moved on with the youngest four children to Tadmor, where he got work on the Nelson to Glenhope railway line. Roy went to yet another school while Laura worked in the hop gardens. Olive, who had never liked William Knowles and had trouble accepting her mother's actions, went home to Awaroa.

Ivy had been walking out with William Roberts, the palace car driver she'd met while she was at Haven House, and in January 1903 when she turned 20 they were married. He owned the bus in partnership with a man called Edmondsen, but after their marriage he sold his shares and bought a horse-drawn cab.

Roberts was a diabetic whose frequent bouts of illness stopped him from working very hard. The couple settled in a small house with a few acres of land, and Ivy soon found herself having to give up her own job because she was expecting a child. She did her best to keep the house going and grew a garden, but they were very poor and once again produce from Meadowbank found its way over to Nelson.

Adele's divorce came through and on 12 March 1903 she and William Knowles were married at Motupiko, their witnesses the local butcher and another labourer.

Soon afterwards they moved to Palmerston North to live, taking only little Evered Hadfield, who had just turned six, and Reginald Knowles who was eighteen months old. Laura and Roy, aged fifteen and eleven, were left behind staying with the Wilkinson family and working in the hop gardens until their father arrived to take them home to Meadowbank.

CHAPTER SIX : THE *VENTURE*

1901

BACK AT MEADOWBANK the Hadfield men worked harder than ever. William went back up to the Quartz Ranges at the head of the Aorere valley to work at the sluicing face for Charles Fell, the Nelson lawyer who was left owning the failing project. Fred, Welby and later Bill and Darcy stayed at home to run the farm, and when their sister Olive came home from Nelson she kept house for them all.

The Cunliffes had left the farm at Awaroa and moved back to Wellington, and now the Cracknell boys arrived. They were cousins of the Winters, fresh from England. There were quite a few young people around the inlet in their teens and early twenties, and the Campbell, Sigley, Winter and Hadfield girls were delighted to meet four new young men. They teased them unmercifully.

Lesley, Sydney, Harry and Arthur had been clerks in London and they were used to chatting with girls on city trams and omnibuses, not in such a wild setting as Awaroa. They struggled to keep up and there were gales of laughter from the others as they tore their pants climbing fences, fell off the horses and drenched themselves learning to handle the boats. Once Lesley got lost in the bush on a pighunting expedition and wasn't found until the next day. The search party discovered him on the bank of a stream he'd followed uphill, not realising that it would lead him to the inlet if he'd gone the other way or that if he fired his rifle the sound would guide his rescuers to him.

Mrs Cracknell and the two younger boys established their home in Nelson but Lesley and Sydney stayed at Awaroa, building a house near the Winters, and tried their hand at farming. Like the Cunliffes and the Winters they were well read and educated people and contributed to musical gatherings and

139

conversations. Lesley Cracknell and Welby Hadfield were both enthusiastic photographers and Lesley took indoor photographs of his living room with a magnesium flash. Les worked alongside Fred Hadfield, bushfelling and fencing for Mrs Campbell, Mr Gillstrom and the other settlers in the inlet.

Discipline was strict at Meadowbank, even though the older children were now grown adults, and William expected them all to work just as hard and as conscientiously as he did. When he was away he sent home instructions for the running of the farm, and once when Fred protested that moving the sheep across the inlet to graze on Cave Hill was physically difficult, the mail brought a terse reply. The sheep were to be moved, even if they had to be rowed across one at a time in the dinghy.

The cave at the bottom of Cave Hill was an ideal holding pen at shearing time, although the sand got into the fleeces and blunted the shears. It was also a source of wonderment to the children, and a good shelter in a storm. The floor was higher or lower at different times over the years and the marks of ancient campfires could still be seen at different levels up and down the walls. The natural slope of the cave roof provided a good draft for smoke to escape.

One night when William was away at the goldfields Fred met the steamer off Awaroa as usual to get the mail and supplies. The captain handed him a letter for his father, and Fred realised it was from Adele and should be delivered with some urgency.

His journey that night became a legend in the district. He took the supplies and mail back to Meadowbank and set off out to sea again in the heavy 17-foot dinghy they used as a workboat. He rowed around to Mutton Cove and called on the Mackays to borrow a sail, but there wasn't enough wind and he had to row all the way to Collingwood which took him all night. The captain of the *Wairoa* couldn't believe his eyes when he went out on deck early the next morning and saw Fred, whom he'd last seen at Awaroa the previous night, rowing steadily past the wharf and up the river. Fred rowed on up the river and when it became too shallow, he tied his boat up and walked on up through Mackays Pass and past Bainham to where his father was working at the sluicing face not far below Boulder Lake.

After Fred had delivered the letter and stopped for a meal and a talk with his father he set off for home again. This time the wind was with him and he managed to set the sail and enjoy the trip home. The captain of the *Wairoa* said later the sight of Fred's little dinghy ahead of him on the moonlit water, sails filled with a steady breeze and the lone man sitting upright in the stern with his hand on the tiller, was an unforgettable sight. Fred arrived at Mutton Cove very early the next morning, went ashore and left the sail neatly folded back on the verandah where it belonged, and that's how the Mackays knew he had come safely home. The whole round trip took him a day and two nights.

Not every sea voyage was so uneventful. In 1901 the cutter *Planet,* with Captain Jack Johnstone in charge, got into trouble off Awaroa, William, Fred and Will Winter rowed out over the bar to guide her in and she sheltered in the inlet for some time while repairs were carried out. On board *Planet* was Hugh Oliver, a young American who was to have a significant influence in the life of the Hadfields.

Hugh was taken home to Winters' house, where he quickly made himself popular with everyone, and by the time *Planet* sailed again he had formed a particularly close bond with Christiana Winter. He had been working on the scows trading between Nelson, Collingwood and Puponga, where the coal mines were just opening up, and long after he had sailed for home he kept writing to the friends he had made at Awaroa.

Fred was across at Awaiti again in 1901, fencing for Mrs Campbell. He felled logs and sold fenceposts, and then he got a contract with the Collingwood County Council to form the first road from Wainui to Awaroa. It was a benched track, including part of a rough horse track from Totaranui which came out just behind Dick Hancock's house at Wainui.

Welby and Darcy worked on the road contract and Fred paid them wages. They were camped in a tent in the hills behind Wainui, and each night after dinner they would talk about the next day's work.

"We'll be back down to rock again soon," Welby said cheerfully. "Time for some more fireworks."

"Fred said not to use the gunpowder unless we had to," his brother reminded him. "I think there's hardly any left."

"Enough though, if we set the charges carefully. And it hasn't rained for a week so the ground will be dry enough."

"We'd best look in the tin when it's daylight," Darcy said. "We might have to tell Fred on Sunday to send for some more."

Welby loved setting the explosives and blasting rock from their path, and as they sat over their last billy of tea he couldn't resist getting the tin from his kitbag where he kept it well wrapped up away from the damp night air. As Darcy cleared a space on their tiny bench at the doorway of the tent he opened the tin and shook the contents slightly to assess their weight.

"You're right, it's lower than I thought. Light a match and pass it to me."

"Careful," Darcy breathed as he struck the wax match well away from the tin of black powder.

Welby took the match carefully and held it well above the old tea tin, his face close as he peered down at the contents. Then the flaming match head fell off the stick in his hand and the world disintegrated around him.

Darcy screamed as he saw his brother's head disappear in a huge orange fireball. For a second the flames seemed to fill the whole tent, lighting the night and framing the scene in stark black shadows. Then there was a dull bang and Welby threw himself at his brother, knocking him back into the ferns as their whole camp erupted in fire.

It was all over in a few moments, the flames dying as quickly as they had flared up. Both men were in agony, arms and hands flayed raw and burning with pain. Darcy groped blindly for the water bucket, sobbing with relief when he found it still upright and plunged his hands into it, gasping with the pain.

"Welby," he screamed. "Welby? Are you all right? Can you see?"

Water was the first priority, water to plunge their blistered hands and arms into while they could still bear it. Sobbing, they found their way to the little stream behind the remains of their camp and rolled onto the grass edge, splashing their clothes and their faces in the ice cold water.

Neither could bear to light a match, even if they could find one. Shivering with shock and pain, lungs seared with the harsh smoke of the explosion, they stumbled to their feet and tried to work out what to do. The nearest homestead was the Pratt's house at Totaranui. Fortunately both had their boots still on, so as the moon rose and the night air chilled their wet clothes they set off to find help. Every step was agony and as the branches and ferns of the bush scratched against their damaged arms both men sobbed with pain. They stumbled into the porch at Totaranui more dead than alive, ghastly figures that frightened the two young lads left alone at the homestead while their parents were away.

The lads did what they could, cutting burned clothing clear of the wounds, helping the injured men to lie down on soft linens and easing water between their scorched lips. But there was no one else in the bay and no steamer due for two days, and by dawn there was nothing to do but help Welby and Darcy on with their boots again for the long walk home to Awaroa.

Welby got the full force of the explosion in his face, and although his eyes were all right his ears and face were badly burnt, his hair, eyelashes and brows singed close to his head. Both had badly burnt hands and arms, Welby's flesh raw to the elbows. When they finally made it to Meadowbank they collapsed, too ill to be moved again. The doctor in Nelson was contacted and instructions were sent by steamer. Olive took over the nursing and changed the dressings, an ordeal which took several hours each day. Welby was the most badly injured but Darcy elected to stay with him rather than going out on the steamer. It was a long while before either of them could use their hands again.

When William was away Fred was the man of the house, and he acted more like a stern father than a brother to the younger Hadfields, ordering their tasks each day and handing out beatings for misbehaviour. Everyone worked to keep food on the table, and as much as possible came from the land. Fish was plentiful, and as always fishing was one of the regular chores.

The catch was often recorded in Fred's diaries, along with sheep tallies and other farm records. One day the men dragged a net in the deep hole in the channel and got 45 moki, another day they hauled 143 big schnapper from a set net in the harbour. Their best haul was 215 fish, and there were days when they had hapuka, herrings and even crayfish. Fish were always shared around the inlet, and what couldn't be eaten fresh, smoked or fed to the pigs would end up as valuable garden fertiliser.

The old sow Queenie finally died, but the boys managed to catch another wild pig, a half-grown boar, and bring him home to fatten. They put him in a pen and he seemed to settle down quite well, but one morning when they went out to feed him he was gone. There was no hole in the sty big enough to let him through, but they found a few hairs on top of the fence and realised he had jumped out and escaped.

At the end of the week Fred sent Laura, Darcy and Roy off to the other side of the harbour to find the missing pig and fetch it back They had no guns, but took the dogs with them.

"Well, we weren't too keen but it was something to do." Laura explained to her daughters years later. "I kept to the ridges but the boys went down in the gullies. After a long afternoon's hunt I heard the dogs barking and went down the hill a short way and found them with the pig bailed up with his head between two rocks in a small creek bed.

"We told the dogs to hold, and one of my brothers tied the rope that he had brought round the pig's two back legs and pulled. Out in the open he rushed like a mad thing; ready to rip anyone to pieces who was in the way, but the rope took care of that and after a while we had him tied up ready to carry him home, but we couldn't as he was too heavy."

After a while the hot, tired trio heard Fred calling from the dinghy and to their relief he climbed up and carried the pig to the boat. It had been a long afternoon tramp but now the tide was in far enough to row them all home across the inlet. The pig never got out again, and a few months later they killed him and salted down the meat.

Sawmilling had begun in earnest. William and Fred encouraged the industry, giving the men who established the mills house room and supplies and selling them cheap timber. A consortium of men set up their own company, Thomson, Hunter and Co, and leased William's land at Awapoto to mill the timber off it. Maurice Hunter, Alexander Thomson, Magnus Manson, George Sigley and Charles Hockey were the principals, and with their families there was soon a sizeable population up at Awapoto. On July 2, 1903 the scow *Oban* brought the sawmill in to the bay, and the *Wairoa* towed the sawmillers' punt from Motupipi. Soon there were bullock teams working deep in the bush dragging the timber out, and bush that had been cut through forty years earlier was cut again, the old tracks re-opened and new stands of rimu and birch found. Fred sold 3634 feet of white pine at six shillings and sixpence per hundred feet, and another 1339 feet of rimu.

He also supplied the sawmillers with meat twice a week and helped build the shop and school, in the paddock in front of Campbells house, and a wharf near the mouth of the river. When the Campbells left Awaroa for Nelson the Mackays bought their house, William and Adele Hadfield's original home. Soon there was also a post office at Awaiti, formerly Awapoto and now more commonly called by the English translation, Little River.

The population of Awaroa was at a new height with the sawmill at Little River and sawyers at Waiharakeke, and the Hadfields made the most of it. Fred and Roy butchered meat for sale and William grew vegetables and raised poultry. Butter, eggs, fruit and vegetables were shipped out of Awaroa and there was also a growing demand for firewood and fenceposts. The *Transit* began to come in and out of the inlet regularly to load timber. When Laura, now fifteen years old, came home from Nelson with Roy she took over the housekeeping and Olive went up to Little River to work with Mrs Campbell as a dressmaker. Later she went to Scotts at Totaranui, earning wages to contribute to the household. Young Roy worked around the house and garden and helped where he could.

At Little River there were Sunday services held regularly at the little schoolhouse and parties and dances at MacKay's house. Down at the mouth of the inlet there were enough men to field a cricket team, and that summer there were lively games, picnics and parties to break the monotony of the shearing, dipping and haymaking work that went on through the hot dry days.

When Roy got back to Awaroa after his mother remarried he was too young to leave school, but he found further attendance impossible. After the Hadfields had moved away in 1898 the little Awaroa school had been closed, and the new families were settled around the sawmill, up at the head of the inlet near William's original home at Awapoto. The new school that was built up there was too far for Roy with the tides against him at least one way each day, so he gave up and went to work on the farm, butchering the meat and tending the garden and the animals.

William was kept busy building boats, and everyone pitched in to help when timber for knees and ribs needed to be found and hauled out of the bush. He still worked away from home for quite long periods to keep cash coming in for essentials like copper nails.

There was a bigger project under way too. The Hadfields started work on their own trading scow, to be called the *Venture*, in the little tidal creek between Meadowbank and the Winters' farm. Roy spent his twelfth birthday deep in the bush helping the men get wood out for the scow.

Her timbers included kahikatea, rata and beech from Totaranui and Awaroa. The bends and knees were rata roots, the deck beams squared off from birch logs and all the masts and spars came from white pine cut out of the swamp at Little River and man-handled back to the other end of the inlet. One huge piece of rimu was salvaged from a tree that Harry Hadfield had cut down years before. Much of it had rotted, leaving a piece of heart rimu about fourteen inches by ten inches and about 50ft long that was to become her keel. The project took over two years. Money was a problem, and work on the Venture was held up for long periods while the men worked on other projects. After the hull had been built they needed rigging and deck gear so they began to look around the district to find what might be available.

The Hadfields built a number of small boats, including a double-ended dinghy that was used around Awaroa and Totaranui for many years and later used on Lake Rotoiti. The boys were all strong rowers and they travelled long distance. When there was a breeze from the land they would sometimes row or sail to Nelson and back again. There was still no land access to Awaroa, but all the settlers were well used to travelling up and down the coastline, and journeys to Collingwood or Riwaka were not uncommon.

There were plenty of visitors in and out of Awaroa too, seafaring men who would seek out William's company and yarn with him for hours around the dining table at Meadowbank. The crew of the *Asa* were favourites and when they acquired a phonograph on board William used to enjoy joining them for the evening to smoke his pipe and listen to the music.

As well as the working scows and trading vessels there were yachts like *Oyster,* belonging to the Glasgow family, who would come into the bay for cherries, milk and eggs. The Hadfields and Winters were always ready with their hospitality but if half a crown was proffered in payment for fresh produce it was seldom refused.

In January 1904 the notoriously unstable scow *Oban* capsized off Torrent Bay and was seen drifting slowly past Awaroa upside down. There was consternation and the men put out in their boats to see what had happened, but fortunately her crew was safe and unharmed. They were so familiar with the vessel's instability and the accident had happened so slowly that they were able to walk over the side and around the hull as she went over. For years afterwards they boasted that they hadn't even got their feet wet.

A few weeks later Fred took Laura and Darcy with him and they headed off to the Takaka Show in the eighteen-foot workboat they all called the *Old Tub*. It was one of those glorious summer days, with just enough wind to take them safely around Separation Point and into Waitapu before mid-day and the three of them had a wonderful afternoon and evening. For Fred and Darcy the interest was in the sheep and cattle on exhibition, the farm equipment and the woodchops, but Laura wandered happily around the grounds with her eyes on what the other women were wearing. She had a flair for design and she was already a competent dressmaker. The A&P show was a chance to show off new hats, stylish buttoned boots and extravagant sleeves. While there were still a few old-fashioned bonnets in evidence, many of the women were wearing large-brimmed boaters dressed with ribbons, and their skirts were cleverly cut to flare out from their belted waists.

They went to the dance that night, and although Laura had no shortage of willing partners she was more interested in the swirl of skirts around her than the conversations of the young men she met. The next morning she sat dreamily in the bow of the *Old Tub* while Darcy and Fred took turns to row along the golden coastline, cursing the wind that was too light and fickle to fill out their sail. When they got home to Meadowbank Laura flew to her sketchbook to record the dresses and hats she had been admiring. She knew exactly what she wanted to do to earn her keep, and as she went about her chores in the kitchen she wondered just how she could get away from her role as cook and housekeeper and become a dressmaker's apprentice.

Fred went off to Nelson in Mercer's oil launch to see Mr Gillstrom and came back happy. With his father's help he had bought the land at Big River and arranged to pay it off, so now he could run his own sheep there and work for himself. It had formerly belonged to the Ricketts family, and their house was still there a bit further up the river, derelict now, with a big snowball tree at one side and a gum at the other. Further down towards the sea there was an old whare which Fred's father and Gillstrom had done up to stay in. William still owned land at Little River and between their three properties the Hadfields ran enough sheep to keep the mill workers in mutton.

A granite quarry was established at Tonga Bay. A Bark Bay section which had been owned by the Huffams was bought by the Tonga Bay Granite Company Incorporated. Machinery, plant and materials were ordered from England and the company went into production in 1904. It was a boon for the Awaroa families not only because of the growing demand for their produce but also because of the new people who came into the district.

Bessie Winter, who had been teaching at Umere School at Karamea, married John Connor in 1904 and the couple came back to Awaroa, to the joy of her family. Her husband found work at the Tonga Quarry and so did her brother Will Winter. Tonga Bay granite was used for the church steps and the Queens Garden gates in Nelson and for the new chief post office in Wellington. The scow *Ngaru* was kept busy transporting the stone, while other scows brought supplies.

Fred was kept busy with his roading contracts, undertaken for the Collingwood County Council and supervised by County Clerk William Baird. The roadworkers would set up temporary camps and Roy would make regular trips to supply them with meat and produce. There were often other visitors too, to see how the work was progressing, and William, Fred, Welby Bill, Darcy, Will Winter and Syd Cracknell were all part of the road gang at one time or another, depending on what other work was available.

When the sawmillers lost their punt in heavy rain, the Hadfields set to and built them another one and in less than a week they were back in business, bringing the sawn timber out from Little River to the Awaroa wharf at high tide so it could be loaded onto scows and taken away to the market.

The collapse of the timber wharf was another saga. The timber wharf was out at the edge of the channel near the sawpit, where the scows could come right in to it on the tide. One cold showery day in mid-June Albert Gibbs and Magnus Manson were stacking timber ready for the next boat, working hard to keep themselves warm. While others ferried the loads out to them by punt the two men on the wharf stacked it higher and higher, ignoring some ominous creaks and groans from the wharf beams.

The tide was nearly at its height when Albert heaved a plank too many onto the stack. There was a sharp crack as a beam snapped, and the whole structure started to wobble dangerously. Mag Manson looked around and realised the danger first, but Gibbs stood irresolute. Then the whole wharf collapsed and Gibbs dived overboard, disappearing from sight for a moment and then reappearing in the water swimming for his life to get out of the way of the punt and the baulks of timber swirling around in the current.

It was a costly accident. Most of the timber was salvaged over the next few days but it was deeply ingrained with coarse sand, not fit to be shipped out to the finishing mills, and it was sold cheaply to the farmers around the inlet. The story was told and retold, and Will Winter wrote a poem about it to entertain the community and survive the years.

"...Then in the days of winter when the air is cold and raw
And the bushmen talk together as they ply the crosscut saw
When hat and coat are laid aside and the largest pipe is lit
And the logs are cut in twelve foot lengths for the vertical to split
While Tommy drives the engine and Hockey drives the truck
While Thompson's bullocks merrily go splashing through the muck
Then in their conversation oft is the story heard,
How the Awaroa wharf went down with Alf and Mag aboard."

Awaroa families at the landing, Awapoto. Timber and flax were loaded aboard the scows here or punted down the inlet to the Awaroa wharf which stood in deeper water.

A week later there was another incident in the inlet, but this time it was a tragedy. It a Friday evening, 24 June 1904, and Laura was expected home on the *Lady Barkly* after a visit to Takaka. With her were two Awaroa men, Charles Robinson and a labourer called Emil Bang who worked at Sigley's mill.

It was a clear moonlit night but the wind was strong and the sea rough. Fred rowed out in the heavy workboat just after eight oclock to collect the three passengers and the usual supplies for the inlet. The transfer went well, and as usual Fred shipped his oars and tipped his hat in salute as the *Lady Barkly* pulled away. He was soon hard pressed to row back against the falling tide, the wind taking the dinghy side on and swinging it broadside to the waves.

Bang, who was a strong, fit man, insisted on taking an oar to help pull the boat over the bar but it soon became clear he didn't know much about handling small craft and the ride got rougher. Laura and Robinson clung to each other as Fred set his course and pulled desperately, calling instructions over the noise of the waves. For a few moments it looked as if they would make it and then Bang's oar caught a wave and slewed the dinghy broadside on to the tide rip. Before any of them had time to think they were in the water, the heavy boat upside down and the supplies all around them in the darkness.

Fred caught his sister's floating skirts and dragged her towards him choking and spluttering. "Hold onto the oar," he managed to yell and he looked around for the others. Bang was too far away to reach but was swimming quite strongly, and Fred yelled to him to follow. Then the two Hadfields kicked out for the beach below Cave Hill on the north side of the inlet, knowing they had to get out of the tide rip if they weren't to be swept out to sea.

Laura caught a glimpse of someone clinging to the dinghy, then concentrated all her energies on struggling to keep her head up in the freezing water. Her clothes dragged her down but she hung on to the oar for all she was worth, sobbing with relief when she felt her feet touch bottom and the current lose its strength. They sank down onto the sand, coughing and spluttering, and then Fred was back on his feet calling out to the others.

"Bang? Robinson? Over here!"

His voice was lost in the wind and rain and he peered across the darkness. He thought he heard an answering shout and tried again.

"Over here!"

There was a splashing in the water but it seemed to be moving away.

"He's got into the channel," he told Laura in despair. "He'll never make it. He's gone the wrong way."

They lay shivering and exhausted for what seemed like an eternity, their clothes trapping the rain and chilling them until they began to lose their strength and they could do nothing but huddle together to try to survive.

Back at Meadowbank William and the others waited for Laura with anticipation that turned to unease. Olive fussed with the kettles and William poked at the fire, neither voicing their concerns.

"I'll go and look for them down on the beach," Darcy said suddenly. "They might have missed the channel and grounded and then they would have to drag the dinghy. Come on, Roy."

But they were back indoors almost as soon as they had left.

"Dad, the dogs are barking like mad," Roy said anxiously. "Something's wrong."

There was no sign of Fred or the others down at the beach and anxiety turned to urgency as William and the boys ran to Venture Creek where their boat *Lorna Doone* lay above the tide line, ready to launch. Cautiously they rowed out into the darkness, stopping every few strokes to hold the lantern up and call out. It seemed like hours before they heard an answering shout, threadlike on the wind.

"They're across the other side," Darcy had to cup his hands around his mouth and lean close to William's ear, and his father nodded agreement.

"Carefully then, both of you. I'll row and you must watch and listen for all you're worth. There's something terribly wrong and we won't help by drowning ourselves."

Laura and Fred were frozen when the men found them, and Darcy took the oars while William chafed his daughter's hands and cradled her in his coat, trying to warm her. He wanted to put them ashore but there were two men still out there and time was everything. Fred huddled in the bow, his father's greatcoat over his wet clothes and they rowed, stopped and called out, straining their ears for an answering shout. The tide was running out and they knew the men would have been swept out with it so they headed out to sea. Soon Roy was shouting that there was something in the water.

It was Charles Robinson, miraculously clinging to the upturned dinghy about a mile offshore. He had managed to cast off his heavy overcoat and boots and was using the last of his strength to hold on until the tide turned. They dragged him on board and headed for the homestead, Laura nearly dead with cold and exhaustion. William put Laura and Robinson ashore with Roy to help them up to Meadowbank, where Olive was waiting with the fires roaring and warm blankets ready.

William, Fred and Darcy searched the dark waters again, following the coastline and straining to see the still-missing mill worker. They picked up the boat Robinson had been clinging to and managed to right it and get enough water out to tow it back over the bar, and then went out again, searching the beach and the rocks but with no success.

"Best go up and tell Alex Thomson the man's gone," William finally conceded. "Get some dry clothes first though."

But Fred set his jaw and headed up the inlet to break the news. It was not until the accident was reported at the mill that he went back to Meadowbank to thaw his aching body. He and Robinson searched the beach again that night, and again at first light but the tide was still in and the water too deep to see anything. About nine o'clock all the mill hands came down to join the search, walking the shore line and rowing up and down in the *Nipper*. William, Welby, Fred and Charles Robinson went out over the bar in the big workboat, and there in about ten feet of water they found the body.

"Made stretcher of oars and timber and carried body to the school," William wrote in his diary that night as he finished recording the tragic events. "Sigley went to Takaka to inform police of accident."

The mill had been silent that day, and would be until after the inquest, due to be held on Monday. Fred, Welby and Charles Robinson went out again to drag the seabed for the missing luggage, stores and mailbag from the accident, but found nothing.

William had immediately offered his house for the formalities and Olive, Laura and the Winter women were all busy baking and cleaning, preparing for the influx of visitors. There were shocked men and women to comfort, but more than anything William dreaded meeting Mrs Bang, who would want to hear at first hand how her husband had been drowned when the other two passengers were saved.

Albert Emil Bang was 28 years old, a native of Denmark who had married into the Nalder family at Motupipi. He left three children and a sister, Mrs Christenson who lived in Collingwood. She had not come to Awaroa but Mrs Bang and the children arrived with Mr Langridge, the JP who conducted the inquest. He publicly commended Fred Hadfield for his bravery in saving his sister's life, and all the Hadfields for their part in rescuing Robinson and trying to find the other missing passenger.

William felt an overwhelming relief that his own children were safe and the accident had not been their fault, and his heart went out to the bereaved family of the drowned man.

William heard from England of another death, one that took his mind far back into the previous century and his own youth. His aunt Emma Bloodworth, the woman who had been like a mother to him on that quiet farm at Empingham, had finally died and his cousin Fanny wrote with the news. It was nearly fifty years since William had seen her, and he realised with a shock that she must have been just a young woman, barely in her thirties when he had taken his meals at her table with the other men after the morning milking. It had been to Aunt Emma that he had turned that dreadful day the news of his brother's death had come, and now his own son Fred was a grown man.

That night William took Fanny's letter with him, not to his usual seat overlooking the inlet in front of Meadowbank, but around the side of the house to the garden, and he walked among the flowers searching for the first bulbs of spring. It had all started in Aunt Emma's garden, and now as he picked his best sprigs of daphne and sniffed their sweet scent he could see her as clearly as if he was fourteen again.

Welby was married to his childhood sweetheart Laura Cunliffe. She had been living in the comfort of a well-appointed home in Wellington and spending her summer holidays at Awaroa, and when the joint farming venture between her parents and the Winters proved unprofitable the whole Cunliffe family returned to Wellington.

Laura had always loved Awaroa and Welby Hadfield. Their brothers and sisters all remembered their days in the little school room, when Welby would pull her pigtails and toss notes to her. "I'm going to marry you one day, Laura Cunliffe," he'd tease when she tossed her fiery curls at him.

They were a match for each other, adventurous and full of jokes and laughter, and neither of them had ever had eyes for anyone else. When the time came Laura had no hesitation in leaving her more cultured city life and her music and painting to live with Welby Hadfield. She spent her first Christmas as a married woman down at Meadowbank, and that year there were six of them to sail the *Old Tub,* with a new set of sails Fred had just finished making, around the point to the Takaka Show.

Shortly after they were married, both in their early twenties, they went down to the Buller River where Welby had found work on a gold dredge. Laura was a striking-looking woman with masses of red hair, and a strong person both physically and mentally. She revelled in the outdoor life and was already a crack shot and an accomplished cook and an artist. Now she learned to handle a saw, to live in a tent and to cook over an open fire. The couple always intended to make their home at Awaroa and worked hard to raise enough money to buy their own land there.

The men who worked at Tonga, about 1909. This group includes John Connor (second from right) who married Bessie Winter, Charlie McGrath (front left) and Will Winter with Ivy's son Henry Roberts (back left).

Unloading a new boiler from the *Advance* at the Tonga granite quarry

There was another wedding in the family, this time between Olive Hadfield and Harold Nicholls. Olive had been working at Langridges in Takaka, Harold was a labourer who worked at the mill. He was a good man, related to the Cracknells, and the couple married with William's special blessing. The previous year had been an eventful one for all the Hadfields, but particularly traumatic for poor Olive. She had been a typical eighteen-year-old, working at Langridges in Takaka, enjoying parties and dances and looking forward to romance. Then one winter night when she was going home from a dance she was waylaid and raped by a Takaka man. It was a terrible shock to the girl, especially as her mother was too far away to help her through the trauma, and she went back home to Meadowbank where William did his best to comfort her. It was a great relief to him when he saw the gentle affection between Olive and Harold blossom into courtship and he did everything he could to encourage the match, knowing it was the best way to heal his daughter's heartache.

Ivy and William Roberts had presented William and Adele with their first grandchild in 1903, and William had lost no time in visiting them to meet and welcome little Henry Roberts. He was thrilled to have a grandson, but worried for his daughter when he realised just how ill her husband was and how poor their circumstances. He visited when he could, and made sure there was always fresh produce for the family and a few pounds to be slipped discreetly to Ivy so her husband's pride was not hurt. It was no surprise to anyone when Roberts died in 1905, and Ivy was left widowed and penniless.

William immediately brought her home with his grandson to Meadowbank. Ivy was a capable housekeeper and soon to Laura's great joy it was her turn to leave home. She went out to work in Takaka as Olive had done before her, setting off in her best clothes with Mrs Manson. Her father gave her half a crown, and borrowed another ten shillings from Welby for her and she started working for Mrs Beardmore in her dressmaker's shop.

Now there were only five of William's nine children left with him at Meadowbank. Welby and Olive were married, Laura was working in Takaka and Evered was with his mother in Palmerston North. Fred, Bill, Darcy and Roy worked from home although Bill and Darcy were often away labouring further afield, and Ivy ran the house for her father and brothers. Little Henry Roberts, now two years old, was the joy of his grandfather's life.

Young Roy was not allowed to go out to work while Fred needed him to help at Meadowbank, and Ivy had no independent means of supporting herself and Henry, so brother and sister went into partnership milking five or six cows and making surplus butter to sell to the granite workers at Tonga. Little as it was, this was the only money these two ever had while they lived at home.

Over at the Winters' household there was some excitement early in 1905 when George, now eighteen, decided to follow in his sisters' footsteps and go teaching. He was appointed to start a new school at Puponga, a coalmining settlement at the base of Farewell Spit in Golden Bay, and he arrived with the desks, chairs and books to set up classes. For young George, with no training or experience save what he had learned from his sisters, and for the children of the settlement who had not had a school there, it was a mutually daunting experience. George lasted two terms and left thankfully, replaced by Miss Bessie McKay who at least had a new schoolroom, an organ to play hymns on and a newly-elected school committee who supported her.

Fred Hadfield and Will Winter were also interested in Puponga. They found a derelict scow lying in the mud there, her rigging still intact and slowly deteriorating. *Orakei* was a 68ft deck-loading scow built of kauri in 1882. She'd come down from Auckland and traded around the bays until she was left beached at Puponga where her custodian was a territorial seal living under her hull. Fred and Will Winter bought her for £5 and were happy with their bargain. Will formally joined the *Venture* project as a partner, paying £80 for his share in the scow and with the new injection of capital they were able to send to Auckland for a set of sails.

They sailed across to Puponga for a second time in the *Old Tub*, this time with William to help and advise, and they made the *Orakei* seaworthy enough to make the journey home. She was still full of mud, crabs and debris and wallowed sluggishly across the bay one calm night under a jury rig, the *Old Tub* towing behind. *Orakei* was stripped out at Awaroa, her fittings adapted to fit *Venture* and get her ready for sea. It was a long term project and it would be another four years before *Orakei* left the inlet again.

Venture was launched in January 1906, a festive occasion for everyone at Awaroa. She was 46 feet long and nineteen tons, and her hull gleamed white with fresh paint. Flags were draped over her decks and an ensign hoisted, and Welby took a photograph from across the creek.

"Well, boys?" William Hadfield asked them with quiet pride.

"She's a fine ship, sir," Will Winter answered. Fred made no answer but simply nodded and climbed on board again to busy himself with some rope that had not been coiled properly. A meal was spread out under the trees overlooking Venture Creek and Ivy sighed when she realised the boys were nowhere in sight.

"Better tell Captain Fred the ladies are waiting with his dinner," she told Will Winter tartly. "And tell those young brothers of mine there'll be no running away to sea for any of them while there's work to be done at home."

On her first voyage *Venture* carried timber on account for Baigents and limestone for Lukin, both Nelson merchants who had promised support for the new venture. Furniture was taken to Tonga, and coal, stone, timber and sundry freight was carried. Picton cement went to Tata Island, sacks of pollard and chaff were hauled, and after those first few trips the men could afford to buy some comforts for the little galley, a lantern and a billy, a teapot, kerosene and nails, an account book, potatoes and honey. *Venture* was a centreboard scow, built to get up and down the creeks and inlets on the tides, and she made an attractive picture as she sailed out to join the rest of the Blind Bay trading fleet.

It was a light-hearted and happy Fred Hadfield who berthed *Venture* on her third trip to Nelson one Friday in February, but at the wharf he and his young brother Bill were met by a stern-faced official.

"What's this?" Fred asked, puzzled.

"Read it for yourself," was the reply. "I'm sorry Mr Hadfield, but regulations is regulations."

"Memorandum from Collector HM Customs, Nelson, to M F G Hadfield, Schooner *Venture*," Bill read slowly over his brother's shoulder.

"I hereby give you notice that your general transire is revoked as from today, and also that the schooner *Venture* is under detention at the Port of Nelson and must remain in port until a master has been appointed and until the registration of the vessel has been completed. WB Montgomery, acting Collector." He frowned. "What does he mean, Fred?"

"He means to collect money, young Bill," Fred said bitterly. "I'm not a properly qualified captain and *Venture* is not a properly registered ship, and until we satisfy their rules and pay their bills we're not allowed to go about our business."

"But that's not fair. You're the best skipper there could be, and it's your boat after all."

"Maybe not fair, but it's business," Fred said dourly. "The wind might be free, but nothing else is, and even the wind can't be harnessed it seems without the filling in of papers."

Venture remained at the port while she was measured and checked over, and Fred drew on his slim savings to pay the harbour dues. He sent a note home on the steamer to his father and Will Winter to explain the delay and to ask their advice about a new skipper. When *Venture* sailed again she had Captain Watchlin as master, and Bill Hadfield as crew. Fred stayed in Nelson to recruit new customers, aware that the captain's wages would have to be paid from the profits. He was a ship-owner now, and the pressure was on.

Launching the *Venture*, Awaroa, January 1906

Venture and *Matakana* at Nelson
Glasgow Album, Copy Collection, Nelson Provincial Museum

CHAPTER SEVEN : ADELE KNOWLES

1903

ADELE HADFIELD'S NAME was seldom spoken at Awaroa but her influence lingered. Her children remembered her as sharp, independent, resourceful and very strong-minded, and as they grew up each of them found themselves striving to keep up her standards and ways of doing things. Many said she was fey, and her grey eyes saw through pretence and hypocrisy very easily. Her husband William was a quieter and gentler man, deeply hurt by the breakdown of their marriage. He and their children worked to rebuild their lives without her, feeling her presence still in the home they had built together.

Laura wrote to her mother regularly, and through her William and the others sent money and small gifts for Evered whenever they could. As the youngest daughter Laura was possibly the closest to Adele, loving her unconditionally as a child loves her mother without any real awareness of the adult complexities of the last two years. Laura had also grown close to baby Reg, whom she had played with and cared for, and for her the parting was hardest of all. She sent news from Awaroa to her mother and to Grandma Snow, and although she didn't often share her letters with her sisters she always passed on news of Evered.

After they were married in 1903, William and Adele Knowles went to Palmerston North where he found work as a labourer in the council gardens. Adele became pregnant again and in December 1903 she had a daughter, Florence Adele Knowles. She was still a firm mother, running her household with an iron hand and demanding high standards. She did not allow drink in the house, and was not very impressed with her new husband's reluctance to work. After 20 years as one of the hard-working Hadfield of Awaroa, she had very little patience with weak minds and idle hands.

Adele and William Knowles with their children Reginald and Florence

Adele had always gone to church when she could, enjoying the social contact of Sunday services at Awaroa and the rare church meetings she was able to attend at Riwaka or Nelson. She had not been involved in church life while she was at Haven House, but when she moved to Palmerston North she found herself drawn to the Anglican parish of All Saints and took the children regularly. All Saints was a wooden building in the town centre and Adele enjoyed the Sunday morning walk with little Floss in her pram and the boys trotting along beside her. Often she persuaded her husband to come too, and although their clothes were not new or fashionable she always made sure they were clean and respectable.

When Floss was six months old Adele arranged a christening service at All Saints. It was a fine sunny Saturday afternoon and her heart was filled with joy as she stood by her husband and watched the young curate solemnly bless each of the children in turn. Florence Adele Knowles was the first, and after her parents had prayed for her to grow in truth and light her father held her in his arms, cuddling her tenderly and leaving Adele to bring each of the boys forward in their turn.

Little Reg was too young to understand why the man in the white robe was sprinkling water on his forehead but Evered, now seven years old, was gravely proud to play his part. Adele had explained to him that he had never been baptised as a child because they had lived too far away from any church. Awaroa was beginning to fade from Evered's memory now, mixed up in a jumble of other more recent and exciting experiences. He attended Sunday school at All Saints and went to church with his mother, and the ritual of prayers and hymns was familiar to him.

. It was 2 July 1904 when the children were christened and their names entered in the parish register, Evered as the son of boatbuilder William Hadfield of Awaroa, Reginald and Florence as the children of William Knowles, labourer and his wife Martha Adele Knowles.

Adele looked up at the high roof as the pedal organ thundered through the final hymn. The ornamental cutout shapes on the rafters reminded her of gulls soaring over the Awaroa sand at low tide, and the heavy wooden beams were jointed like the knees on one of William's boats. For a few moments she felt a pang of regret for the life she had once known and the steady, strong companionship she and her first husband had shared. Now she was the elder partner, the rock on which her little family rested, and it was up to her to be strong for all of them.

She soon found her strength taxed to the limit. William was drinking heavily, and that winter he became more and more morose. His small income was stretched to the limit paying rent, as the couple had no capital to buy their own house. They found a home in Bourke Street, and as winter turned to spring Adele dug over an old garden plot in the backyard, planting potatoes and spring vegetables. She taught Evered to hoe and weed the ground and there were many nights when the family sat down to vegetable soup and floury dumplings for their tea.

Knowles stopped going to church with her, and he complained that the children got on his nerves. Adele's housekeeping skills were tested as she lived more and more frugally, sitting up late in the evenings to mend and darn the family's clothes. She and the children were much happier when William had gone off to work each day, and she began to dread his return home in the evening, never knowing when he would be violent and abusive. Each payday she waited anxiously for his wages, knowing he was not handing all of it over but keeping some back for his own drinking and tobacco.

"I can't work on this muck," William exploded one night when he looked at the bread and vegetables and the single mutton chop on his plate. "A man needs good meat. What do you do with the money?"

"I spend it as well as I can," she retorted. "But the children have needs too. Evered has to have new boots if he's to walk to school any longer, and his pants have split because they're too small for him, he's growing so fast."

He looked at her across the wooden table with its darned linen cloth. "Then you'd best ask his father for them, hadn't you?"

She pursed her lips. "Evered is part of our family, William."

"He's no son of mine."

"What are you saying?" she asked, appalled at the bitterness in his tone.

"I want you to send him back to his father," Knowles said flatly. "I can't afford to keep him."

Little Evered sat quietly, his lip trembling. His mother's face was white with anger and she rose and went to stand by him, her hand on his shoulder.

"Evered is my son, William. His home is here with me."

"You call this a home? What kind of home is it when a man has to sit down to this?"

He swept the food to the floor with an angry gesture. There was a crash of broken crockery, and knives and forks went flying. Little Reg screamed in fear and Adele put her arm around Evered protectively.

"How dare you?" she demanded. "What kind of father are you?"

"Not his, at any road. Nor Reg's father either, by my reckoning."

He pushed Evered out of the way and took Adele by the shoulders, shaking her fiercely. "Whose brat is he, Adele? Some other soldier's child, or some sailor's perhaps? I know what a fine time you had there at the port after I was gone. Your first husband was well rid of you, wasn't he?"

He shoved her viciously away from him and left the house.

Adele sank into the one comfortable chair in the room, taking Floss and Reg into her arms to rock and sooth them while Evered stood white-faced and shaken at her elbow.

"It's all right darling," she whispered, looking at his frightened face. "He's just very tired tonight. He's been working so hard."

"You won't send me away will you Mummy? I promise I'll be good."

She reached up and touched his teary cheek. "No darling, I won't send you away. Not ever."

William Knowles didn't come home that night, and she waited anxiously for him the following evening, knowing it was his payday. She fed the children without him and put them to bed as early as she dared, and then she brushed her hair and washed her face, determined to work hard at overcoming the growing rift between them. It was nearly midnight when he came in, dirty and dishevelled and smelling the worse for drink.

"There's my good and faithful wife," he sneered. "Sitting up waiting for me. Well, here I am, and I know what you're waiting for too."

He reached for her breasts and fumbled at them, slobbering on her neck with beery kisses, and her heart sank. She tried to push him away but he became more pressing, pinching her arms as he pushed her back into the chair.

"What do you want to do, wake the children?" he jeered, in a cruel parody of her remonstrances. "You weren't always so stand-offish, my pretty lady, nor so particular about who you took to your bed, were you?"

Adele tried to fight him off but he pinned her down, fuelled by rage and drink. She heard one of the boys stirring in the other room, and realised that the noise was disturbing them. Any moment now one of them would come out, and she could not face the scene that would follow. Reluctantly she allowed herself to be dragged to the sagging double bed, where she endured her husband's pawing and thrusting in leaden silence, praying only that Floss would not wake from her cot at the foot of the bed before he had finished.

That night was the lowest in Adele's life. While Knowles snored drunkenly beside her she sobbed quietly until dawn, knowing that she could never love him again.

In January 1905 Adele obtained a separation order in the magistrate's court, on the grounds of persistent cruelty, citing physical and mental abuse. William admitted the charge, but told the court he had been provoked.

"There can be no provocation to justify any man in being guilty of cruelty to his wife," the judge remarked sternly after he had listened to William's rambling accusations. There was no likelihood of the couple being able to resolve their differences and live happily together, Adele's counsel told the judge, but he was reluctant to issue the separation order. He wanted the case adjourned so an attempt at reconciliation could be made, and in the end Adele had no option but to agree. Her husbands wages were £2 a week, and the judge ordered that 25 shillings a week be paid in maintenance until the date of the next hearing. With that Adele had to be content.

She was appalled at the prospects before her, and for the next few weeks she practically starved herself as she struggled to feed her children. The rent came out of her meagre income first, then came some milk and eggs for the children. They ate vegetables from the garden and she drank her tea weaker and weaker, wondering how she would manage when winter came and she had to find wood for the fire as well as the kitchen range. In spite of the scandal of her name and circumstances being published in the court reports, she managed to keep up her Sunday attendance at All Saints, facing down her critics with all the dignity she could muster. Under the kindly influence of Archdeacon Harper there were occasional gifts of food or secondhand clothing for the children.

William came back one night, sober, clean-shaven and remorseful, and against her better judgement she let him in. When dawn came he was back in her bed again, promising to mend his ways and help her look after the children. It was the children who were the problem, he told her. He loved his daughter dearly, but no man could find it easy to take on a stepson, and Evered was now old enough to leave his mother and go home to his family. As for Reginald, William could not quell his doubts. He had only Adele's word for it that he was the child's father, after all, and a woman who could commit one act of infidelity could surely commit others.

But Adele was unyielding. The children stayed, she told him, and although William Hadfield sent money for Evered whenever he could, the boy's welfare was as much the concern of the Knowles family as that of the other two. As for Reginald, he was a Knowles and a child of their love, in spite of his illegitimacy, and that was the end of it.

For nearly eight weeks they lived together again as man and wife, but William's weakness for drink was his undoing. He came home one payday empty-handed, his money poured into the throats of his fellow workers, and when Adele remonstrated he hit her hard enough to fell her to the ground. She fled to barricade herself and the children in their bedroom for safety.

Her blackened eyes and bruised cheek sobered him the next morning, but in spite of his tears and protestations she had had enough. They met again in court, before the swelling in her cheek had subsided, and his lawyer told him he was very lucky she hadn't pressed charges of assault. Maintenance was set at fifteen shillings a week and Knowles went on a drunken bender which ended with him taken into the care of the Salvation Army, penitent and very distressed.

Adele was unable to make ends meet on this lower income. She moved to a cheaper house in Bourke Street, and began to take in laundry and to clean shops and office buildings to earn money. William repeatedly accused her of unfaithfulness and refused to accept Reginald, born out of wedlock while he was in South Africa, as his child. He doted on his daughter but wanted Adele to be rid of the boy, and to send Evered Hadfield back to his father, and although the Salvation Army officers who counselled him worked hard to achieve a reconciliation, he refused to back down on these points. For her own part, Adele resolved to make her own way in the world and wanted nothing more to do with him.

Knowles was extremely disturbed and sought consolation in religion. He lost his job and moved to Feilding, where there was an active Army outpost, and he found lodgings and work there. He wrote impassioned letters asking Adele to come and live with him, but was met with stony refusals. By January 1906 he was well behind in his maintenance payments and arguing that he should not have to make them up.

"He wants me to put the children in a home," Adele stormed at her lawyer. "I'm a good mother and I always have been, so why should I give them up?"

Mr Fitzherbert raised an eyebrow at the letter she passed across to him. "Because he has not the pleasure and comfort of residing with them, he sees no reason to pay for their keep," he murmured. "We'll see what the judge thinks of that, Mrs Knowles."

Adele was awarded her legal separation order, and William was again ordered to pay fifteen shillings a week plus her court costs. His defence counsel had argued strongly that he was a reformed man, making strenuous efforts to live a life that was above reproach, and that he wanted nothing more than to be reunited with his wife and daughter, but Adele was adamant that his apparent change of heart had not yet been tested and thus could not be trusted.

She was ordered to ensure he had reasonable access to the children, and the judge expressed the hope that their marriage could yet be saved. But Adele left the courtroom with her heart hardened. She had already left one family for his sake, and there was no way she would abandon her youngest two sons for him.

In March Palmerston North was rocked by a dramatic murder in Fitzherbert Street. One Mrs Harris shot her unfaithful lover, with whom she shared a house, and then turned her revolver on herself. When she had recovered sufficiently to appear in court the whole town was agog with the titillating details, how she had gone out and bought the revolver with the intention of taking her own life, how she had shot Fred Murfitt dead in her kitchen and then cradled a pillow under his head and wept over him, how she had lain down beside him and shot herself in the chest so she could die with him, and how a neighbour had rushed in to find her and staunch the bleeding before it could prove fatal.

Mrs Harris was committed for trial, and the evidence was reported in detail in the *Manawatu Evening Standard* on Friday 27 April. The case upset William Knowles, who read the newspaper report over and over again absorbing every word. He had been unwell for some weeks, depressed and unsettled, and he saw dreadful parallels between Mrs Harris's predicament and his own. He had been in court again himself that Tuesday, sued for arrears of maintenance, and his renewed pleas to his wife had been met with a curt rebuff through her lawyer. He received a formal note advising him of a new address and he was deeply suspicious of her motives, fearing that another man was paying her rent. Distraught with jealousy, he went out and bought a revolver.

The next day was a Saturday, 28 April 1906. William went to his estranged wife's new home at 46 Church Street and found her about to leave for work, her children dressed in their outdoor clothes to go with her. He was extremely agitated and the more Adele tried to calm him down and send him on his way, the more passionate and irrational he became. She urged him to move out to the verandah, away from earshot of the children, but he became louder and more violent in his manner until at last he drew out the revolver which he had hidden in his clothing.

Adele was forced to acknowledge that he had the upper hand and she was terrified. She screamed and ran towards the street, desperate to draw him away from the children but she could hear him running behind her. Before she could reach the roadway he seized her from behind, spun her around, squeezed the trigger and shot her down. At least three bullets hit her, one in the heart, and she was dead by the time anyone could reach her.

There were several people on the street, including a woman with a small child and a boy on a bicycle who was sent at once to get help. William Knowles disappeared back into the house, and the men who came running from several directions were uncertain for a few minutes, wondering if there would be more shots fired. Then Knowles came back out and went to his wife's body, holding her in his arms and sobbing. He was disarmed and restrained, a constable was called, and it was left to little Evered who had witnessed the whole thing to try to explain what had happened. When the reporter from the *Evening Standard* arrived panting and out of breath after a tip-off, Evered was still there on the verandah, protecting his little brother and sister and watching with horror as his step-father was led away into police custody.

In those few fatal minutes the calm of the Knowles and Hadfield families was shattered beyond recall.

When Knowles was formally charged a few days later the courtroom was packed. The story was a dramatic one, the scandal on everyone's lips and the two main lawyers, Mr Carty for the defence and Mr Harden for the prosecution, were the stars of the day.

Knowles was described by the court reporter as being "...very dark, beetle-browed and repellent in expression...." while Adele was "a woman of good address, always neatly attired, and evidently desirous of bettering her position."

The *Manawatu Evening Standard* reported the evidence in vivid detail.

"William Macwhinney said that at one o'clock on the day mentioned he saw accused on the verandah of his own house in Church Street. Witness heard screams when he passed the house and on turning round saw Mrs Knowles running towards him. Accused appeared to be chasing her. He caught her and they appeared to struggle. Witness saw smoke and then heard a report. More smoke was seen and another report heard. Mrs Knowles fell into the water table. She did not move and accused turned round and went back to her house. Witness described the steps he took to acquaint the police, details of which have already been published.... He saw deceased still in the water table with several people around...

"Accused was not there but a couple of minutes later came out from deceased's house. He went straight to deceased and kissed her. He remarked. "I am going to have the last kiss: I suppose it will be the last: I expect I will be strung for it." As accused rose from the deceased witness collared him, and a revolver was taken from accused's coat pocket..."

Knowles pleaded guilty and his counsel argued that he was insane at the time of the murder. He had been living in Feilding for about eight months, attending Salvation Army meetings and worrying about his wife and children. He had recently become more and more upset at the way his wife was living, and had written long rambling letters accusing various local men of sleeping with her. The police and the Salvation Army had become involved, as had a local chemist who prescribed pills for insomnia. Friends who gave evidence said he was unbalanced and could do nothing but brood about his failed marriage and his wife's behaviour.

When Adele's lawyer had tried to deal with him he had asked for a reconciliation and had sobbed and created a scene when the lawyer told him it was not possible. A summons had been issued against Knowles, his wife desperate to resolve the problems and stop his wild behaviour.

Andrew Knowles who was William's older brother travelled from Dunedin to support him during the depositions hearings. He told the court his brother had been kicked in the head by a horse when he was a child, and since then had been regarded by the family as peculiar. He had been a wanderer, running away from home at intervals since he was twelve, and was prone to fits of passion. Their mother had also suffered in the head and died from paralysis of the brain.

The court heard from a Feilding doctor who gave his opinion that the prolonged despondency and brooding fits, coupled with insomnia, were signs of approaching brain trouble.

Adele had in the end been desperate to stop her estranged husband bothering her, and had offered him money to go away. A letter read in court confirmed that she planned to give him £30, which he had promised to return when he could. He was distressed by the idea, and wrote "you were going to get thirty pounds well you can have it, you know I never measured my love by pounds or pence".

She had also threatened him with a horsewhipping if he kept bothering her, and said she had arranged for some cab drivers and express men to deal with him. Knowles told the court he bought the revolver to be ready for the men Adele said would whip him.

"He tried the thing to see if it worked right, he selected a tree in the bush and tried a couple of shots. It seemed to carry faithfully but as there was a house close by and he said a woman came out he went away and intended to go to the range in the afternoon and practice there that was on the Saturday and he had no intention of going to Palmerston.

"He wanted to shoot at the range that afternoon and go to Palmerston on Monday. He bought the revolver as to be ready for the express men and when they came at him he could shoot them. What could he do among so many of them?

"He knew the revolver would be handy if he went to Africa where the nigger war was going on. When he got to South Africa he knew they would take a New Zealander at any time to fight..." the newspaper reported.

On that fateful Saturday morning Knowles dressed in his best clothes and met a friend in Feilding who persuaded him to travel to Palmerston North and see a religious picture, *The Light of the World,* by the famous painter Holman Hunt. They went together by train, and paid their fee to see the painting which was on display at the Municipal Hall for the weekend and which had received a great deal of publicity during its promotional tour around New Zealand. Knowles was quiet and moody when they arrived at the hall, and after a few minutes he slipped away.

When he saw the painting he did not think much of it, he told the court. Of course he knew about Christ laying down his life for the sins of the world but there was not much in that. He was perfectly willing to lay down his life to save his little ones from what was threatening them.

After leaving the picture around midday that Saturday he fortified himself with brandy and went to see Adele who had just moved to a house in Church Street.

He asked her for money, which she refused him, and he wanted to know who was supporting her and paying the bills. She mentioned the name of a man, and told him that her affairs were no longer anything to do with him. Adele was on her way out to work and the couple walked down the path together, arguing bitterly. Knowles accused her of having lovers, she told him she would please herself and he was to leave her alone. He wanted to see the children, she threatened him with the police. The scene became more and more ugly and when Adele, desperate to be rid of him, told him their daughter Florrie was not his child something snapped in his head.

"Well, what next?" asked his Honour.

"I put my hand in my pocket and shot her," replied the witness.

"She screamed when she saw the revolver. I saw the blood well out of her mouth when she fell on the path. I put the revolver up to my right eye. I knew it would send me out at once. I pulled the trigger but did not feel any pain and pulled again. The hammer snapped. The thing went off all right. I pulled it down and looked at it and saw that one chamber had jammed up with lead. I went back to the house to do away with myself. I thought I might mend the revolver if I had time.

"I saw the little boy standing on the verandah and the little girl at the gate. When I saw them everything seemed to come clear as to what I had done. I saw the biggest boy run away and say he has shot my mamma, let us run away. The little boy lifted his sister up on to the verandah and took her down the passage in the house. She fell down and he lifted her up again and went on to the back door.

"I have a memory of them running around the side of the house. I went through the house following the children. When I got to the kitchen table I saw a big knife lying there. I tried to get it into me through my coat and vest, but it was not sharp enough, so I lifted my coat and tried to get it in. I seemed to have lost all power in my hands and they kept jumping on the handle of the knife.

"I seemed to have lost all power in my arms. I thought I had not courage enough to drive it in myself. I put the knife against the fence and tried to fall on it, but the handle slipped.

"Then I remembered the brandy I had purchased and drank it all. Then I thought I heard steps outside and I ran down the back yard..."

Knowles broke down in court and rambled wildly about the devil and the dark side of his life, singing laments and talking of visions he had seen.

His defence counsel, Mr Carty, was the same lawyer who had defended Knowles in the separation hearings and he was familiar with his client's unhappy history. He argued that the murder was not premeditated but a series of unfortunate events. Adele was a strong, powerful woman and Knowles believed she had second sight and that she could do with him just as she liked. He had intended to get away from her, and if it hadn't been for the accidental meeting with his friend in Feilding he would probably have never gone to see his wife that day and would have gone to Australia or South Africa without doing her any harm.

Was there anything else but human infirmity in the whole sorry and sordid tale, was there not infirmity in every chapter of this man's daily life, the lawyer asked? That brooding, that obsession, that one idea of delusion, the proofs that might be little enough to others, but to Knowles they were as strong as holy writ.

It took the jury less than a hour to return a guilty verdict, with a strong recommendation to mercy on the grounds of insanity. Knowles recovered his equilibrium sufficiently to thank judge and jury for their kind and impartial hearing of his case.

"He added that when he left Feilding on the morning of the tragedy he had no intention of shooting his wife. As for the rest he was quite willing to take his sentence and at the last would prove to that gentlemen who said that he was a cur that he was not," the newspaper reported.

Knowles heard his sentence from a Supreme Court judge in Palmerston North on June 6, 1906. Proclamation was made for silence in the court while His Honour assumed the black cap and pronounced in a low and emotional voice, "This sentence of the law is that the prisoner be taken from the court to His Majesty's prison in Wellington and from there to the place of execution and hanged by the neck until he is dead and may the Lord have mercy on your soul."

As Knowles was taken from the court he met his brother and they shook hands and said goodbye, the prisoner expressing regret for the disgrace he had brought on the family.

William Knowles did not hang for the murder of his wife. His sentence was almost immediately commuted to life imprisonment with hard labour and he was held first at Wellington and then at Napier. It was to be many years before the Hadfield family heard of him again.

Martha Adele Ann Knowles, nee Snow, was buried in a simple grave in the public reserve at Palmerston North Cemetery. She was 46 years old and the mother of eleven children. To the last she was a strong, attractive and self-willed woman, the stern puritan streak she inherited from her mother and the Newths at odds with the lively and charismatic personality that had come from her father and the Snow family.

Brought up in the raw new life of the goldfields, married at eighteen to a man nearly twice her age, confronted with all the responsibilities of a pioneer wife and mother, she had in the end chosen to follow her own star and had died for it.

No one mourned her more deeply than her first husband William Hadfield, who had loved her dearly and lost her to another man.

When the news of the tragedy reached Awaroa, William's first concern was for nine-year-old Evered, and Fred was sent at once to Palmerston North to fetch the boy home.

Adele was buried by the vicar of All Saints, the church she and her children had attended since they had first come to the district, and Fred stayed just long enough to settle his mother's few affairs and see her husband committed for trial.

Martha Adele Ann Knowles
1860-1906

Snow Bros Photo

He found the children in the care of the Salvation Army, an arrangement made on behalf of their father and stepfather. Captain George Clarke and his wife had only just been posted to the district and had not known the Knowles family personally, but they were kindly people and the three youngsters were safe and well cared for. They arranged for four-year-old Reginald to be adopted by a couple in their corps, and Fred brought Evered and Florence home with him to Meadowbank.

THE HADFIELDS AND THE WINTERS

FREDERICK and ANN
HADFIELD

GEORGE and MARTHA
SNOW

**WILLIAM WELBY
HADFIELD**
(8/6/1844-3/12/1920)

married
1878-1902

**MARTHA ADELE ANN
SNOW**
(16/2/1860-29/4/1906)

married
1903-1906

William
Freeman
KNOWLES

JOSEPH ROGERS and **JESSIE HOULSON**
(1849-1913) **WINTER** (1850-1912)

ELIZABETH ADA (BESSIE) ——
(m John Conner 4/7/1904)

FREDERICK GEORGE m **JESSIE WINTER**
(Nelson 9/10/1879) (Wales 1979)

WELBY VIVIAN m Laura Cunliffe
(Cwd 15/5/1981)

IVY ADELE m **WILLIAM ISAACS WINTER**
(Cwd 22/1/1883) (1881-5/8/1959)
m William Roberts 1903
- Henry 1903

WILLIAM HARRY
(Awaroa 25/9/1884)

CHRISTIANA WINTER
(1884-9/4/1933)

OLIVE FRANCIS
(Awaroa 2/4/1886)
m Harold Nicholls

GEORGE WINTER
(1886-19/4/1926)

LAURA MAY
(Awaroa 7/1/1888)
m James McLaren

ROBERT WINTER
(1888-5/6/1925)

DARCY CLARENCE
(Awaroa 1/12/1889)
m Rita Coyle

ROY HUBERT
(Awaroa 15/1/1892)

EVERED ROGERS
(Awaroa 4/3/1897)

REGINALD KNOWLES
(8/10/1901)

FLORENCE ADELE (FLOSS) KNOWLES
(29/12/1903)

171

A road gang at work. Les Cracknell second from left, Will Winter at right

There were not many pigs around Awaroa in those early days although as the settlers cleared more land around Wainui and Totaranui the pigs moved back across the hills. The first pig Roy shot was over the hill at the back of Meadowbank soon after he bought his shotgun. He made short work of the pig after the dogs had sniffed it out, and he cut the hind legs off and staggered home with them, arriving just on dusk very pleased with himself. His day's work wasn't over, however. His brother sent him back for the rest of the meat.

Between his contracting work, farming and running the *Venture,* Fred worked hard. He paid Darcy's wages on the farm and Bill's on the *Venture,* while Roy, William and Ivy were kept busy at Meadowbank. When Roy turned sixteen Fred started paying him a shilling an hour for the work he did. Like his father and the other farmers and businessmen, Fred kept a daily diary in the pages of *Lucas's Almanac,* printed in Nelson and filled not only with local advertisements and shipping timetables but with information about the moon and tides, weights and measures, history and geography and a hundred other useful things to know.

The road from Wainui to Awaroa was finished by 1906 and a benched track carried on around the inlet. It opened up new options for the Awaroa families who no longer had to rely on the steamer twice a week, and soon there were more visitors than ever. No one in the Hadfield household had spare time for visits to town, but when Ivy became ill soon after the Boxing Day regatta Fred rode to Takaka to see the doctor for advice. He made the round trip in just under seven hours, noting the record time in his diary with satisfaction, and he and William followed the doctor's instructions by taking Ivy out to the steamer *Wairoa,* bound for Nelson where she could be given the care she needed.

On 19 January 1907 Captain Bruce sailed *Venture* in to Awaroa. The next day Olive and her boys arrived on the steamer and suddenly Meadowbank was full of children again. Henry Roberts was the eldest, just turned three, then Florence, Frank and baby Roy Nicholls, five months old and more than ready for the attention his mother's family lavished on him. While the women were busy with cooking and washing William found himself enjoying the little ones, sitting on the verandah in the sun while they played around him, or down at the beach while they sat in the water and splashed each other. He had been away so often when his own children had been toddlers he had never really learned to play with them, but now he discovered a new happiness in his grandchildren.

William had noticed the wistful look in his eldest son's eyes when their scow came in over the bar, and that night after the others had gone to bed he stood up and suggested a turn outside.

"We're managing well on the farm these days,"he said mildly. "Young Darcy's a strong lad, and now that Evey's here to help around the house and garden there's not much Roy and Darcy can't do between them."

"I've got the sheep to manage," Fred muttered in the darkness.

"Aye, but Will's happy to work up at Little River, and we've finished shearing and the hay for the season."

The old man gazed up at the summer sky, still grey and faded at the corners as if reluctant to admit the stars had light of their own. "There's something about a sunset at sea, you know, that's different to the way it looks from the shore."

When *Venture* sailed again Fred was on board, and the next few months were some of the happiest in his life. They loaded coal from Puponga and took it to Nelson, then left for the pa at Riwaka to pick up fresh-cut flax for the mill. To Waitapu for timber, back in to Awaroa to top up the load, then a run of 4 hours and 20 minutes down into Nelson Harbour.

Venture's centreboard allowed her to get in and out of the smaller tidal estuaries and they worked up and down the coastline carrying what they could, firewood for the Lightbands, limestone from Tata Islands, totara from Waitapu. They carted timber for Baigents, loaded flax at Pakawau, unloaded machinery and topped up with more firewood, constantly moving between the wharves at Nelson, Awaroa, Waitapu, Collingwood, Pakawau and Puponga.

It was early June before Fred brought her back into the inlet empty and put her into the creek by the school with her sails neatly furled and her decks scrubbed clean. She'd been trading for 18 months and it was time to paint her and renew damaged timbers. He and William worked side by side again, enjoying each others' company. When they finished repainting *Venture* they worked on *Orakei*, hunting through the bush at Big River to find timber for her new keel.

It was time to evaluate their position as ship owners and plan the next move. *Venture* had proved herself well and Fred was pleased with her and with himself. They decided to put a derrick on her deck, anchored at the base of the mast, and they set up a double-ended two-man wire rope winch.

"She looks lovely," Jessie called when she walked to the slipway one Saturday. "I wish I were a sailor too."

Fred stepped back from the white hull and grinned at her. "Don't you know ladies bring bad luck to a ship?"

"What about your aunt Ada Wheeler? She sails with her husband."

"Ah, but she's the captain's wife."

There was a moment of silence and Jessie's cheeks went pink. William busied himself around the far side of the hull, smiling as he turned away. High time these two were married, he thought, while the girl could still flummox his son and bewitch him. They'd be staid and middle-aged soon enough.

Fred and Will Winter took *Venture* out for a sail the next day. It was Sunday, and Ivy and Jessie packed picnic baskets and dressed in shady hats, stepping carefully across the deck as the men looked after them with elaborate courtesy. William smiled at the contrast between them as he stood on the bank with the little ones.

Jessie Winter wore a dark blue pinafore dress with a blue and white checked blouse. She had pink ribbon and white lace at the neck and cuffs and a blue ribbon in her hat. Her brown hair was pinned back neatly and she was every inch a gentlewoman, more at home in the drawing room than the deck of a scow in spite of all her years at Awaroa.

His own daughter Ivy Hadfield was just as elegant as Jessie in her best Sunday dress but with rougher hands and strong shoulders. She could handle a sailing dinghy as well as the boys, and bossed her family around in a way Jessie would never dream of doing. She was her mother's daughter, firm and determined. William watched as the two women settled themselves on the deck and the men busied themselves with ropes and tackle. Ivy could do worse than Will Winter, her father thought with a grin. She was only 24, and he was a good man, strong enough to handle her.

Flossie was Adele's daughter too, with that same streak of determination that could so easily spill over into anger, and from the beginning she and Ivy were at loggerheads. Nothing the little girl did seemed to please her half-sister.

One morning when she was four she caused a huge uproar in the back yard. The dogs were barking and hens and turkeys screeched and gobbled, trying to fly over their paling fence and into the vegetables. William heard the commotion from the cowshed where he was mending a railing, and as he rushed towards the orchard where the disturbance was coming from, he saw Ivy fly out of the house behind him, wiping her floury hands on her apron.

The scene that met their eyes was one of carnage. Flossie and Henry were chasing the turkey chicks, laying about them with strong manuka sticks and beating them until they fell. At first William thought they had been attacked by the adult birds and then he realised the children were the attackers.

Ivy screamed to them to stop and grabbed little Flossie, snatching the stick from her hands and raising it to strike until William stopped her. Something in the little Florence's eyes warned him it was not just temper or devilment, and gravely he asked the children what had happened.

"We're helping you, Grandad," Henry piped up. "Flossie said to."

"Why, child?" he asked her.

"We're killing all the dirty bad ones for you."

He looked around the yard and realised what she was saying. The dead turkeys were all dark grey or black, the white ones were left untouched. He told Ivy not to punish the children. They were only four, after all, he reminded her gently, and he led them away to wash their hands and play down at the beach.

Fred took *Venture* down to Tonga that winter to load stone for shipping to Nelson. It was a precarious business, even with the new derrick, and the punt was holed in the first few weeks. Fred fixed it there on the beach, but when in August a stone fell through *Venture*'s deck and broke a beam and two floors he had to bring her back to the little boatyard for repairs.

He was kept at work splitting posts and laying the tramline to the mill, and in September *Venture* began taking loads of flax and supplejack to Nelson and bringing sheep back for Black's farm. Olive and her husband moved to Waiharakeke where Harold found work in the sawmill.

Will Winter was working over at Little River cutting flax, and Fred soon organised his brothers into the job too. The mills were busy around Nelson and Tasman Bay and there was money to be made. It was hard, blistering work,

Blocks of granite at the Tonga Quarry, waiting to be unloaded at the wharf. Tonga granite was used on building projects in Wellington, and the quarry was at the peak of its production about 1910.

Newton Nalder photo

even in winter, the sticky gum bleeding over hands and clothes that were permanently damp with wading through the swamps. The flax was bundled and then sledged down to the landing stages, ready to be shipped away.

The work gang was Bill Hadfield, Albert Reeves and Darcy, and often there were itinerant Maori labourers employed with them. The flax they cut was on William's land at Little River and Fred paid him a royalty of six shillings a ton. He paid the men seven shillings a ton for cutting the flax and they tried hard to get it loaded out green because the longer it sat ready on the landing the more it dried out and lightened in weight. Fred seldom worked on the flax but would split fencing timber and manuka firewood to make up a load for *Venture*.

After Black arrived in Awaroa he started a bark mill. Birch trees were felled in the spring and the bark stripped and stacked ready for grinding in late summer. The grinding mill was powered by a secondhand 8hp motor previously used for flax milling at Puramahoi, Waitapu and Wainui. When it had been ground to powder, the bark was bagged up and sent to the Nelson tannery where it was used to dye leather. Roy worked for a while sledging the bark out of the bush to the mill but he gave up bagging at the mill after trying it briefly. The job was too dusty and unpleasant. He applied for a lease up near Fred's land at Big River and was granted 500 acres. With Welby's and Bill's help he felled about fifteen acres of trees, then looked about for more land.

Roy got the engine bug. He'd first seen a motor-powered boat in Nelson nearly ten years earlier and since then had wanted to get about Awaroa some way that was easier and faster than rowing. When he was seventeen he finally had enough money saved to start the project so he bought a boat at Marahau. It was an old dinghy from the *Queen Bee*, wrecked on Farewell Spit twenty years before, and it took Roy five hours to row from Awaroa to Marahau and do the deal. He towed his new boat home behind the work dinghy, leaving it at Bark Bay to retrieve later on as the last haul round Abel Head against the wind and tide was too much for him.

He bought his first motor from Jack Reed for £25 and shipped it home on *Venture.* It was an 8hp Racine, the first in Nelson and it had done service in the harbour pilot boat for years. By the time it came to Awaroa it was old and worn out and needed a new magneto, but Roy got it going eventually and he and Fred used it for years. It was a motor with a history, as it had once towed Captain Voss's *Tilikum* out from Nelson to carry on his sailing trip around the world. Roy sold it to Hunters but eventually Fred got it back and it was retired to sit under the trees at Big River.

Boat owners like Nalder, Westrupp, Ricketts, McNabb, Lukins, Tregidga, Ercolano and Reeves were frequent visitors to the inlet and there were scows and cutters in and out all the time, carrying freight or sheltering from the weather. The cutter *Gannet* came for a load of timber, and the *Jessie Logan* was in for shelter. *Maid of Italy, Vindex, Transit, Southern Isle, Matakana* were all instantly recognised as they passed or sailed in. *Venture* was among them, and her sails off the entrance were always an exciting sight.

It was not all plain sailing for *Venture*. She arrived once from Motueka with twelve drowned sheep on board after a rough passage, and Fred had to turn out and skin them to salvage their hides at least. It was blowing too hard to take her up the river to the landing on that occasion so the flax had to be punted down to her. When she finally arrived at the Wainui mill with 559 bundles of flax on board they could not unload them because the tide was too low.

On another occasion Fred punted timber from the mill down to the scow *Morning Light,* owned by Captain Kirk. He overloaded the punt and it sank under him, but he managed to secure the timber and salvage it when the tide dropped. It was loaded aboard *Morning Light* and shipped out, but Fred was not popular with the eventual purchaser whose saws were badly blunted by the coarse golden Awaroa sand caught up in the rough-cut planks.

Bill Hadfield was also in trouble one day, he and Moreland Gibbs fighting over ownership of a timber jack used to lever stumps out of the ground. They came to blows in a bitter and angry fight that quickly drew a crowd but Bill was well able to defend himself. He was farming the land that his father still owned at Little River, with some more leasehold property that William was negotiating to buy. Bill was torn between land and sea, however, and a few years later he shipped out of Nelson as a sailor.

Welby and Laura had their first baby, James Welby Cunliffe Hadfield, in the February of 1908. Laura went home to her family in Wellington for the birth and it was Easter before they brought him back to Meadowbank to show William and the others.   They decided to lease some land on the true right bank of Big River and they set up house there on the river flat opposite Fred's land, Laura working alongside Welby to establish a garden and tend their animals. Their home was on the site Joe Taylor had picked out years before, and although his house was gone the atmosphere was sylvan, trees and flowers he'd planted merging into native bush. Streams and swamp attracted the birds and it was an attractive setting for Welby and Laura who were very happy.

Laura Hadfield was home again too, with her fiancee Jim McLaren. He'd known her since Haven House days, when he'd been friends with her brothers and had loved to meet them all down at the wharf and show off on his bicycle. Jim lived at the Albion Hotel down by the waterfront, and he worked at the Anchor Foundry. His father was a craftsman, selling wickerwork and supplejack products, and over the years he became a frequent visitor to Awaroa to collect supplejack which he would weave into strong round coal baskets, four foot across, with rope handles for use on the ships.

When the little girl the McLarens had known as a twelve-year-old turned up in Nelson again she was a polished and sophisticated woman of twenty. Her dressmaking skills had brought her in touch with society women and her years of housekeeping at Meadowbank had made her a very competent manager and housekeeper. She and Jim were soon courting, and in 1908 they were married in Nelson, Laura in a white wedding gown she had made herself.

They settled down happily in Russell Street. Jim had been at the Foundry since he was eleven, and he eventually became the engineer there. As their family grew they kept returning to Awaroa for Christmases and holidays, maintaining the close bond between Laura, her father and Meadowbank. She had always loved the inlet and she still went out to swim, row or fish every chance she got.

1908 was a busy year for the Hadfields. *Orakei* was launched on Friday 14 August, two weeks before Laura's wedding. She was still a bare hull, stripped of her mast, rigging and gear, but she had a new keel and floated soundly in the water. She bore little resemblance to the sad mud-filled hulk Fred and Will Winter had sailed into the inlet nearly four years earlier.

Survey gang, about 1910. Darcy Hadfield, second from left, worked with the surveyors at Awaroa and then on the West Coast.

Re-launching *Orakei,* the scow Fred Hadfield and Will Winter bought derelict for £5. *Orakei* was built in 1882 in Auckland and raced with other scows on Auckland Harbour, winning regattas in 1897 and 1898. Bought by the Puponga Coal Company to carry machinery from Nelson to Puponga at the turn of the century, she then lay idle until she was taken to Awaroa in 1905. She was re-registered in Nelson 1910-1921 as a deck-loading schooner, sold to Millar and traded around Tasman Bay, taking timber from Croisilles up the Matai River to Miller's Acre.

Darcy and Bill had both been taking their turn to crew *Venture,* Roy worked hard to help Fred, and William had done most of the work on *Orakei.* Now it was time for the older boys to find work further afield. Darcy went off with a survey party and their father was left at Meadowbank with Ivy, Roy, Evered, Flossie and Henry. They were kept busy in the orchard and the garden, supporting their little household by selling produce around the inlet, Tonga, Totaranui and further afield.

Uncle Stanley Snow arrived for a two week visit. It was the first time any of the Snows had been to Awaroa since Adele's death and the first time Stanley had seen his niece Florence.

Stanley was only a few years older than Fred, and as the two men worked side by side in the bush they talked about Floss and what was to become of her. Stanley looked around the isolated inlet in dismay, trying to see it through Hadfield eyes.

"Adele hated it here, you know that, don't you," Stanley said abruptly. "It's no life for a woman, not these days."

"Jessie's happy enough here."

"Happy enough to have a hard-working husband like you, I daresay," Stanley commented. "As your mother was, I don't doubt. But it's not enough for a woman."

He slashed at the bush, and the air was heavy with the unspoken things that lay between them. They were clearing an old fence line, and they worked in silence for a while, sweat pouring from them in the hot sun.

"I'm not saying anything against your father, mind, he's a good man." Stanley said at last. "Nor your mother either, and we'll talk no more about her. But this life of yours was too hard for Adele in the end.

"You be careful your Jessie doesn't change her mind and want to move to the town."

It worried Fred more than he wanted to admit. Jessie was a vivacious, laughing woman with a quick mind and she and her brothers and sisters lived in a world of music, books and discussion Fred could never be part of. The conversation with his uncle kept returning to his mind, long after Stanley had left the inlet.

He took Jessie up to Big River and showed her what he had been doing to the land. It was a Sunday, and she wandered along the riverbank in a big shady hat, stopping to admire the new fence and to pick the daffodils that still clumped in the grass where the original house had been, now burned down. A young gum tree sprouted on the site.

The Ricketts boy who had died in a shooting accident and been buried near the house years before, and the wooden cross that had borne his name had long since disappeared. Now there was just a grassy mound, with a little cairn of stones to mark the grave. Jessie knelt and carefully pulled the weeds from around the stones.

"He was only thirteen, Fred," she said softly. "How his poor mother must have grieved."

"It's a hard place to bring up children, Jess," he said soberly.

"And a magic place, too." She took his arm, her eyes shining. "Oh Fred, we will be happy here, won't we?"

"I'll not manage to build us a very grand house, not at first any way."

"And I'll not need one. My dear boy, don't you see how impatient I am to be married?"

She stood very close to him, fresh and lovely, her eyes full of sunshine and her skin smelling faintly of rose water. Fred kissed her gently, but shook his head. He was just as anxious to be married as she was, but he didn't want her living in the primitive way his sister Olive did, nor to have the kind if life Welby's Laura seemed happy with. His Jessie was a lady.

High tide at the head of the inlet, 1898. Fred and Jessie made their home on the true left bank of the Awaroa River, Welby and Laura on the right.

Photo by T W Cane, courtesy Glasgow family.

It was a fast trip home, four hours from Waitapu to the inlet in *Venture*'s dinghy with a single big sail up, and by evening Fred was home with his wife and two- day old son Clifford Frederick Hadfield.

Jessie's confinement had been a shock to Flossie, who like most children of her day had no understanding of how babies arrived. When she got up in the morning and went into the kitchen she was surprised to find Laura washing the newborn boy at the table.

"Is that your baby?" the little girl asked.

"This is Jessie's baby," Laura answered, but Florence shook her head.

"Jessie hasn't got a baby."

"Now she has."

Florence took some convincing, but by the time Fred got home she was getting used to the idea, and she was kept busy helping as best she could while Jessie recovered her strength and learned to nurse the boy. Fred spent the week close to the house, putting scrim on the walls and building a new outhouse with Welby's help, and then as the tides rose on their next cycle he left with Roy and Albert in Welby's launch to get *Venture* back to work.

"I'll be back as soon as I can," he promised Jessie. "It should take us only a day or so at the outside. I'll be here for Easter Sunday, at least, and we'll take our son down to Meadowbank."

It was to be another ten days before he got back home. They re-launched *Venture* on Good Friday, their mood lightened even more when Darcy called at the wharf to see if she was in. He was on his way home to Awaroa but *Venture* still had supplies to unload and a cargo to pick up from Collingwood. They arrived on the falling tide, bought the stores they needed and loaded *Venture* that night, slipping out about ten as the tide rose again.

They ran around the point as far as Astrolabe where they lay all the next day, becalmed. The wind picked up in the early hours of the 29 March and they were able to run on down into Motueka to unload and head for home. They were hoping to make Awaroa by midnight, but once again the weather was against them. The wind came up south east, and Fred decided it was too rough to get into Awaroa so they dropped their anchor off the point and settled down to a rough night. The seas built up around them and the wind increased to gale force again. There was no option but to slip the anchor, marking it with a buoy, and run for Separation Point where they could round into shelter.

Roy walked home over the hill from Motupipi, preferring to feel the land under his feet again and anxious to let the family know they were all right. It wasn't until the first of April that Fred picked up the anchor off the point and sailed back into Awaroa to see his wife and baby again.

Venture wasn't the only vessel in trouble on 29 March. The scow *Kohi* capsized along the same coast that night, her crew managing to stay on the hull until the seas abated.

Fred went ashore again after that trip and he, Will and Roy worked together on the farms, dipping Fred's flock of 245 sheep, sowing grass seed on Will's newly cleared land. Fred was killing two sheep a week on average. Roy bought land at Little River and they cleared bush for him, and for Bill Hadfield who was also farming there.

"My Dear Fred and Jessie," Martha Snow wrote from Picton just after Clifford was born. "I just wish to remind you that you owe me a letter. I think it is about six months since I wrote last so I hope you will answer this at once. I hope you are all well. I remember you every day in my prayers (more especially Little Flossie) that she may grow up in purity and godliness. I would like to know how your father and all the family are, also Mr Winter's people....

"...Why do you not come and see us? I am sure it would do you good and you might do some business here. I suppose your boy is quite a wonder now, able to sail a boat and muster the sheep and sundry other clever things, be sure to tell me his name.

"Is Mr Perrott there now, if so tell him I wish to be remembered to him. I wish to be remembered to the Winters also, and tell your Father I am tired of wishing to hear from him and getting none. With kindest love to you all. From your Grandma, M Snow."

"That's your great-grandmother, Cliffie," Jessie told the baby as she nursed him before the fire. "You're a lucky boy, to have a great grandma and I hope you can meet her one day when you're bigger." Jessie had known and liked Adele, and although they never talked of her she made sure there were little drawings and notes from Flossie included in letters to Grandma Snow.

There was a newcomer in the bay. Bill Samuels was a very black skinned West Indian and at first his appearance startled everyone. The Robertson boys over at Wainui first met him swimming in the creek, and the sight of his glossy black body with eyes and teeth gleaming white in the water scared them so much they were back on the bank before they had time to think straight. Samuels and his wife, who was a white woman, lived at Gilbertson's old place on the west point and he worked as a labourer for the farmers around the inlet.

Always a gentleman, Bill Samuels quickly became popular around Awaroa. No one ever knew how he came to be there but he was a good worker and no one questioned his status. He was known to be a blue-water sailor, a ship's carpenter from the *Latimer,* and he had a recipe for smoking fish that he said he had learned from an old uncle in Barbadoes.

Bill Samuels, the
Jamaican sailor who
worked for the Hadfields
at Awaroa, with Mr and
Mrs Newton Nalder.
Newton Nalder photo

There was a story which quickly did the rounds that he and William Hadfield had been out fishing and he had caught a groper which slipped the hook just before they could land it. Samuels had been over the side in a flash and disappeared under the water, only to surface triumphantly a few seconds later with the big fish hugged tightly to his chest.

He enjoyed church services, drowning out the other singers with his rich baritone, and later he acquired a cylindrical phonograph and recorded his voice and others on the wax cylinders so they could be played back.

Fred and William Hadfield got to know Samuels very well because he worked on *Orakei* with them. A skilled seaman who had come ashore to work in the flax mills, he helped them rig her and get her back into service, and he also worked for Fred logging and fencing. They moved *Orakei* up the creek, put her new mast in and worked on her blocks. In May Fred went to Wellington to buy new gear for her, and he, William and Bill Samuels worked on her through the winter.

The little boatyard at Venture Creek was a busy place that winter. Welby was building himself a launch and the others were working on *Orakei* and on

Venture which was slipped for painting again. The children loved to go down below the scaffolding and look up when Mr Samuels was working on *Venture*'s hull. They were fascinated by the soles of his feet which were much paler than the rest of his skin.

One night after *Venture* had been refloated Fred took Floss down with him in the dinghy to see Mr Samuels, who had been left on board to move her over to the wharf when the tide turned. It was a magical winter night, when the stars hung heavy and fish jumped in the shadows at the edge of the water. Fred was at the oars, rowing quietly and smoothly while Floss sat in the stern and trailed her fingers through the water.

Even before *Venture* loomed up out of the darkness they knew where she was, because Bill Samuels' rich voice rolled out over the water. Fred shipped his oars and let the dinghy glide smoothly to *Venture*'s side, catching the anchor rope and carefully pulling them against the hull without a sound. They sat for a long time entranced, listening to the uninhibited and joyful music pouring out into the dark night, as Bill Samuels sang alone and unaccompanied, the parlour songs of the day interspersed with hymns and spirituals and with the older songs of the sea and his people.

When the songs were finished and the moreporks and weka took over, Fred took care to make the kinds of noises they would make if they had just arrived. Years afterwards he recalled the magic of that night and the power of the music that rolled across the water.

In July Welby, Will and Fred took *Orakei* to Croiselles to load timber and then sailed down to Nelson where she waited in port for a fortnight to be measured by Customs. Now there were two working vessels in the Hadfield fleet. Samuels shipped aboard *Venture* for Waitapu and *Orakei* sailed for Croiselles again.

Ivy Roberts and Will Winter were married in September 1910 and they lived in a tent at Tonga Quarry where Will worked a granite saw. The quarry was a big operation that year. Tonga Bay granite had been used to face the imposing Public Trust building in downtown Wellington, and demand for the stone was at its peak.

The Wilson brothers now owned the 500 acres of land, plant and machinery at the quarry. There were four cranes, two in the quarries, one in the machinery house and one at the wharf. A frame saw cut the stone into slabs and there were planing and moulding machines, all powered by a 35hp steam engine and boiler. The little settlement consisted of a number of cottages, a wharf and a reservoir and a regular mail service had been organised.

Will Winter and Ivy (nee Hadfield) with Ivy's son Henry Roberts at their tent home at
Tonga Bay, where Will worked at the granite quarry.   *Courtesy Tui Winter*

The sawmill at Waiharakeke where Harold and Olive Nicholls lived
From a glass plate photo by Syd Cracknell

Back at Awaroa Fred worked on at Big River, building a chimney and putting up a cowyard, and with Bill and Welby he felled bush and worked on road contracts. By October the sale of *Orakei* was completed and Fred paid his eight shillings to come home on the steamer *Wairoa* with new towels for the house, new boots and singlets for himself, treats for Jessie and his pockets full of lollies for Floss.

They shore 178 sheep on Fred's property that year and more on his father's. They mustered for Winters and started cutting Roy's bush. Welby's boat was launched 2 December 1910, the day after Darcy's 21st birthday. There were celebrations for both events, with cherry pie and cream as always, and afterwards Darcy left Awaroa for Auckland where he found work as a carpenter, his boatbuilding skills standing him in good stead.

Fred arranged to sell off a large area of standing bush to Henry Baigent, who had been pressuring him for some time to allow his mill into Big River.

"I should like to have a mill in that locality as I am sick of continually cutting small patches and then having to move the mill, it doesn't give the mill a fair chance to pull up," Baigent wrote. "When I put in a mill I expect to cut everything that can be got at a reasonable expense.....You can rely on my making a cleaner cut of the bush than most millers would do. When I put in a mill I do not expect to leave anything worth sawing."

There was very little choice about selling the timber that year, as Henry Baigent indicated very politely at the close of his letter. "I can't forward a cheque as requested because you have no credit balance."

Laura and Welby had a baby daughter, William's first grand daughter. She was born on January 7, 1911, and when Laura brought her to Meadowbank William was overcome with joy.

"What have you named her?"

"Eva Mahala Ann," Welby told his father proudly, and there was a moment of surprise.

"Not a family name?"

"Eva for my sister," Laura told him softly. "And Mahala's a new name, for a new and very special little girl. We wanted a daughter so much, and she's so lovely, isn't she?"

The next time *Venture* came into Awaroa there was a small package for William, and the next Sunday afternoon he put it carefully in his pocket and sailed up the inlet to Big River. He had sweets for Jim and little Allen Herbert, who was already known as Bert to the whole family, and a basket of golden apricots for Laura. After he had been greeted by everyone and sat down with a cup of tea and a plate of fresh scones in front of him he reached into his pocket and handed Laura a little velvet box. Inside was a gold locket on a gold chain, with a tiny red stone glowing on the front of it.

"My mother's name was Ann," he said quietly, "and little Eva is my first grand daughter. She's very special to me."

"As you will be to her," Laura told him gently, and she lifted the baby from her bassinette and laid her in her grandfather's arms, slipping the dainty little locket around her neck. "Thank you."

The Hadfields all went to the Takaka Show in Welby's new boat, putting in to Waitapu and taking the bus up to the showgrounds. It had become a regular annual event for Fred ever since he sailed his workboat around Separation Point to Waitapu to attend the first Golden Bay A and P Show, but this was the first time he'd been around the point in a motor launch.

The families were no longer isolated at Awaroa. They had a road, a post office, telephone and telegram links, and now they had new motor boats instead of sailing dinghies they could take part in Golden Bay social life and could enjoy the best of both worlds.

The granite quarry wound down the following year and Will and Ivy Winter moved back into Meadowbank to live with William and housekeep for him. Roy bought the land at Tonga where they had been living. There was 220 acres of land still owned by Harry Hadfield, still happily market gardening in Blenheim, and Roy bought it from him for £100. In the new year Fred started working on it with him, clearing and burning it ready to farm. Roy sold his Big River property to Syd Cracknell who was also working for Fred at the time.

Roy was soon disheartened with his prospects. He did his best but he had always found the bushfelling and flax cutting around Awaroa was too heavy for him and when a survey party came into Awaroa with Albert Waters in charge he was taken on as a chainman. He went off down to Karamea with the surveyors, and found work around Nelson and Motueka, eventually settling to a dairy farm at Takaka.

There was a letter from Adele's sister Laura Smith in the mailbag, and William passed it around the family so everyone could share her news. She and her husband William were both schoolteachers now, and were to go off to Niue Island to establish government schools there. They asked if they could visit Awaroa before they left.

William Smith was the first schoolteacher at Awaroa, and his former pupils cleaned and dusted the empty schoolhouse for the visit, giggling as they remembered their days in his classes. He had left the inlet long before the Winters and Cunliffes arrived but Jessie had found the odd record in his handwriting when she had taught there in her turn.

The Smiths were popular visitors and they were interested to see the changes at the inlet in the twenty years since they had been there. They were good company for William and spent long evenings talking with him at Meadowbank, and they also found a welcome at the Winters' house where both George and Christiana were interested in missionary work. They were learning Maori from books and with the help of Jim Perrott. George hoped to find work teaching Maori children in the North Island.

Adele was never discussed among the Hadfields but Jessie, who had known and liked her, was intrigued to meet her sister and to hear the news of the Snow family. She made a point of inviting Laura Smith up to Big River for a day, and when the two women were alone they found they had a good deal in common.

"That little niece of mine's a Snow all right," Laura chuckled when Floss was out of earshot. "She's got my sister's stubborn streak."

"And her looks too. I thought that was from the Newth side of the family?"

"It's quite a combination, isn't it? Mum's looks and Dad's personality. Addie always said that her Welby was more a Snow than a Hadfield, and Laura May as well. I always think that's why she's named after her aunts."

"And Fred?"

"Oh, your husband's a Hadfield through and through, my dear, don't you worry about that. It's not a bad thing either, if he takes after his father."

She smiled as Jessie poured another cup of tea. "I remember when we were girls and William would come to Glen Howard. It seems such a long time ago. Do you know, he was such a gentleman we didn't know which one of us he was courting until he proposed. We all got a surprise, I think. Addie thought he was after me, not her."

"Your life would have been so very different," Jessie said softly.

Laura chuckled. "Maybe I would have run away with my schoolteacher just the same."

She realised she had shocked Jessie, and put her cup and saucer down quickly. "Oh my dear, don't mind me. I'm very fond of my brother-in-law, and always have been, and I still can't get used to what happened to poor Addie in the end. You look after her little girl, and don't worry about her too much. What Addie chose was between her and God, and not for us to wonder at."

She changed the subject to Niue Island and her new life there, and they talked about the plans for the new school until it was time for her to go.

"What did you and Auntie Laura talk about?" Fred asked that evening, and Jessie bent her head over her sewing.

"Oh, the usual things. Teaching and babies. She's promised to write to us with descriptions of her new home."

"That's nice." He poked at the fire and got up restlessly. She waited for him to speak again, but he got his account book out and busied himself at the table, and after a few minutes she went and stood behind his chair, her hand gentle on his shoulder.

He leaned back against her for a moment, his head brushing her breast, and sighed. "She looks so much like Mother."

In February 1911 *Venture* went ashore on the rocks at Bark Bay. Young Newton Nalder raised the alarm, walking across the hills from Torrent Bay to knock at the door at Meadowbank and tell them she was stuck fast and slewing with the tide. He was left to walk all the way back again while Fred, Welby and Syd Cracknell went down in Welby's launch, and helped the crew to make her fast. The next day Harold Nicholls went with them, and after ten hours of hard work they managed to get her onto the beach and paid the crew off.

Venture was quite badly damaged, her keel rubbed on the rocks where she'd been caught and skewed around with the falling tide. There was nothing to do for a few days except keep an eye on her until they could work out how to get her off the beach and back home again.

They had to replace her keel, a huge job which kept her out of action for months and strained Fred's resources. He kept working on roading contracts for the council, timber and flax for the mills and whatever other forms of income he could generate.

Working the scows took skill and management. The men had to load and unload according to the tides, and their patterns of work were geared to the timetables of the boats and their skippers. A load of fenceposts or flax had to be cut and sledged down to the landing stage ready for loading, and when the scow came up the river it was often a race to turn her round or get her ready for the next tide so she could leave. Welby's launch was a godsend because it meant the scows could be towed and manoeuvred rather than having to sail inside the inlet.

There were still problems with the deck-loading scows. *Matakana* was loaded with posts once and the men found her sides were not big enough to secure the load so they had to take all the posts off and restack them. The job took three men a full eight-hour day.

Welby's launch was the first of several motorboats built at William Hadfield's Awaroa boatyard and used to ferry passengers and produce out to the steamers. This photo of Fred's workboat, built just before the war, was taken on a rare family outing.

Laura and Jim McLaren had a daughter in April 1911 and they called her Nina Adele, her second name in memory of her murdered grandmother. It was as if Laura and Welby had broken the run of boys in the family. At the end of May Jessie went off to Nelson with Ivy and little Clifford and on 21 July she gave birth to her first daughter, Mavis Jessie Hadfield. The baby was William's tenth grandchild and the third girl of her generation.

Jessie was nursed by Mrs Campbell, competent midwife and family friend who had moved from Awaroa to live in Nelson. The birth was a difficult one however, and Cliff was brought back to the Winters while Jessie stayed in Nelson with the baby. After a few weeks Fred got a telegram to say that his wife was ill, and he hurried to Nelson on the steamer.

Jessie was attended by Dr Barr who had known the Hadfields for years and had been Adele's and William's family doctor. He knew the family history well enough to be quite blunt with Fred. Jessie's trouble was nervous, not physical, and she was to stay away from the inlet until she was recovered enough to live there again.

Fred remembered Uncle Stanley Snow's warnings, and the stories about his mother's nervous fits, and he became quietly determined that history would not repeat itself. He had always loved his mother deeply, and although he'd been shocked by her divorce and second marriage he'd not been able to judge her as harshly as his sisters had. He remembered long weeks and months of his childhood when his father was away working, and Adele left to cope on her own. Now for the sake of his own marriage he decided that he would swallow his pride and accept help when Jessie needed it.

He took her to the hospital where she was admitted for rest and care. Fred and the rest of the family soon realised that she needed more than just a few days there. Her sisters-in-law all pitched in to help and after he had registered Mavis, he and Laura Hadfield, who had come over to help with the children, set off for home on the steamer. They took the baby to Olive at Waiharakeke while Jessie rested in a villa at Ngawhatu Hospital, where the beautiful gardens, spacious grounds and restful atmosphere gradually helped her to feel well again.

The Hadfields had good friends in Nelson, many of them people who had known Adele and the loneliness she had suffered at the inlet. Jessie's letters were soon full of church and family news, telling of visits from Mrs Lukin the merchant's wife and Mrs Gilbertson who had lived at Awaroa. The McLarens looked after her well and her own family visited whenever they could. She saw the Gillstroms and the Estcourts, went to tea with her friends and took the children to the gardens, and eventually she was able to return to Laura's house and become a day patient at the hospital.

For Jessie and Fred it was a time of stress but also of closeness. Fred missed her and looked forward to her letters. She wrote brave and loving messages, always addressing him as My Dear Boy, and worried about how he was managing without her. He sent her money whenever he could and reassured her that everything was fine at home. He planted an orchard of apples, pears, plums, peach and apricot trees which came in on *Venture* from John Hale's nursery in Nelson. As he set the trees out and protected them he imagined his children one day picking the fruit and Jessie bottling it for the winter, and he knew she had the strength to get through it all and come back to him.

Jessie's father came to see her and her sisters Christiana and Bessie wrote and visited when they could. She kept with her in Nelson two photographs from Wales, taken by their mother's brother Colin Houlson who had been a photographer in Abergavenny, and as she convalesced in the warm Nelson sunshine that spring her thoughts turned to Wales more than once.

One photograph was of Raglan Castle, big stone towers twined with ivy and ancient well groomed lawns and hedges under it. The other was a shady lane at Abergavenny, banks of oak trees either side of a simple dirt road curving gently into the distance. How far she had travelled along life's road, Jessie thought, since she had left Wales with her family as a little girl of eight.

Jessie Hadfield (nee Winter) with her family in 1910. From left: Christiana with Floss Knowles, Robert, Mrs Winter, George, Jessie with baby Clifford Hadfield.

While she was away Fred used locally-milled rimu to finish the house at Big River. He understood more now about what had happened between William and Adele, and he was still afraid that his marriage might break down the way his parents' had. He was determined Jessie was not going home to the little whare in the bush.

He and the boys moved the furniture and possessions from the whare into the new house while Jessie was away, and he built new furniture for them. The house had a kitchen with a dresser, a table and a fireplace at the end, and a big dining room with an open fire, a rimu table and chairs and a couch. Fred pasted wallpaper over wooden boxes to provide for extra storage. Two bedrooms opened off to one side, and there was a back porch. The foundations were laid for a front verandah, although that was never finished.

Jessie did not return to Awaroa again until Fred fetched her home on Christmas Day, and then she stayed with her parents down at the entrance until the new year. It was a Meadowbank Christmas that year, the family gathered around the big table under the fruit trees with William at the head and Laura McLaren, over from Nelson with her family, supervising the cooking. Jessie sat in the shade and Fred fussed over her and stayed close by her side.

Early in January he took his wife and family back up the river and they went straight into the new house. With Flossie, Cliff and baby Mavis home, the family was together again. They began calling their son Kiwi, an affectionate nickname that summed up their hopes for their new life at Big River.

Jessie found changes at Awaroa since she had been away and there was a lot to catch up on. Fred's uncle Harry Hadfield had been to visit, delighting his nephews with stories of the inlet in the early days. Roy had bought the Tonga Bay land from him and they had all walked over the old ground again.

Baigents' mill had still not moved into Awaroa to cut Fred's bush at Big River. Lewis Baigent and Fred had been corresponding for over a year about the mill, and about *Venture*'s contracts to move timber from it. The damage to her keel had forced her off the run at a time when Baigents were expanding and there was pressure to get her mended and back at work.

Jessie laughed when Fred read her the next letter from Lewis Baigent.

"This Collingwood mill has only been sawing about half time for some time back despite our trying all means to hurry it along. The price of butter etc is very high and the millhands are making enough to keep them out of the cows alone hence do not care whether the mill works or not. We are sorry we have been so long getting through this last piece of bush and will not be sorry to see the last of Collingwood. Will probably be over your way shortly. Yours faithfully..."

"The poor mill hands," Jessie laughed. "Your Mr Baigent sounds like a real slave driver."

The mill finally arrived on *Venture* and was unloaded up the river past the two Hadfield houses. The men built huts up the river and worked systematically with a steam hauler, and Jessie and Fred made sure they had enough butter and vegetables to keep them going so they were not distracted with having to be farmhands on the side. It was a good arrangement for both parties. The men appreciated the fresh produce, and for Jessie and her children there was some life and activity around the farm for a change.

In the winter of 1912 Mrs Winter died. She was buried in Nelson and soon afterwards Jessie's father began to look for a house in town. None of the family was in good health and Christiana was not able to manage the household on her own, while the men had trouble keeping up the farm. It was obvious they would have to leave the inlet. They would be sorely missed, not only by Jessie but by William Hadfield who had enjoyed the quiet companionship of Joseph Winter through difficult times and troubled years. The Winter family had been at the inlet nearly twenty years and together with the Cunliffes and the Cracknell boys they had formed the little community the younger Hadfields had grown up in. Now there would be only a handful of people left at the mouth of the inlet.

In the middle of all this gloom there was good news from Darcy in Auckland. He had taken up rowing as a sport, which caused great amusement at Awaroa where everyone had done it as a chore and a way of life. Darcy, Fred, Welby and the others had never thought anything of taking one of the heavy old sailing dinghies and heading for Nelson to the show or a dance. They'd always taken a sail but invariably had rowed at least one way.

Although he was a strong rower, Darcy had never stood out over his brothers and Fred could still beat him in a straight race. No one in Auckland could, however, and he wrote to say he'd won the sculling championship on Waitemata Harbour. There were newspaper cuttings sent down to pore over, and the Awaroa family were amazed and very proud when they realised Darcy was becoming a sporting champion.

The Winter family outside their orchard to greet Fred and his younger brothers. The trees were planted by Fred's uncle Harry Hadfield 1863-1894.

Courtesy Tui Winter

There was a big photograph they'd brought out with them, a family portrait taken in the studio and blown up as big as a painting. There was her father, a young-looking man with a well-trimmed beard, and her mother looking stern with little Christie sitting on her knee. Jessie was seven, with short hair and frills around her pantaloons, and young Will stood looking serious and uncomfortable. Jessie loved the photograph because it was so big. It was almost like being a little girl again and having her family there in the room with her.

Bessie, the eldest, already looked like her mother, and Jessie felt comforted by that, as if the coffin Fred had made had not been able to hold every part of her mother after all. She looked at the locket Bessie wore in the photograph, and fingered her own, given to her by her parents. It was to go to her eldest daughter Mavis when she was twelve, chubby little darling that she was.

"Look Mamie. Here's your grandpa Winter, and Auntie Bessie and Uncle Will, and Aunt Chrissie," she told the little girl, holding her up to the sepia photograph. And here's your Nana, and I thank God she saw you and Cliffie before she died."

"Talking to yourself, Jess?" She whirled around and laughed when she saw her sister-in-law by the open doorway, a big enamel bowl in her arms.

"Welby's been doing the hives," Laura said, whipping the cloth off with a flourish. Dark gold honey dripped from a big clump of yellow wax, filling the kitchen with its scent. "How's your bread? My boys have got themselves sticky and sick with crusts and honey, so we came to share."

They sat there on the verandah watching the children play. There were cornflowers, marigolds and roses around the house, and the apple trees were laden on the hill. The valley dripped with summer.

"I hope so much for another girl," Laura said softly as she watched Mavis smearing a honey-covered crust around her face. "I've been having an easier time, so it might be another daughter."

"Lucky you," Jess patted her own bulging front. "This babe's a boy I've no doubt. He's already kicking me heartily and my back aches as it did with Kiwi."

"Jess," Laura began, but she stopped and turned away to watch the boys. Floss was in the field with Fred and Evey, and James and Allen were racing up and down the paddock playing horses, little Cliff shrieking and screaming as he ran wildly around them. He was not yet three and her own sons were five and four, but there was something different about Jessie's boy. His pretty face was still a baby's, sweet and beguiling, and his blue eyes held his emotions like sunshine and clouds across the sky, with no hint of understanding.

Clifford Hadfield 1910-1917

"Kiwi's a blithe spirit," Jessie said fondly. "He's a little wild creature, isn't he?" Sometimes in this heat I have such a struggle to keep his clothes on him, and he hates to be shut inside. He would run free as air if I let him."

But as that summer progressed Jess found it harder to run after the little boy, and when it was her time to go to Nelson for her confinement she became more and more concerned about how to manage. Laura McLaren gave birth to a daughter early in February, and wrote to say she'd called her Bethany Olive. Welby's Laura was to go home to Wellington with her boys for her confinement, due a few weeks after Jessie's own.

Laura came over late in February to bring Jessie fresh fish Welby had caught in his net. They were moving house, the first one built too close to the river and caught in a flood. To Jessie's amazement and envy her sister-in-law was still brimming with health and vitality, her bulging stomach hardly slowing her down at all. Her skirts were still wet and muddy from a clumsy step out of the dinghy Welby had rowed her across in.

"Can't stop," she cried at the doorway. "Welby's taking us down to Meadowbank to give Dad some fish too. I haven't been away from the river for ages. Don't you feel restless?"

"I just feel exhausted," Jessie confessed. "I wish I had your energy."

When Laura had gone she slumped down at the table, too listless even to start cleaning the fish. Their glassy eyes turned her stomach, the limp fins and tails revolted her and when the flies arrived to hover around the fish she covered them up with a cloth, unable to cope. When Fred came home he found her rocking helplessly, her hands on her heavy belly, and when he took her in his arms she burst into tears.

"I miss Mother very much," she whispered forlornly. "I feel so alone and so tired, and I can't go to McLarens this time."

"It's the heat, and the running around you've been doing," Fred told her. "How would you feel about leaving Kiwi behind this time?"

"Oh Fred, I couldn't. And how could you cope?"

"Floss could care for him. She's ten now, and a strong capable girl."

Jessie shook her head. "Dear Boy, you're so good to me, but it wouldn't be fair to Flossie. It's too much for her, and for you too. If only there was someone who could come and look after you all while I was away."

Fred stared into the fire, his mind busy. It was the end of February, the hay all cut and the shearing done, and the winter pasture was growing nicely. Jessie had made jam and bottled fruit and there were sides of bacon hanging above the fire, dried mushroom and tomatoes in jars in the pantry and pumpkins ripening nicely in the garden. She'd made soap from the mutton fat and lye, fighting the nausea of her pregnancy as she'd stirred the brew with a long wooden stick. March was an easier time than any other, but there was always the *Venture* and the road contract, fence posts to cut and flax to haul. Mr McLaren would be ready for another load of supplejack soon, and there were Harley's sheep to look after. Jessie was right, he couldn't possibly stay at home for all the long weeks she would be in Nelson.

"What about asking Dad to take the boy?"

"Oh Fred, Cliffie would be too much for him, and Evey is too busy to run after him all day."

"Ivy and Will would have him."

"Ivy's got Henry and little Neil to care for. I'd be so afraid Kiwi would run away and get in the water, or go down to the mill and get in the way of the men."

He woke in the night and realised she was not in the bed beside him. He slid carefully out without waking the baby asleep at the head of the bed or Cliff turning restlessly in the cot beside him. He found Jessie sitting in the big rocker by the fire, a shawl wrapped around her shoulders and her hair hanging down in a long plait over one shoulder. He poked the fire up and set the big kettle across it, then he took a kitchen chair and sat down facing her, her slim white hands captured in his work roughened ones.

"Kiwi shall stay here, Jess. I'll go down this morning and ask Mr Perrott if he'll come up and stay in the whare while you're away."

James Perrott lived in this cottage on Silver Point. Photo taken 1920

T Pratt photo

Wild pork and bacon were welcome additions to their diet
and Fred went hunting whenever he could.

Now there were only Fred and Welby, Ivy and Evered left at the inlet. Evered was the only one still single and he lived at home with his father, working on the Little River road contract. *Venture* was busy with the timber and flax.

Sigleys had built a big house over by the mill, where Mrs Sigley and her girls cooked for twelve mill hands and they were always busy with the Post Office on the little verandah. The road was now up to the standard where a horse and gig could get in to Little River and then around to Meadowbank. It was a long trip but possible in most weathers. The population was now concentrated on the east side, around the saw mill, rather than at Little River.

Horses prospered in Awaroa where sheep did not, for although the grass was lush after the initial burning off, the potash was soon exhausted and much of the land was found to lack cobalt. Horses were used for sledging foods up from the boats, for harrowing or transporting people over the track to Wainui. The sawmill used bullocks at first to pull the logs out, but by 1910 they had all been replaced by steam haulers.

Laura Hadfield with her daughter Ada, born 1913. "I was reminded of Romney's *Diana the Huntress*," schoolteacher Ella Flower wrote of Laura (nee Cunliffe) with her luxuriant red hair.

Courtesy Ada and Joan Hadfield

In 1913 the Takaka County Council allocated £35 for a rough horse track from Awaiti to Big River, and Fred undertook the labour contract. He tendered £49.7.6d for another job, with an additional 27/6 for each culvert.

Fred's regular work gang was Syd Cracknell, Bob Allen, Will Winter and occasionally Bill Samuels. Roy, Evered and the others worked for Fred when they were home. They did fencing contracts and worked on the roads, and contracted for each other, cutting grass seed for Roy, fencing for Baigents. In the summer of 1913 *Venture* shipped out eleven bales of wool, 40lb of potatoes and a great deal of flax. She also took hides, walnuts and other saleable goods to Nelson from the Awaroa farms.

Bill Samuels was the fastest flax cutter in the inlet, his good friend Albert Nalder a close second. They would grab a clump of flax, tuck it under an arm and then cut it with a sharp half sickle. The clumps were sheaved and carried to the wharf, and when there was enough and a scow was ready the sheaves would be loaded onto a punt and taken down the river. A shilling a ton was the going rate and a good man could earn ten shillings a day. The faster he worked the better, because fresh flax was heavier, and the regular flax cutters kept their own tallies.

Fred bought a punt from the Hunters at Totaranui, and used it to take timber down from Little River to the *Venture* when they couldn't get right up. Rimu, matai and birch went out in large quantities. On one trip in August *Venture* left for Nelson with 3500 super feet of rimu and 1500 of matai for Baigents, on another 1600 for Robertson Brothers. *Lady Barkly* was still plying the route between Nelson and Collingwood on a regular basis, but now she was sold to the Burfords and renamed *Hina*.

Evered turned sixteen and had a sweetheart, Eileen Sears. She came to Meadowbank to stay, and they sat out on the porch in front of the homestead and watched to sea, planning a future together. Evered carved their initials with a penknife in the cabbage tree his elder brother Roy had brought back from the West Coast when he was on the survey gang.

Evered and Eileen had met through Roy, who was courting a young lady in the Moutere valley and often took Evered along with him when he went out to dances and socials. It was a long trip out from Awaroa, down to Riwaka by boat and then a long bicycle ride over gravel roads to the Moutere. Roy was working in the hopfields at the time, and often Evered worked with him. On one trip the front fork on Evered's bike snapped and broke, stranding the pair miles from anywhere. Roy cut a manuka stick to length and wedged in inside the hollow tube of the fork, lashing it firmly in place with flax, and the bicycle not only got them to the dance but got them safely home again the next day.

Eileen was popular with all the Hadfields and visited the McLarens in Nelson regularly, delighting the little girls by whistling popular music hall tunes as she came up the front path. She and Evered were still young and there was no formal engagement but everyone in the family knew about their romance and approved of it.

Les Cracknell in his house near the mouth of the inlet. Cousins of the Winter family, Les and Syd came to the inlet from London and made their homes there. Les died in WWI.

Photo Syd Cracknell

Fred Hadfield with a load of supplies from the boat. Horses were always very important at Awaroa where they were used to carry heavy loads and work the farm machinery.

"Time we thought about a school, Jess," Fred said one night at Big River. "I'll be off up to Sigleys after tea to see what they think about it."

She was startled. "Cliffie's only three, Fred."

"Aye, but Floss is nearly ten and she's hardly learned her letters at all, and Welby's Jim is five. And there'll be Mavis and our Bill, and Bert and Ada and no doubt a few more before we've all finished. Sigley's girls could do with some schooling instead of hanging around the mill workers all day, and there are the Brunings over at Little River whose children are nearly old enough. I'll be bound he'll like the idea."

The Sigleys had previously gone to school at Little River, in a one-roomed schoolhouse built for the mill hands by William and Fred Hadfield years earlier. Evered had also managed to get there often enough to learn his letters, going up with his brothers each day when they went to cut flax, and helping them after school until it was time to come home. Once the Sigleys moved across the inlet the school closed and the little building soon deteriorated and fell down.

By the end of 1913 Fred had built a little one-roomed schoolhouse across the paddock from his house at Big River and Freda and Zena Sigley came over most days to join Floss and Jim Hadfield at their books there. It was a tiny room, shaped like a box and clearly inadequate, but it was a school.

Blackberries and gorse were a major problem now and the men spent days cutting them down. Fred bought pigs from Manson for the Big River property and he would let them run loose, calling them in each evening to be fed and put away. Floss and the boys across the river learned to be wary of the pigs on the beach and in the bush, as there were often wild ones mixed in amongst the domestic stock.

Fred worked hard every day, but he had his own priorities. When Jessie told him early in August 1914 she was pregnant again he spent the whole day making a new cot. William came up for dinner now and then, his little dinghy sailing up to the landing with both main and jib set taut.

Olive Nicholls and her boys came from Riwaka for Christmas, and Christiana Winter came from Nelson, but when everyone else went picnicking at New Year, Fred and Syd Cracknell were busy with the hay. Fred got permission from the Council to erect telegraph poles between Totaranui and Awaroa, so now it was possible to send and receive telegrams from the little post office at Awaroa rather than going across to Totaranui each time.

In 1914 there were rumours of war. The news came to Awaroa as most news did, told by one man to another long before the papers arrived to confirm it. People visited each other more than ever, taking comfort in conversation.

The threat of war loomed over them all. For the women and girls, especially those with husbands, sons and sweethearts of army age, it was a worrying time. It was apparent to everyone that all the young fit men would soon be leaving.

One of the first casualties at Awaroa was Violet Sigley, one of the elder daughters from the mill. Whether it was the talk of war, the oppressive isolation of the inlet, the restlessness of the age or some other emotional trigger, she became distressed and upset, and on 18 July 1914 she took a rifle and shot herself. A few weeks later war was declared, the mill closed and the first of the Awaroa men called up.

Fred and Jessie slowly began to come to terms with a tragedy of their own. Little Clifford, affectionately known to everyone in the family as Kiwi, was not developing mentally and became harder and harder to manage. Matters came to a head early in 1915 when Jessie's fourth child was due and she took the two children to Nelson with her on the steamer. In her heart she knew she would have to deal with the problem and it worried her greatly.

"Dear Fred," she wrote. "I thought you would like to hear from us as soon as possible. We are here safely, which is a comfort, isn't it? We had a good trip, very smooth, but as Cliff was frightened by the noise of the engine I took them all into the cabin, where he was soon comfortably in a bunk and fell asleep before very long.

"The others were more trouble, wanted to see Dad and didn't like it very much: Bubs was cross too but fell asleep at last, and Mavis stayed awake until about half past eight. Mr and Mrs McBurney got aboard at Tonga with their children, so I should have had company if I hadn't had to stay with the little ones. ... .

"...George was down to meet us and so was Laura, but all the children were asleep so we thought perhaps the best plan would be to stay on board all night especially as George was doubtful if we could get a cab and they might charge 18/- at least. (Cliff is sitting on the table shaking it, so excuse writing).

So I lay down again and had a few naps, broken by squeals and grunts from a lot of fat pigs just outside the cabin. The bunks are very hard too when you stay in them all night and it was very hot and stuffy; however morning came at last and Laura came down again and we went up there.

"We arranged for a cab to come for us at ten o'clock. Of course Cliff was all over the place; just as we were getting on our hats to go he disappeared, but we discovered him in the next garden just after the cab arrived. Poor little Mamie started to cry when she saw us driving off without her, but I hope she has settled down by now.

"I wish Cliff would settle down too, he doesn't like it if you shut the doors and windows, but he is all over the place, climbs over the gate in a twinkling. I think he will not be so restless in a day or two…"

She was to have her baby at Mrs Gledhill's nursing home, and as usual spent the last few days of her pregnancy shopping, sewing and catching up on family news. Cliff's erratic behaviour could no longer be ignored, however. He ran away at every opportunity, and when they shut him in he banged his head against the windows so hard he cracked one. George and Christiana finally persuaded their sister to seek medical advice.

Jessie took Clifford to see Dr Barr, who examined him carefully and said there was nothing physically wrong. He recommended the boy be sent to an institution where he could be properly trained and where he could be kept from hurting himself. It would be best for the whole family, Dr Barr said, if Clifford was sent away. A home for Mental Defectives had been established in Richmond, and in February little Kiwi Hadfield was registered as an inmate.

It was an agonising decision for Jessie and Fred to make, but she realised she would soon be unable to handle the little boy, who rolled around violently through the night and wandered away whenever her back was turned in the daytime. He couldn't communicate with other children and seldom responded to adults, and Jessie accepted that the doctors could not do anything for him.

"I don't quite know what I expected, unless it was a miracle," she wrote to Fred. "I hate to think of him shut in there, he's always been so free." Exhausted by the stress and broken nights, she told him of the arrangements that were to be made for little Clifford, and a few days later she reported that she had left him at the Richmond Home. She and the children visited him frequently, finding him miserable, crying and trying to get away from them one day, calmer and happier the next.

"But I don't think there is much chance of improvement up there, why should there be; only he is kept out of harm's way. But I don't like him staying there, perhaps I know too much about it; perhaps I imagine too much…

"I want to cry, but I'm always telling the children that it is no good, so must try to practice it."

Ralph Gordon Hadfield was born 19 March 1915, a fine, strong baby, but Jessie returned home to find their financial situation worsening. Cliff's care now had to be paid for each quarter, and there were other demands on their slender finances. Fred's sister Olive Nicholls wrote from Riwaka to ask for help. Her husband had been in ill health for some time before he died, and she and her sons were nearly destitute. She could not afford shoes for the boys, and had trouble keeping food on the table.

Now there were more children ready to start school at Awaroa. The Education Board wrote to Tod Sigley refusing to build a school but offering to pay rent if a suitable building was available, and one day Fred and Welby went back up past Meadowbank to take a good long look at the old school building their father and uncle had put up over twenty years before. It was a kitset building, the timbers numbered and still sound, and it would be ideal if it were not in the wrong place. Fred measured it up and they realised if they knocked the verandah off it would fit on the big punt they used for the timber. Fred went back to Sigleys with a new proposition, and Welby started looking for a site.

The school was moved, and there was great excitement when the new schoolteacher finally arrived on the *Wairoa*. Mr Edgar Ford took up his position in September 1916, and taught until he was called up for military service, when Miss Lewis took his place. The new school was between Welby's house and Sigleys, and the children from those two families walked to and from school while it was the turn of Fred's children to be rowed across the river each day. New books arrived from Jackson and Co in Nelson, and Floss Knowles, Freda and Zena Sigley were the eldest in class, Mavis the youngest.

When Jessie went to Nelson to have her next baby she went to Mrs Jeffries in Van Dieman Street, and Christiana looked after the children and brought them down to the nursing home on Sundays. It was an easier birth for Jessie, and she enjoyed the bustle and activity of the city. When her son was born in November 1916 she called him Nelson Ivan.

"The baker has just called in his motorcar. It stands panting at the gate until he gets back to it," she wrote in amusement. "There is plenty to watch out here on the verandah, the children passing to school, college boys, not many foot passengers, but now and then a motorbike or motorcar rushes past, or a tradesman's cart."

Jessie had a good rest before she and the children came home to Awaroa again. They stayed with Christiana in Emano Street, and the two sisters enjoyed their time together. George and Robert were both out working all day, and enjoyed their niece and nephews in the evenings. Mavis was five, Bill three and Ralph eighteen months old, and the little family was a lot easier to manage now there was room for them all.

While Jessie was in Nelson, Darcy was married in Auckland, and to the joy of his father and the rest of the family he wrote that he'd like to bring his new bride to Meadowbank for Christmas.

Orakei and *Pearl Kasper* raising the sunken steamer *Manaroa* at French Pass about 1912. The *Manaroa* was put ashore by Hautai Island.

Newton Nalder photo.

Tranquillity at Big River. Muriel Hadfield looks across to Welby and Laura's house and the launch *Isis,* bought from Dr Fell and turned into an Awaroa workboat.

CHAPTER TEN : THE WAR YEARS

1916

IT WAS A GRAND FAMILY GATHERING, that Christmas of 1916.

Darcy and his new bride Rita Coyle arrived on the steamer, Olive and her boys came from Riwaka, the McLarens came from Nelson and Roy and Evered arrived home from Trentham camp. Their father was ready for them. The dining room was decorated with greenery and red geraniums, a big wicker basket hung on the wall filled with presents and tents were set up on the lawn.

On Christmas Day 32 people sat down to dinner at Meadowbank and the tables groaned under their feast. There was roast lamb, poultry, peas, new potatoes, beans, ham and tomatoes. There were plum puddings, cherry pies, pints of cream, salads and fruit. The puddings came out of the kitchen on a board carried between two brothers, and were served one at each end of the long table.

Darcy, Roy and Evered were all in uniform and the shadow of war hung over the whole family, the unspoken dread that this might be their last Christmas together. Brothers and sisters laughed and joked into the small hours, children played with their cousins and at the head of the table William Welby Hadfield, now 72 years old, watched them with his mind full of memories. It was nearly sixty years since he'd left England as a lad, over fifty years since he'd first come to Awaroa. Now little Nelson Ivan Hadfield, barely a month old, was the youngest of sixteen grandchildren gathered at Meadowbank.

It was a magic summer holiday. They went out for picnics in the motor launches, swam and sailed, visited the homes at Big River, laughed in the kitchens and talked quietly under the fruit trees. They went fishing, took long walks around the inlet or dozed in the long hot afternoons. William had a smart little sailing dinghy called *The Nipper,* painted bright blue and rigged with both a jib and a mainsail, and he took the older children out in it to race against their parents in *Venture*'s much bigger and heavier sailing dinghy.

They went out in the evenings to spear stingrays, trying hard to spot the dark shapes in the water and drift over near to them without splashing or disturbing them. When they were close enough William or one of the boys would stand up in the bow and hurl the harpoon which had a good stout rope on it. If the strike hit home the ray would take them on a wild ride around the harbour, the wake streaming behind them as they hung on to the sides of the boat and shrieked with excitement.

To the children, their grandfather Hadfield was the kindest and most generous old man, taking time to talk to them and tell them stories of the old days, and rescuing them when they got into trouble. When their Aunt Ivy caught them around the side of the house, cheeks bulging with black heart cherries from the big tree behind the kitchen, they thought they were in for a good shaking at the very least, but their grandfather came to their rescue. He came around the corner brandishing his walking stick and stopped her scolding.

"Ivy, the children will eat as many cherries as they want," he told her sternly.

"Then you won't get your cherry jam this year," she replied pertly.

"That's all right then, it doesn't matter about my jam at all," he said, and the delighted children were told to pick the cherries whenever they chose that summer. Their mothers, aunts and uncles were busy around the house and farms, but their grandfather was always there for the children, telling them stories, teaching them small things or just talking to them as he worked around the homestead garden. In the evenings after tea he would go out and sit on the bench near the dog tree, hands crossed over his walking stick, and gaze out to sea, and anyone who wanted to join him could go and sit beside him to share the view and the mood. He told them stories and sometimes in the evenings his own children would ask him to talk about the early days.

Evered would often draw closer and listen to the stories too, catching up on the family history he'd missed. Once William told them all how he and Harry had climbed the hill above Meadowbank, called Mount Rollinson after one of the first settlers at Awaroa, when they were young lads still.

"We thought our cow might have gone up there." He chuckled. "To tell you the truth we'd always wanted to climb it, so one day we did. It was grand up there." He lowered his voice dramatically. "There were dragons."

"Real dragons?" young Bert asked in awe, and the others followed his glance up to the innocuous-looking ridge behind the house.

"Real dragons. Great big barking things."

"How big?" Floss asked sceptically, and he laughed.

"Well, lizards really, like the ones you find in the logs sometimes, only much much bigger than them. Like miniature dragons with spiky backbones."

"What happened, Grandad?"

"Well, I'm sorry to say we killed them all. They frightened us, they were making a strange barking noise and we'd never seen anything like them before." He looked over at Evered. "I think now they were tuatara lizards. I've never seen them in the inlet since, but I've heard tell of them on some of the little islands near Croiselles."

The story was a popular one and the next morning an expedition of little boys and girls was mounted, armed with sticks to kill the dragons. They had a fine game on the bank behind the sawpit.

All too soon the first of the visitors left. Photographs were taken, promises exchanged, hands shaken and cheeks kissed, and those left behind on the beach waved until the boats were out of sight, The family separated again, all too conscious that Darcy, Roy and Evered and many of their friends would spend their year in uniform and at war.

Awaroa was a quiet, uneventful place during the war years. Magnus Manson died and was buried in Takaka, and Jim Perrott moved back to his whare at Silver Point after more than a year at Wainui. *Venture* was laid up, and the last stack of dressed flax lay abandoned, rotting at the Little River crossing, the market no longer there for it even if there was transport. The steamers were no longer running so regularly and the mail was brought through by road, Tod Sigley riding out to Tarakohe twice a week to bring the heavy mailbags to Wainui, Totaranui and Awaroa.

Fred worked on a new road contract, south from Awaiti. He sat up late at night poring over the specifications Takaka County Clerk William Baird sent out to him.

"At peg 8 a bridge culvert shall be built across the creek, 18ft between the sills. Two sills 12"x10" 12ft long drift bolted together to be bedded down solid and level on each side of the creek. Four stringers 12"x8" spaced 2ft 9" apart to be securely drift bolted to the sills and covered with 6"x3" decking 12ft long securely spiked on to stringers with 7" spikes. Two guard pieces 6"x6" spaced 10 feet apart to be securely bolted down through the stringer. All timber shall be best heart of Black Birch free from knots and shakes."

"I wish my heart were free from knots and shakes," Jessie laughed as she read over his shoulder. "But how bland our life would be then."

On 20 March 1917 little Clifford Hadfield died at the Home for Mental Defectives in Richmond. Fred and Jessie grieved for their firstborn son but his death was not the blow it might have been. They had long since come to terms with losing him, and with Floss and four little ones already in the house and another one the way they had little time for mourning.

Roy wrote from sea, on his way to France. Darcy and Syd Cracknell were in England, Evered was in camp in New Zealand.

Darcy wrote from camp in England in July 1917. Everything was strange and exciting to the New Zealand soldiers, and Darcy and Roy were especially fascinated with the destroyers that came out from Plymouth to escort their troopship in. "They would come close alongside us and give their orders, then all of a sudden they would give an extra kick and would be round our bow and on the opposite side in a minute," Darcy wrote. "When they turn round they lay right over on their sides. They can twist about very quickly and turn right round in less than two lengths when they are travelling at about 25 miles."

An enemy submarine was sighted in the channel but quickly submerged again, and when Darcy got to camp he heard that the 22nd company had been luckier. They had seen a submarine sunk by the allies.

The New Zealanders were quick to notice the number of British girls doing men's work, driving milk carts and bread trucks, sweeping the streets and working in the factories. Flowers were plentiful, food less so, and Darcy noted with approval that there were vegetables being grown on every available piece of ground. His training camp on the Salisbury Plain was very close to an air training field and every evening he and the other soldiers were treated to a free airshow as the pilots learned to loop the loop and staged mock attacks. The training was brief and intense, and by Christmas he was in France.

That Christmas was a sad and worrying one for the family back home. There were presents ordered from the shops in Nelson, but the steamer did not arrive in time and the children were terribly upset when they realised they would have none of the goodies they had enjoyed the previous year. Jessie sat up most of the night making little gifts for them out of what she had to hand, a rag doll from a cast-off shirt for Mavis and little stuffed animals for Billie and Ralph. There were some raisins and walnuts in their stockings and recycled Christmas cards, and as they sang the old familiar carols their parents found it hard to keep their spirits up and be joyous.

It was a very different Christmas for Darcy too. The previous summer he'd been at Meadowbank, swimming, sailing and fishing. Now it was winter in France, and a heavy fall of snow forced the cancellation of a Boxing Day sports programme.

Darcy and Roy, two of the three Hadfields from Awaroa who served overseas in World War One, with their father William Welby Hadfield.

The Kiwi soldiers had joined with Tommies and Canadians in fighting off their officers in a fast and furious snowball fight instead, then some of them decided to storm the little bridge which was their camp boundary.

"They tackled the police guarding it and drove them off, and then they toured the town giving everyone a hot time but it led to no trouble and they all came home again to tea," Darcy wrote in a letter home.

He was sent behind the lines to do a course in observation and sniping. Although his poor education handicapped him he found his experience with the survey gangs an advantage in the mapreading and compass work, and he enjoyed the challenge. He met one of Westrupp's boys and one of the Morrisons from Nelson, and back in England Roy met up with several men from Takaka.

By August Darcy was at the front line and in the thick of the fighting. He wrote to his father that he had met plenty of Huns. "I was glad to get among them, for the chance to strike a blow to pay them out for bringing me all the way over here away from my wife. It seems hard to say you killed a man, but when you think of what they have done you can't have any mercy for them..."

Life was hard in the trenches, and Darcy told his father he hadn't had his clothes off at night since he arrived in France. They had no blankets but lay down where they could, their oilskins under them and their greatcoats over them.

"The trench isn't a very nice place when it is raining I can tell you, after you have had a few days tramping about in the mud a foot deep, without any place to lay down for a rest. You can make a hole in the bank big enough to sit in with your legs doubled up in the mud in the trench for everybody to walk over. Then it is almost impossible to sleep with the shells bursting all around you. If you dig in too far, the bank is likely to fall in on you. It is hard enough to keep the bank up against the shell fire at any time. I had often heard about what a bad time the boys had in the trenches but had no idea how bad it really is."

Darcy caught a shrapnel wound in his head, his life saved by his tin hat. He was invalided back to England but then sent back to the front as soon as he had recovered, and was there until bronchitis beat him in the last few weeks of the war and he returned to England to convalesce.

Roy was also sent to France. He trained on the Lewis gun and in trench warfare, and his first day at the front was memorable because of the unpleasantness of hiding in a shell hole close to decomposing corpses.

In September 1917 he and his Lewis gun crew were advancing on a series of concrete pillboxes when an enemy grenade landed at their feet. "The gunner was going round in circles like a stunned fowl, but I was not that bad. I tried to help him back to the first aid post but he was too much for me and I had to leave him, and the poor chap never got back but died there."

Roy was sent to a French hospital where the shrapnel was dug out of his legs and foot, but he was also shell-shocked and spent some time in Brackenhurst Hospital back in England. A few months later, however, he was back at the front, facing the Germans who had made a stand near Beauencourt.

"I had the woodwork stripped off the barrel of my rifle by a bullet that afternoon," he wrote later on. It was to be a hot few days for Corporal Roy Hadfield, who with two others was posted to guard his company's right flank. The ground was too hard to dig more than a rudimentary and shallow trench, and the three men were out of sight of the main body of soldiers.

Unbeknown to them the company commander decided to fall back from the ridge, and the three men with the Lewis gun were forgotten for the next 24 hours. One was badly crippled, but Roy kept his head and led them safely back to their own lines. "We had been given up as lost and we had a job to convince the look-outs who we were and had to go through the routine of being taken in for interrogation after being disarmed."

Roy remained in France until the war ended in November 1918, when he and his company took part in a long route march to the German border. He was awarded the Military Medal for his service at the front.

Evered was held back in New Zealand with measles and did not get away until mid-1917. He went to Egypt and Palestine, and his letters home were filled with descriptions of touring in rickshaws, bargaining in bazaars and a visit to the famous Cinnamon gardens near Colombo. He visited an ancient mosque and paid a shilling for a 30lb bunch of bananas before embarking again on the troopship *Tofua*.

They were joined by the Australian ship *Canberra* and entered Suez where they left the ships and went into training camp. Like Darcy they were close to an air training field, and Evered wrote that they did not feel very safe with about twenty aeroplanes going through their manoeuvres overhead.

Scarlet fever broke out in the camp and Evered became Provost Sergeant, responsible for enforcing the quarantine. It was a good job but did not last for long, and early in 1918 he was in training with the mounted rifles in Ismailia. It turned out to be a fascinating lesson in ancient history. Evered wrote to the family back at Awaroa.

"We have a splendid chaplain here and on church parades he takes for his text various happenings around our camp and Egypt generally, and they are much more interesting when you know the lay of the country and what hardships they must have had travelling in caravans across these sandy wastes in those days. We are also studying up the Old Testament and the references that are in it to various Biblical places about here. The Testament is the best guide you could have to Palestine and Egypt, and already we have found a lot of information in respect to the locality of our camp."

Evered was sent to Cairo for a course on bayonet fighting, and he took the opportunity to see the sights and keep a detailed diary. He saw the irrigation projects on the Nile delta, and visited the great pyramids, the Dead City and the Sphinx. He was interested in the intensive agriculture on the Delta, where four crops a year were grown on the richly sedimented ground, and he watched the annual pilgrim caravan set out for Mecca. In Jerusalem he met up with a chaplain who shared his interest in Biblical history and he took intensive notes as he was shown around the city. He spent time at the village of St John the Baptist and in Bethlehem too, and found that by keeping his eyes open and asking questions he had rich opportunities to learn about the things around him.

"I would like to give you a full description of everything, but it would mean me leaving the army to do the writing it would entail, so Fred, I'm afraid it had better wait until the war is over," he promised.

For Evered the war was an enriching experience, in spite of his contracting malaria and spending the last months of it in a base hospital. He came home full of wondrous stories and he brought back exotic souvenirs, including a tiny scarab beetle with brilliantly shining wings for Jessie.

The letters from the front were pored over by kerosene lamp and candlelight all around the inlet. Jim Perrott would row over to Meadowbank to sit on the verandah with William Hadfield and talk over the latest report from France or Egypt, and up at Big River Fred and Welby would meet on the riverbank and wonder about the strangeness of the seasons and the crops on the other side of the world. They would talk across the river for hours, squatting one on each side and shouting across the water while their children wandered upstream looking for duck eggs.

For the womenfolk the war made little difference. They were anxious for their soldier boys and did their part by knitting and letter writing, but their daily round of cooking, washing, gardening, preserving and making butter went on unchanged. There were occasional parties at the Sigleys' house, patriotic concerts got up by the girls as much to brighten their lives as to raise money. The post office was run by Sigleys at that time and Freda and her mother had an anxious time dealing with the telegrams and war news that came buzzing in Morse code down the wire to the little settlement.

At Awaroa the work went on...

Les Cracknell died in the war, and Bob Allen, who had worked for the most of the Awaroa farmers over the years, lost a leg but the Hadfield boys came through relatively unscathed. The Cunliffe boys were at war too, and Laura was uneasy when she heard that Frank had been wounded. Then came the telegram they all dreaded. Laura's younger brother Willie had died at Gallipolli and all the families felt for her. Mrs Cunliffe came down to Awaroa and the two of them spent a few weeks quietly drawing strength from each other and from the children.

Laura went to Wellington to have her last child, a daughter Joan Edna Eila born in April 1918, and a few months later Muriel Christiana was born at Fred and Jessie's home at Big River.

Jessie had intended to go out to Nelson for the birth, as she had always done, but the steamers were erratic and Muriel came unexpectedly early. Fred raced down to get Mrs Samuels to help, but she was lying down with a migraine and it took some time for her to get ready. Fred fumed and fretted but could not hurry her, and then when he got her back to the dinghy and pushed it off he found it had sprung a leak in the planking. By the time she and Fred arrived back at the house they found Laura there, hastily summoned by Floss. She had arrived in the nick of time and turned the newborn baby upside down with a hearty spank to get her breathing.

A telegram was sent to Christiana Winter in Nelson to tell her that her new niece and namesake had arrived safely. Christie sent Jessie a parcel by the steamer, a little china sugar basin for Muriel, and when the minister was next down at Awaroa he christened the little girl with water sprinkled from the basin.

In October that year Fred was milking in the cowshed under the trees when a thunderstorm struck the valley. A bolt of lightening hit the bail next to him, killing the cow and setting the wooden rails on fire. It was a miraculous escape for Fred and the other two cows, all knocked down but otherwise unhurt. He kept a section of the burned rail for years and would show it to visitors and tell the story over and over again.

Peace was proclaimed 12 November 1918. It made little practical difference at Awaroa, but there was relief in everyone's hearts. New Year's Eve was especially lively and joyful, and all through the following year there were parties and welcomes as the boys came home.

Ella Flower came to Awaroa in 1919. It was her first posting as a teacher and she was straight from secondary school. At sixteen she was only a year or two older than the elder Sigleys, Hadfields and Brunings who were her pupils.

Ella found Big River a strange and lonely place. She arrived at night, the transition from the steamer to Welby's launch confusing in the darkness, and as they went back up the inlet on the tide she could see nothing of her new home. She sat in silence, wondering how the men could navigate through such inky blackness, but then when her eyes got used to the darkness she was comforted by what she thought were lights burning in houses all around her. Daylight revealed the truth, that there were only two households by the river. Fred and Welby had been burning gorse on the hillsides and what she had thought was candlelight was nothing but the flickering embers of their fires.

Miss Flower was welcomed into Welby's and Laura's home, where she found white muslin curtains around the bed and a bowl of French marigolds on the dresser. The furniture, like everything else, was home-made, and the young teacher learned to do without the amenities of town. She had time on her hands to sew, and with her first pay she bought new clothes and fabric by mail order, a few yards of silk poplin, material for a blazer, a white Panama straw hat and two pairs of pure silk stockings.

She stayed with the various families, a few months at each place, because boarding the teacher was part of their obligation to the education board and the committee ensured it was shared around equally. When it was time for her to move to the next house the teacher would pack her things in her wicker hamper

To the children he was a frail, sad figure in the end, full of gentle dignity. The young McLarens knew he would die soon, and Bethany watched in awe as he seemed to grow smaller. She knew that the Bible said "Suffer the little children to come unto me" and she could see that soon her grandfather would have shrunk small enough to be a child and go to Jesus. Laura nursed him until he died on 3 December 1920, a year to the day after Evered had drowned.

They brought William home to Awaroa and buried him beside Evered, under the trees at the back of his beloved Meadowbank. Jim Perrott led the funeral cortege, hat in hand and silent with grief at the loss of his old friend.

William Welby Hadfield had lived at Awaroa for 57 years. He left his eight surviving children and 22 grandchildren a legacy of memories, a home and a garden by the sea.

He was remembered not only as a pioneer settler, farmer and boatbuilder, but for his manners and values as an English gentleman.

The graves at Meadowbank. Evered Rogers Hadfield, William Welby Hadfield and Allen Herbert (Bert) Hadfield were buried here, and a memorial stone has now been added for William Welby's son Roy Hubert who died in 1986.

HADFIELDS AT AWAROA - THE THIRD GENERATION

WILLIAM WELBY HADFIELD and **MARTHA ADELE ANN SNOW**
(1844-1920)   (1860-1906)

FREDERICK GEORGE
(9/10/1879-11/1/76)
m JESSIE WINTER 1908
Clifford Frederick (15/3/1910-20/3/1917)
Mavis Jessie (21/7/1911)
William Rogers (8/3/1914)
Ralph Gordon (19/3/1915)
Nelson Ivan (6/11/1916)
Muriel Christiana (8/7/1918)
Colin Houlson (3/1921-10/11/1923)
Dorothy Joy (Aug 1922)

WELBY VIVIAN
(15/5/1881- 4/8/1950)
m **LAURA CUNLIFFE** 14/2/1904
James Welby (14/2/1908)
Allen Herbert (1/6/1909-1931)
Eva Mahala Ann (7/1/1911-11/9/1912)
Ada Frances Vivian (9/4/1913)
Frank Roy Lane (7/5/1916)
Joan Edna Eila (1/4/1918)

IVY ADELE
(22/1/1883-24/1/1961)
m WILLIAM ROBERTS 1903 (d 1905)
Henry Thomas Roberts (1903)
m **WILLIAM ISAACS WINTER** 1910
Neil
Una

WILLIAM HARRY
(25/9/1884-March 1969)
m NELLIE REDFERN 4/4/1931
Adele Dec 1934

OLIVE FRANCES
(2/4/86-4/10/1967)
m HAROLD NICHOLS 17/3/1905
Francis Charles 4/5/1905
Harold Roy Williams 31/8/1906
m JOHN ALEX ADAMS 21/8/1919
Earl Welby 8/7/1920
Nevil Alexander 12/8/1922
Ian Lenard 3/7/1925
Shirley Adele 14/10/1926
Graeme Evered 14/6/1929

LAURA MAY
(7/1/1888-6/10/1982)
m JAMES STEPHEN (JIM) MCLAREN 26/8/1908
Evered Stephens Hadfield 13/8/1909
Nina Adele 15/4/1911
Bethany Olive 10/2/1913

ROY HUBERT
(15/1/1892-27/9/1986)
m MINNIE ALBERTA BARLOW 2/3/1926
Bernard Roy 4/4/1931
Roger Evered 4/6/1932

DARCY CLARENCE
(1/12/1889-22/9/1965)
m RITA COYLE 29/8/1916
Jean 22/11/1920-29/9/1956
Darcy Victor 19/2/1927
Rex Arnold 9/6/1933

EVERED ROGERS
(4/3/1897-3/12/1919)

CHAPTER ELEVEN : FLOSS

1920

WHEN FLORENCE KNOWLES was fifteen she left school to work on the farm with Fred. It was hard, heavy work and she hated every minute of it. Like every young girl she dreamed of romance, fine clothes and parties, and with her best friend Freda Sigley she tried her best to brighten up her life.

During the war there were patriotic concerts, and when each man left for the front there were farewells. When the boys came home there was fun and laughter again for a short time. Zena Sigley was a great organiser and a good pianist, and their pleasures were simple, unsophisticated games and charades with lots of nudging and giggling. One evening Florence was got up as Sleeping Beauty, laid on a bier with her eyes closed and her hair and clothes beautifully arranged. One by one the young men were invited to come in and try to waken her with a kiss, but the moment their lips touched hers Freda, who was hiding under the bed, jabbed their legs with a hatpin. The girls shrieked with laughter at the expressions on the young men's' faces.

Another time a young man was taken out of the room and blindfolded and then told to fold his arms. Freda painted a tiny face on the back of his hand and Florence draped a woollen shawl and bonnet around it. When the young man was led back into the drawing room he looked as if he was cradling a baby in his arms and his audience found it hilarious.

Laura's brother Frank Cunliffe was a popular visitor at Big River. He was a handsome and charming man with a good tenor voice and he would stand by the piano while Zena played. The song the girls loved best was very romantic. "I did but see her passing by and yet I'll love her til I die." Everyone sang at such evenings, and when they had farewells for the soldiers they always closed with "God be with you til we meet again."

Laura, Olive and Ivy were close, and all three sisters were concerned about what the future would hold for Floss. They had all at some stage been under the stern control of their elder brother, and they could sympathise with her plight. Like their mother, each of them in their own way had been desperate to get away from the old-fashioned, hard and socially-limiting life of the inlet. Jessie had always been kind to Floss but left her upbringing to Fred, as her legal guardian and the head of the house, and she never intervened in the decisions he made. When Floss was fifteen Laura decided to act, and she wrote to Fred asking for her to come to Nelson where she could be guided into a suitable job.

"I thought if she got a place for part of the day and came home at night for a while I would have more control over her than if she went to a stranger altogether. I would undertake to look after her and see she didn't mix with people who would do her harm... and I will see she goes to the clerical school and learns any of the subjects most suitable for her. I thought if she could work up a bit she could get into an office after a while."

"...Also I would like her to come over before peace time as it would be something for her to see, and it would be a pity to miss it if it would be convenient for her to come."

Like the rest of the family, Laura was anxious about William Knowles who they all knew would sooner or later be released from jail, but she was more concerned to help Floss gain the social and practical skills she would need to get a good start to her own adult life. She discussed her plans with her father and sisters, but in spite of her carefully-worded arguments she could not win her brother around. Fred felt it was best that Floss should stay at Awaroa and help him on the farm.

It was a lonely time for Floss. She worked long hours beside Fred, doing a man's job as a farm labourer. She lifted, hauled, dragged and chopped, and the days she hated most were those when there was no other urgent work and Fred decided to sharpen the knives and axes. Then she would stand for hours turning the hand wheel on the grinder while he put a keen edge on all their tools, ready for the next round of fencing, ditch digging, shearing, ploughing or harvesting.

Fred was always been a hard taskmaster. He expected Floss to work hard without complaining, and was quick to blame when she did something wrong. She suffered badly with migraines and with toothache, and when she was finally forced to take an afternoon off school, the first day she had ever missed, Fred had no sympathy for her headache but reproached her for spoiling her perfect attendance record.

None of the folk at Awaroa had any dental work done, and when Floss left the inlet she had to have many of her teeth extracted because they had abcessed. She also suffered badly in childbirth in later years because of the heavy work she had done as a young girl. Fred was determined to take care of his Jessie and protect her from the harshness of working outside in all weathers, so he was content to have her run the household and look after the children. Floss was a fit, strong girl who could cope with what needed to be done on the farm. There was no question of paying her wages, as it was understood she was working for her keep.

Fred let his cows wander and they would show up at milking time. Once Floss and Mavis had to go looking for them and they searched the bush until they got lost. When the moon rose they realised they were on top of a cliff and couldn't get down safely, and it was nine at night before a young farm labourer, Tommy Hume, heard them calling out and was able to guide them home. Jess was frantic with worry when they finally came in.

Another time when Fred was away from home a terrible storm blew up and the roof came off the hayshed. Jessie hugged the frightened children as thunder crashed around the hills and the rain beat down all around them, but Floss knew she had to brave the storm or they would lose the whole winter's feed. She and Mavis struggled out into the night with a storm lantern, and together they climbed to the top of the stack with a big tarpaulin which they managed to tie down with ropes. The job took far longer than it should have because of the howling wind, and both girls were drenched to the skin and blue with cold when they finally staggered indoors again, but Floss knew she had done the right thing. Fred would have expected no less from her.

Fred and Jessie didn't take part in many of the social activities around the inlet. Fred had little music in his soul and was always concerned about the next job to be done, while Jessie seldom went far from her home and garden. She played the piano and her brother Will Winter was an accomplished fiddler. He always had a mouth organ in his pocket, and loved music, but apart from hymns on Sunday it was left to Welby and Laura to provide the liveliness and laughter.

Welby also worked away from home a great deal, fishing, boatbuilding and contracting. Laura and her boys ran the farm, tended the garden, and looked after the pigs and the bees. Laura had an outdoor brick oven and made pastries and cakes, as she'd learned from her father the baker in Wellington, and on more than one occasion Ada was sent scrambling up the hill to find her father and deliver hot apple turnovers for his lunch. She would tuck them into the leg of her bloomers to leave her hands free for the climb, and when she found him they would stop and sit side by side, enjoying the treats.

Laura sewed on an old hand-turned machine, as Jessie and all the other women did, and when peace was declared and the boys were due home from war she sent away for some fabric from a Laidlaw Leeds catalogue and made Floss a pink party dress with a matching petticoat.

Her kindness was amply rewarded when she saw the look on her sister-in-law's face. Floss was accustomed to wearing hand-me-down dresses with the hems turned up, and heavy lace-up boots for her work on the farm. Her bloomers were made from old calico flour bags, the brand names still legible on the sides. She was so overwhelmed by the new dress that she hung it at the foot of her bed so she could touch it and feel the fabric next to her skin, and she looked forward to each Sunday so she could wear it again.

Floss went to Nelson to see the peace celebrations after all. Her half-sister Ivy took her and they stayed with the McLarens and had a great time. For Floss, who had never been away from the inlet before, it was the most exciting thing that had happened in her life.

It was also the time when she found out what had happened between her mother and father. The family tragedy was never spoken of and Floss had grown up accepting that she was a Hadfield and that their mother was dead. Her migraine headaches were attributed to the usual adolescent growing up and she was taught to endure them without complaining, but when she was in Nelson with Laura and Ivy she plucked up the courage to tell them about a recurring nightmare. Her sleep was disturbed by uncomfortable and frightening dreams, always ending with a loud explosion like a gunshot which woke her in fright so she sat bolt upright in bed, trembling and shivering.

"Hush, my dear, hush," Laura whispered when it happened for the second time during their visit. Floss was sleeping on the couch in the living room and Laura was up for a glass of water. She hugged her half-sister close, concerned about her sweaty pallor. "Are you ill?"

"A bad dream," Floss gulped. "I'm sorry I disturbed you."

"It must have been a very bad one." Laura looked at the girl closely. "What was it about?"

"It's always the same. People yelling, then a loud bang. It frightens me. I don't know what it's about."

But Laura did, and her mind was racing as she soothed Floss back to sleep, talking about the dance they had all been to and the nice dresses the women had been wearing. When she finally relaxed, her thoughts diverted to dreams of handsome young men and pink satin, Laura left her but she tossed and turned on her own pillow until morning when she could discuss the problem with Ivy.

They decided it was time to explain to Floss what had happened to their mother in 1906, and as compassionately as they could the two women told her the whole story, how her mother had been shot while she and her brothers watched, how Fred had gone to get her and how she had been brought home to Meadowbank where William had cared for her.

They explained that her real father, William Knowles, was in jail serving a life sentence for murder. She need not be frightened that he would come back, as he would probably be moved to an asylum when he was released.

Floss had always known she was different, and now as she stared from one sister to the other she began to understand why.

The story filled many unexplained gaps in her life, and at last made it clear why her family had always seemed so anxious to shelter her from the world.

Florence Knowles, daughter of Adele and William Knowles, who was brought up by Fred and Jessie Hadfield at Big River.

"What was he like, my father?" she asked at last.

"A smooth-talking wastrel," Ivy snapped, her lips pursed, but Laura stopped and considered the question carefully.

"I was only thirteen when he first came to Haven House. Younger than you," she said softly. "He was a lot of fun then. He told us such wonderful stories, of travelling with a circus and seeing the country.

"Mother was different when he was there. She laughed and joked, and sometimes she would forget to send us to bed on time because there was music. She seemed to be younger, somehow."

"But why did she leave Haven House if she was happy there?"

Ivy frowned. "That's not for you to understand or worry about, young Florence. Our mother made her choice, and she suffered the consequences."

"Mother and Father were divorced," Laura explained as gently as she could. "Mr Knowles took Mother away up north with him, and Evered went too. That's when you were born."

"So my name is not really Hadfield?" Floss's eyes widened with shock.

"He did the right thing by our Mother," Ivy confirmed. "They were wed decently. She wouldn't have stood for less, at least we can thank God for that."

The two older women exchanged glances over the girl's head, knowing their tacit agreement to leave part of the story out had been the right one. Poor little Floss had enough to cope with already, without tales of a bastard brother disturbing her mind even more.

"So, your name is really Florence Knowles, but you're part of our family and always will be, and it's best you forget all about Mr Knowles. You'll never see him, and you mustn't think about it again."

"But why did he shoot Mother? Was it because of me?" Floss asked tearfully. "Didn't he like me?"

Laura looked at her compassionately. "Mother loved you very much, Floss, and she would be proud of you now, God rest her soul. You must strive to be a good girl always, and not let her down."

"And now you must go to sleep, and never speak of this again," Ivy added. "Our Fred and Jessie were good enough to take you in and treat you like their own, and they'll not be pleased if you reward them by mentioning Mr Knowles in their house. Do you understand?"

Floss gulped, understanding much more than had been spoken that day. The nightmares stopped, although for the rest of her life she was never completely able to come to terms with what had happened. She had been only a child of two when Adele died, but she was never able to rid herself of a feeling of blame for the tragedy.

Back at Awaroa Floss gained some comfort from Jim Perrott, who had been her friend and confidante since she was a child. He had known her mother from the time of her marriage and had seen many things happen at Awaroa, and it was to him that Floss turned with the questions she was unable to ask the Hadfields. He told her all over again about Adele and her life at Awaroa, and shared his memories of the happy days when she had lived at Meadowbank. From that time forward he referred to Floss by her real name of Knowles, not Hadfield, and she made it clear to everyone she wanted to use that name.

She turned to religion for comfort, as her mother had. She went to the Church of Christ services with Laura McLaren in Nelson, and came back to Awaroa enthusiastic to start a little Sunday School, which she did with Jessie's help. Over the next few years Muriel Green and Freda Sigley both taught Sunday

School in addition to their normal teaching duties. Floss still worked from dawn to dark beside Fred, but now she looked forward to Sundays.

While Floss toiled on Fred's land, Laura worked just as hard on the farm across the river, and by the time her eldest boy Jim was twelve he was planting alongside her, and cutting posts for his father. Laura regularly took her end of the crosscut saw, and when they built a new house after their old one flooded she worked with the boys under Welby's directions. They moved house several times in those years, their first house on the river flats flooded and then put onto skids by Fred and Welby and dragged to higher ground by their team of horses. When it flooded a second time they built a new one, and their first house, dragged even further away by Fred, became a woolshed.

The family moved their possessions from the old house to the new as soon as it was habitable. There were four bedrooms, a kitchen and bathroom and a panelled dining room, with linoleum right through the house. The bathroom was not finished until years later, and the children all bathed in the big tin bath in front of the fire even after they'd moved, their parents doing the same later in the evening.

For Laura, climbing into the rafters of their half-finished house with a hammer in her hand was another adventure, learning to fix the joists another skill to be learned, and she and Welby laughed and joked as they worked together. She also learned to swear, and blamed her husband for putting her in situations where she inadvertently used rude words in front of the children. They shared the hardships as well as the good times, and their marriage was always a partnership between equals.

When she became impatient with the salt water stains on the hems of her skirts she shortened them as the stitches rotted. In spite of the heavy work the women did in places like Awaroa it was still not acceptable for them to show anything above their ankles in public, and Laura earned Fred's grave displeasure when she began to cut her hems off shorter, but she pointed out that she couldn't go pighunting with her skirts dragging on the ground.

He was even more displeased when she cut her long red tresses short, and so was her husband. Laura had suffered for years from migraine headaches, so bad they forced her to bed for days at a time. A visitor suggested the weight of her luxuriant waist-length red hair, carefully pinned and twisted up on top of her head each morning and plaited each night might be the cause of the headaches and in desperation she cut it short. The family was aghast but Laura, freed from the migraines, was unrepentant. She wept when she cut her hair, long since childhood, but when that was over she never grew it long again.

Laura was a capable and independent person who could row, swim and shoot as well as any of the men, but she never lost her femininity. She started notching her gun for each pig she shot after reading cowboy books, and she was adept at melting lead and making her own shot. It was a skill she passed on to her daughters. Years later when she watched a cowboy movie she was unimpressed with the standard of marksmanship "What puzzles me is how they keep missing their men. I wouldn't," she declared.

Welby came home one night shivering and ill, and Laura pulled the couch up to the fire and called for the girls to fetch blankets for him. It was the beginning of a rheumatoid arthritis, and although he recovered from that first bout it became increasingly obvious that he could no longer do the heavy labouring and contracting work he and Fred had been used to. He began to stay closer to home, tending his bees and going out fishing in the little launch *Isis*. He and Jim regularly took the loads of firewood to Motueka for sale in her.

The two families didn't have a great deal to do with each other. Laura and Jessie got on well, and the children went to school together but there were so many chores at each place there was little time to socialise. Welby was no longer able to work for Fred, and he spent his time fishing, tending to his hives and helping around the farm and garden. Sometimes he would go out in his launch to set a net or a longline, and occasionally he would fish with explosives, a plug of dynamite flung in to bring the stunned fish to the surface and then everyone would scramble for them.

Fish was shared around the whole inlet, because it had to be eaten straight away. Apart from smoking it, which they often did, there was no way of keeping it. Food was bought and sold between the families, as it had been in William's day, and a careful account would be kept. Fred would note down each day how many hours each man had worked on the road or scrub cutting, how many pounds of butter went to each household, how many pounds of mutton or bacon. Produce was sent out to Olive and Laura and their families, and board was charged and paid whenever a single man or a schoolteacher stayed in any of the households.

Fred and Welby worked hard to keep the produce flowing out of the inlet and the income coming in. Mr McLaren came for another load of supplejacks, and a new sledge track had to be cut to get the cut vines down to the inlet. There were slips on the road to clear, Harley's sheep to muster and shear, more posts to be taken to Shag Harbour and goods to be sledged for Mr Buttress who arrived in the bay. Pigs, honey, hides, walnuts, fruit and vegetables were sent out by steamer and as the timetables became more erratic and the steamers less frequent after the war the pressures became more intense.

Little Ada Hadfield went to Wellington when she was five, to stay with her Aunt Eva's family and go to school there. Welby didn't want her to go, but he and Laura were stretched to the limit running the farm with Jim and Bert, and looking after young Frank. Laura was expecting another child and she was adamant that her daughter should have a better start in life than what was on offer at Awaroa.

Ada felt very homesick that Christmas, and she had trouble explaining what the matter was. She missed the ritual of the Christmas eggs. Laura and Welby had few gifts to give their children. Birthdays were always marked with a cake and something special for tea, and the highlight of Christmas morning was an egg for each child, lovingly painted by their mother with beautiful scenes, flowers and decorations. Her Auntie Eva worked hard to make that Christmas morning in Wellington a special one for the little five-year-old cousin, but the splendours of a decorated tree and piles of gaily wrapped gifts did not compensate her for the lack of a Christmas egg. She believed the hen laid them ready-decorated, and to her they were the most miraculous part of Christmas.

After Ada went home to Awaroa there were always presents from the Cunliffes, who had realised for the first time just how hard Welby and Laura struggled to provide treats for the children. There was always food on the table and the family had the necessities of life, but few luxuries. The following Christmas a 60 lbs tea chest arrived on the steamer, full to the top and with a smaller box filled with gifts for the children packed in amongst the dark tea for safety. It was the best present Laura had ever had, and she shared it around the little community, filling everyone's tea tins from her giant hoard.

Venture was still up the river, and Fred would sometimes set her sails to air them. The children used to climb aboard her now and then, enjoying the musty smell and exploring the fascinating things still left in her four-berth cabin. The big emergency rockets were still on board, and so were the emergency canisters, with floating lights in one end and hard, dry biscuits in the other.

The mill workers' huts were still up the river too, and Muriel tasted condensed milk for the first time when her brothers took her up to explore them one day. They poked through the debris, finding unopened tins that were too tempting to resist, and spent a blissful hour taking turns to dip their fingers into the sticky mess.

The boys spent one whole summer holiday making a new canoe to get them across the river to school. The first boat they had was a heavy one, chopped out of a hollowed out log by Syd Cracknell and now waterlogged and barely useable. When Welby's children had crossed the river to the first schoolhouse

Venture below the landing at Awaiti, where she used to load flax for Nelson. She was laid up after the war and sat quietly in the river for years before she was taken back down to Venture Creek near Meadowbank.

Fred ferrying Joy and Muriel across the river to school in a dugout canoe

he had made them a punt, and when Flossie first started taking the children across to the new school she still used it, but it was hard to handle and they often arrived wet. Now Nelson and Ralph got stuck in with their father's help and made themselves another canoe, long and light, and it served for as long as they remained at school.

Crossing the river involved "fairy money" a concept that puzzled the children for a long time. There would be little extra treats and luxuries now and then, a new book, store-bought biscuits, lollies or hair ribbons for the girls, and Jessie would tell them in her soft Welsh accent that she had been paid the fairy money. It was ferry money, an allowance paid by the Education Board to the parents who had to ferry their children to and from school each day. When Laura had rowed her children across the river regularly, she used the ferry money to buy seeds for her flower garden.

Fred was still chairman of the school board, but by now there were few other board members. There was trouble among the parents and two distinct factions developed, the Hadfields on one side and the Sigleys, Brunings and Gibbs on the other. Fred felt that he, Welby and Will Winter were doing all the work while the other men were simply out to cause trouble. Not surprisingly, they were just as adamant that they were entitled to a say in how teachers were appointed and supervised and how things were run, especially when it came to deciding who should have the income from boarding the teacher.

In desperation, Fred wrote to the Board to clarify the regulations. Was it true that mothers could be entitled to vote for the school committee too? Should men whose children had not even started school yet be allowed to have a say? Was the Board aware that there was a family at Awaroa who had taken a boy from a receiving home? What should he do if he could not get anyone to agree?

There was no chance of a quorum, and after postponing the school committee elections once, the Education Board finally decided such a committee was unnecessary. In 1919 Fred was appointed commissioner of the school.

"It is with regret that the Board notices a certain amount of ill feeling between parents in connection with school affairs, especially in small communities. Why it should be so is difficult to comprehend, but we are satisfied to have the assistance of your good self so far as the management of the Awaroa household school is concerned."

It was a position which carried all sorts of responsibilities, from supervision to general maintenance. The school board was responsible for arranging the teachers' accommodation, purchasing textbooks and exercise books which were sold to each pupil, and keeping the schoolhouse in good repair.

When Fred wrote and asked for disinfectant one spring when there was a spate of infections, he was sent a quart of Jeyes Fluid, "to be mixed 1:100 with water and sprayed directly over desks, floors and walls.

The Commissioner of Crown Lands surveyed off an acre of land which was gazetted as the school site, and the pupils were encouraged to plant trees and shrubs and grow a garden as part of their lessons. When Miss Flower left after the war Miss N Brown taught for a while, then Miss Myrtle Smith was appointed but she failed to take up her position, putting the board in a spot. In August 1920 Freda Sigley was appointed as teacher, and Fred reacted sharply, telling both her and her parents she was unacceptable because she had not been trained for the job.

"Floss is just as qualified as you are, and a year older," he told Freda, and he wrote to the Education Board to say he did not want a local teacher and would prefer it if Ella Flower could come back. There was an angry exchange of letters before Miss Sigley took her place at the teacher's desk.

"Please see that the pupils attend school," Fred was told, and a few months later he was warned that if the parents did not stop interfering with the way the pupils were being taught, the school would be closed.

Getting the right teacher was a matter of pupil numbers, and it was worth money to the Awaroa community to have a large roll. Parents provided all class texts, copy books, drawing books etc, the committee provided chalk and ink, and boarded the teacher. If the parents could promise in writing to send ten children regularly, they would no longer have to provide free board and lodgings, and the teacher would pay for her keep. A salary and allowance of £150 and an initial school grant of £14 was a powerful inducement.

"If the attendance of ten children is guaranteed for the school it will be possible to send almost immediately a teacher who, however, will not be a male," the Board wrote in 1920. It was to be several years before a male teacher was appointed again, and in its last few years the roll dwindled until there were only a few Hadfield children left.

Miss E Brown was the teacher in 1922, and school inspector Gilbert Dalglish reported that "This small school is in good hands..." She was capable, well-trained in larger schools, and the ten children in her care prospered and learned well. Under pressure from the Education Board, Fred and the other parents replaced the old iron chimney with a brick one and enlarged the playing area. The next year the teacher was less competent, and Fred managed to have her replaced. There was no question of his authority in the matter.

"Miss M E Green has been instructed to take charge of the school after the term holidays," he was told. "I regret to find that Miss Whelham has not given satisfaction and has apparently been defying instructions from you. She will of course finish at the end of the month and will no doubt find it difficult in securing employment again."

Muriel Green had a roll of 13, the highest ever achieved at the little school, and her report from the school inspector was correspondingly high. Much steady work had been done, he noted, the pupils had made good progress and their attendance was commendable. Like Ella Flower, however, Miss Green found it was sometimes an uphill battle trying to keep the childrens' minds on their books.

Teaching "...has been uphill work as frequent changes of teachers has militated against the regular progress of the pupils, and their general knowledge is limited owing to lack of communication with the outside world..." Mr Dalglish also noted with irritation that something should be done about the thick pall of smoke coming into the schoolroom from the still-inadequate chimney.

The Sigleys left the bay in the 1920s, and with the mill closed and William Welby Hadfield gone, the spirit seemed to go from Awaroa.

The old man had known of his illness for some time and he made his will in Takaka a few months before he died. County clerk William Baird and his wife Catherine, long-time friends of the Hadfields through their dealings with roading contracts, witnessed the will which named Fred and Ivy as the executors.

William's will was a simple document, distributing his few personal possessions among the older members of the family. Fred was bequeathed the family pictures and oil paintings in the dining room at Meadowbank and his father's private box, the sea chest he had brought with him from England all those years before and which had stood in his room with his most treasured papers and possessions in it. Ivy Winter who had kept house for him for so long was given the French clock and the rest of the furniture and effects, and Darcy and Roy were each left a walking stick, Darcy's a handsome whalebone stick and Roy's one with a black elephant head handle that Evered had brought home from the war.

Florence Knowles was acknowledged and remembered with a legacy of £20, to be given to her when she was 21. William had always cared for and been kind to his late wife's daughter, acknowledging her as part of the family although she was no blood relation of his.

He asked that Evered's grave be secured by the executors for all time, and his wish to be buried beside his young son was carried out, the little graves marked with headstones and kept neatly to this day.

William would have had no idea that his main legacy to his family, the property of Meadowbank, was to cause discussion and dissension over the next four decades before it was finally resolved. He thought he had left them a will that was both simple and fair. He owned several blocks of land at Awaroa and leased others, but the main asset was Meadowbank with its house and seventeen acres. He wanted each of his surviving eight children to have an equal interest in the estate, with the proviso that the executors could sell it to any member of the family on equitable terms to the others.

Fred and his brothers and sisters agreed that Ivy and Will Winter could stay on at Meadowbank as rent-paying tenants. They were all pressed for money and although the farm was worth very little, none could afford to buy the others out. Fred owned his block at Big River but farming it was marginal and he and his family still needed his income from contracting as well. Welby and Laura were struggling to make a living on their leasehold farm, and Laura and Jim McLaren were still renting their house in Nelson. Bill had sold his farm at Little River and was working as a seaman for the Anchor Shipping Company.

Olive was married again, and she at least seemed comfortably off. Her new husband Alex Adams was a widower who was no stranger to the Hadfield family as he'd previously been married to Olive's cousin Edith, Harry's daughter. The Adams family lived at Appleby near Nelson, where he was a dairy factory manager, and Olive's son Earl Adams was born in 1920.

Roy came back from the war to find his farm heavily in debt, the tenant he'd left on it having failed to meet the payments. Dear old Mrs Barlow and her family from the farm next door, where he had boarded before the war, took turns to milk the cows and take the milk to the factory. Meanwhile Roy took Evered's old motorbike and went off down the West Coast to find work, prudently keeping his head down while Fred sorted out his creditors for him.

It was a common plight for the returned servicemen to find themselves in. Roy worked where he could find a job, at a mill near Stillwater, at the butter factory at Appleby, back to Hamama, down the West Coast to Hokitika, Ross, Jackson's Bay, Otira, Cronadun and Reefton, before moving back to Nelson in 1925 for a permanent job with the railways. He married Minnie Barlow, the girl next door at Hamama where he had bought his first dairy farm ten years before.

Jessie went back to Nelson in March 1921 to have her seventh child. By now Floss was old enough to run the household and Jessie took only Muriel with her, leaving Mavis, Bill, Ralph and Nelson at home with their father. They left Awaroa only just in time, and the steamer trip was a rough one. Jessie and Muriel sat up on deck the whole way, avoiding the cabin where many of the women and children were badly seasick. Mr Sixtus brought them tea, and they were relieved to find Laura and Jim at the wharf to meet them.

Jessie was confined at Mrs Kingsley's nursing home in Collingwood Street, only a few doors away from Dr Barr. She called her seventh child and fifth son Colin Houlson, after her mother's family in Wales.

"He is not much like any of the others, he is a bit like you I think," she wrote to Fred. "His hair is dark and a little bit curly and he has a dear little fat face, the rest of him is quite tiny. Nurse is quite proud of him, she says she never had such a good baby."

For Jessie it had become routine to have her babies alone in a cottage nursing home, and her letters home were filled with practical news about shopping and baby clothes and how she was managing on her limited budget.

"I had to get some nighties made," she wrote after Colin's birth. "Mrs Elliott is doing that for me but I will pay her, or else bring the butter jar over to fill. Nurse has a couple too that she would like filled! Butter is such a price, factory butter that is. Chris was very glad of the butter I brought her but it was so soft when we opened the box..."

Fred and the children were ill while Jessie was in Nelson, and she sent cough mixture home and careful instructions. Sulphur mixed with treacle was the best thing, she advised, or taken with milk at night, and a little sulphur mixed with Vaseline was recommended for sores.

It was a low time for Fred, who was still grieving for his father, and his responsibilities as head of the family weighed heavily on him. He was laid up in bed, one of the few times he had ever found himself too ill to work, and he found himself wondering if he was doing the right thing staying on the farm. With the mill closed, Roy and Evered gone and Welby unable to do any heavy work, the land was going backwards, and Fred knew he could not expect to keep Floss for much longer. Will Winter was still around to help with the road contracts but Ivy was impatient to clear up the estate and get away from the inlet, where there was no future for her family. Henry Roberts was now away from home and working, but she and Will now had two younger children, Neil and Una, and both needed schooling.

Fred and Jessie were now in their forties, their children still too young to be much help around the farm, and the days of trading up and down the coast in *Venture* were clearly over. The timber was gone from the inlet and the land was poor, and their increasing isolation from the markets meant it was no longer viable to grow fruit and vegetables for sale. Fred wrote to Jessie while she was in Nelson and asked her to consider leaving Awaroa and making a fresh start in town. He had no idea how he could make a living, but thought his experience as a road contractor might be useful.

Like him, Jessie had never seriously considered a life anywhere but Awaroa. She'd been there since she was a teenager, and he had lived there all his life. She thought carefully before answering his letter, aware that their decision would change the rest of their lives and those of their children.

She was staying with Christiana in Emano Street, enjoying the company of her sister and brothers and the fun of the city where there was a big band contest going on, the various bands playing in hotels and in the streets until the wee small hours. There were drunken revellers out and about, and Jessie was amused at their antics. She realised she had spent long periods in town over the last ten years, and was far more at home in the bustle of Nelson than her husband, but that experience had only strengthened her love for the inlet.

"We have had so many happy hours there, and perhaps some sorrows but a great many joys," she reminded him. "I don't feel like Ivy does about leaving...I think one seems to take root in a place and get fond of it, so perhaps we should do so in another place. As long as we had the children and each other it would be home, wouldn't it?"

"I don't want to be selfish any way, but I think you feel something the same as I do about it...You must do what you think for the best, and trust that all things work together for good to them that love God."

Jessie and Muriel pick fragrant yellow roses from the climber Alister Stella Gray, a gift from her father-in-law William Hadfield. The roses covered the back porch of their home at Big River. At right is the old whare where Jessie, Fred and Floss first lived in 1909.

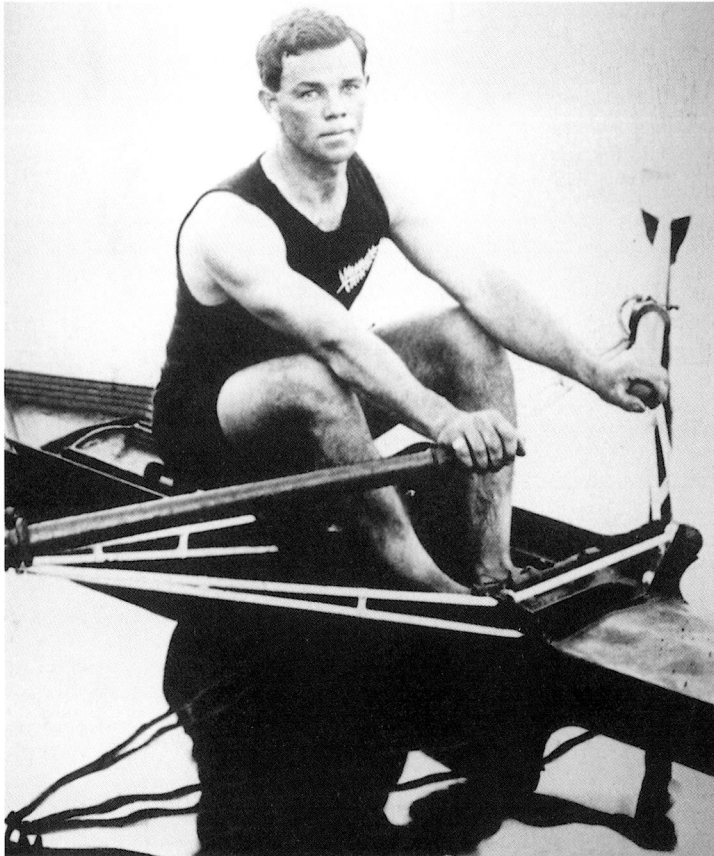

Darcy won a bronze medal for New Zealand at the Olympic Games in 1920. He was the only rower in the four-strong NZ team and the only member to bring home a medal. In 1922 he turned professional and took the world title from Australian Dick Arnst on the Whanganui River.

Auckland Star Collection, News Media Auckland

William lived just long enough to see his son Darcy's greatest triumph, his bronze medal win in the single sculls at the Antwerp Olympics. Auckland was proud of its rowing champion, but the Hadfields of Awaroa were prouder still, chuckling over the memories of Darcy and his brothers rowing up and down the coastline in their heavy wooden dinghies.

Their favourite story was of the time when Bill and Darcy took their fourteen-foot clinker up to Totaranui to pick Welby up so they could all go to a dance. It took the three boys ten hours to row down to Nelson, each taking two hours on the oars and another hour steering. They left on Thursday night, spent Friday and most of Saturday in town and then set off at ten pm to row back home to Awaroa. Darcy was fifteen then, and after he got home that Sunday morning he had rowed back up to Totaranui to see a girlfriend.

Their brother was a champion, winner of the first Olympic medal ever won under the New Zealand flag, but rowing was an expensive business, and after he returned from the Olympics Darcy had to go back to his trade of joinery to support Rita and their children. The shipbuilding industry was in decline and he turned to building houses for a living, rowing with the local club every chance he got.

He came back to the Nelson area in 1921, when he won the Australasian sculling championship on Nelson Harbour. It was a red letter day in more than one sense. Bill Field was operating the 2YA radio station from his Nelson hardware shop and he took advantage of the rowing race to transmit the first live outside broadcast in the country. Hundreds of people all over New Zealand bent their ears to their crystal sets to listen to the news that Darcy Hadfield crossed the line well ahead of the opposition.

After that race Darcy decided to turn professional and so he challenged world champion Dick Arnst to a £200 race on the Whanganui River. Darcy's rowing was the perfect excuse to help his half-sister get away from Awaroa. Floss was a worry to everyone in the family. She made no secret of the fact that she hated the isolation of the inlet as much as her mother had before her.

She had little schooling and no experience of the world, but she felt imprisoned up at Big River, where the only people she saw were Fred and Jessie and the children. Mavis, the closest to her in age, was still only a child while Floss was an adolescent woman, longing for fine clothes and the company of people her own age. Freda Sigley had been her best friend for years and when the two families fell out over the school board and Fred and Jessie stopped taking their family to the monthly church services at Sigleys, Floss felt even more cut off from life.

Adele was never spoken of among the Hadfields, but her presence lingered at Awaroa. Her portrait still hung on the wall at Meadowbank, and sometimes her grey eyes seemed to follow her children as they went about their daily lives. Floss had the same eyes and colouring, and to her half brothers and sisters she seemed much more like a Snow than a Hadfield.

Fred's solution was rigid discipline, isolation from temptation and hard work, and Floss became very unhappy. She had never known her mother or her father, one dead and the other in prison while she was still a baby. Her only real link with her parents had been through Evered, and she felt his death keenly. When William died too she felt she had lost the one person who understood and had been kind to her in her childhood.

When Darcy wrote and asked for her to come to him in Auckland she couldn't wait to leave, and the two Lauras and Ivy encouraged the idea. Between them all they persuaded Fred who reluctantly agreed to let her go. Floss was to be company for Rita and help her with the their daughter Jean while Darcy was away in Wanganui training for his big race.

She was seventeen when she left Awaroa and her sisters helped her with clothes for the journey because she had nothing fit to travel in. Darcy sent the train ticket and Fred and Welby each gave her a pound, the only money she had ever had of her own. Laura McLaren made her a skirt and she bought a new silk blouse, a wild extravagance which got her into immediate trouble with her family but which her soul had been starved for.

Floss enjoyed Auckland and drank in the sights and sounds of the city eagerly. She went with Rita and little Jean down to Wanganui to watch the big race, but got off-side with her sister-in-law when she hung the family's washing out to dry on the balcony of the hotel where they were boarding.

Rita was an attractive and elegant woman whose underwear was hand-made and dainty, with mauve lace and butterflies stitched on as decoration. It had been the talk of the family when she had hung such dainties on the line at Meadowbank when Darcy first brought her home as his bride. Now she was embarrassed enough to see her own dainty underwear exposed to the world, but mortified when Floss's large white calico flourbag bloomers flapped in the wind, the words Lilywhite Flour still clearly visible across the back.

Darcy won the race and became world champion, but he held the title for a bare eight months before losing it to an Australian challenger. Now in his mid-thirties, he went to Australia for a return race but his challenge failed, and he returned to the building trade. For the rest of his life he was active in the sport, encouraging and coaching other promising New Zealand rowers including his own sons.

Fred and Jessie stayed on at Big River, and soon there was another child on the way. Jessie took only the two youngest, four-year-old Muriel and baby Colin, to Nelson this time and the other children stayed home with their father. Jessie and Colin stayed at Laura and Jim McLaren's house while she waited for the birth, and Christiana took little Muriel up to her house in Emano Street.

Jessie found the tiny Russell Street house and steep yard very confining. It was August 1922. The frosts were heavy and the roads too slippery for her to get about, and she suffered badly with swollen ankles. Jim was busy at the foundry, working lots of overtime and often not home until late in the evening.

"I am afraid you also have a lot of overtime lately, but never mind, I will be coming back," Jessie wrote to Fred. "I can't quite say when but it will be nice when I do. I feel a sort of prisoner just now with a little yard to exercise in, but I mustn't grumble, there are many things to be thankful for."

Colin was teething and unwell, and she was relieved when it was time to move into the nursing home. She went to Mrs Moore, who had been a Miss Solly from Takaka and whose husband had worked on the *Venture*.

The new baby was "...a dear fat little thing with such a nice crop of hair," and everyone at the nursing home was charmed by her. "She ought to be called Sunshine, it has been fine ever since she was born," her mother wrote proudly. They decided to call the little girl Dorothy Joy.

Joy was soon thriving, but Colin was a sickly baby and Jessie stayed on at the McLarens. Mrs Bradley, whose own child was a little younger than Colin, came to visit and lent her a push cart so she could take the children out. She spent her days sewing and looking after the children, with outings to church and other social activities. She was still a lively and attractive woman and every night she wound her hair up in rags to try to make it curl, the same as Laura's.

She bought a pram from the secondhand shop, big enough for both Colin and Joy, and she reminded Fred to make room for it in the boat when he came out to meet the steamer and welcome them home.

Olive was also in Nelson and her fourth son Neville was born within days of his Hadfield cousin. Soon after Jessie went home to Awaroa it was Olive's turn to pack her bags for the steamer too, as her husband had been appointed to manage the dairy factory at Rockville inland from Collingwood. They were to live for five years just around the corner from Glen Howard, where Adele had lived before her marriage.

The Snows were still remembered in the district and Olive heard many stories about her grandparents and uncles. Rockville was a busy little farming community, with a school, a store and a blacksmith shop and regular dances and parties in the hall. The McLarens went to stay from time to time, and Alex sent cheeses down to Awaroa when he could.

Colin Hadfield was always a chesty little boy, and when he was two and a half Jessie took him back to Nelson where Dr Barr diagnosed bronchial pneumonia. To her relief she was able to wire Fred that the little boy was improving, but it was a serious illness and the doctor said one of his lungs was still not working properly.

It was a strain on Jessie, and although Laura and Jim were as helpful as they could be she worried about the firewood she was going through to keep the room warm at night. It was November, but there was still a chill in the air. There were shipping strikes, and she was not sure the steamer *Wairoa* would keep on running. It was hard to be in someone else's home at a time like that, she confessed to her husband.

"I would like to send you news of the shipping strikes, you would be interested in it, but I suppose you will hear all about it later on. They always light the fire with the newspaper next morning. Jim would like to talk and tell us all about it as the men talk of very little else, but Laura doesn't like the subject so it is tabooed."

In spite of Jessie's careful nursing Colin got steadily weaker, and finally the doctor admitted him to hospital to be operated on. It was a last chance, he told her. After two days of anxiety it looked as if the operation was successful. Little Colin was looking pale and weak, but brighter than his mother had hoped. Then, soon after she had returned home from an afternoon visit, Jessie got the telephone call she'd been dreading.

"I have to go up and stay with him, and I can't leave Baby," she told Laura through her tears. "What shall I do?"

They rolled the little girl in a blanket and called a taxicab, and Jessie spent an anxious night in the ward caring for her two babies. She walked home the next morning, but was back up a few hours later, leaving Laura to bring Joy up when she needed feeding.

"I can't hold out much hope," Dr Barr told her gently after he and another doctor had examined the frail little body. "But don't give up, Mrs Hadfield. He needs your strength now, and you should stay near him. The next 24 hours will be critical, and if he survives them we might still save him."

Jessie sat on the hospital verandah for a long time after he had gone. So much of her life had been spent there with her babies, it seemed, and every time she had to face it alone.

Then she thought of her beloved Fred, sitting alone by the fire in their little house at Big River. She saw in her mind the familiar marble fire surround, all the way from Wales, and the portraits of Fred's ancestors in their oval frames above it. There would be fresh flowers in a vase, and the bright rag rug that Chris had hooked for her would be spread on the hearth, and she knew in her heart that Fred would be sitting staring into the flames, sharing her vigil as best he could. The thought gave her strength and she lay down on a sofa and slept while the nurses tiptoed about the silent ward.

"Mrs Hadfield?" A nurse shook her gently and she flew to her feet to sit by the cot, but after an hour or two the little boy rallied and slipped into a peaceful sleep, his breath soft and even. Later that night she woke again and he was still sleeping, and she thought the worst was over.

In the early hours of the morning she was wakened again, and this time the nurse's face was grave. Jessie sat by her son holding his tiny hand in hers, hardly noticing the movements around her or the warm blanket wrapped around her shoulders. The nurse left her side and time seemed to stand still for Jessie as the little boy's breathing changed.

She called softly, afraid to let go of his hand, and a moment later he was gone, his hand growing colder and his face whiter as the little chest stopped rising and falling.

She sat there until the nurse gently helped her to her feet and led her away, and after a while they rang for a cab to take her and little Joy home.

The next few days passed in a blur for Jessie. Fred sent messages and money and her brother-in-law helped her make arrangements for the funeral. It was November in 1923, and Colin had been only two and a half years old when he died. Jessie shed few tears at the grave side. She felt numb and empty inside, and wanted above all to go home to her beloved Big River and to Fred.

Ï am not writing a long letter, for I hope to see you soon and that will be better," she wrote to him after the funeral. "Dr Barr has been very good and the nurses at the hospital were very kind too, but of course I missed you at a time like that..." Jessie wept as she relived the last few days, describing to Fred how she had spent long nights at their little boy's bedside, and how kind everyone had been to her.

Back home at Big River Fred had been helpless to support her except in his thoughts and prayers, as his hands were full with the farm and the family. He sent a telegram counselling her to give thanks for Colin's brief life and for his release from misery, and to accept what had happened as an act of God.

"Thank you for the message you sent," she wrote. "I tried to do so, and I know it is far better for dear little Colin, only we shall miss him so..."

"I have wanted you, but still I wouldn't like the children left, after all," she ended. "Hoping to see you very soon now. Love from Jessie."

When she booked her passage on the steamer her heart lifted with anticipation. The moon would be full and she and Joy would be home about midnight, at the top of the tide. As she trudged around Nelson, her skirt heavy around her tired legs and her best blouse sticking to her in the spring heat, she held that vision in her head and it sustained her.

Welby and Laura were also considering their future at Big River. Their lot was harder than the family across the river, because they didn't own their land and Welby was not fit enough to farm it profitably. They made do with very little, keeping to themselves and enjoying the company of their children who were shy with strangers. Jim and Bert worked on the farm and did contracting for other landowners, while Ada, Frank and Joan were all at school.

When her auntie Floss married, Mavis couldn't wait to go off and stay with her in Riwaka. Floss was only seven years older than Mavis, who loved to hear stories about Auckland and the world outside Big River. She cut her hair short, flapper-style, as soon as she left home.

Ralph was a keen gardener, always planting beans, sunflowers or some other crop. Nelson was more like his uncle Roy, a keen hunter and outdoor man. His most treasured possessions were a Scout belt and a sheath knife, and more than once he arrived back from a trip into the bush leading a young goat. Fred taught his sons to be handy with knives and axes and they were kept busy chopping wood for the stove and the copper, while the girls worked inside or at the washing. The children were brought up strictly, the boys taught to keep their hands out of their pockets, the girls forbidden to whistle.

Mavis, the eldest surviving child of Fred and Jessie, was a dedicated follower of fashion.

"A whistling wife and a crowing hen would drive the devil out of his den," Fred told Muriel when she tried to learn from her brothers. On Sundays they wore their best clothes and amused themselves with books, conversation and hymns, occasionally with a picnic or a visit. There was no work on Sunday but no swimming either, and Jessie wore her Sunday brown dress with matching braid and a crepe-de-chine collar tacked back on after each careful washing.

Mondays were washing days, and the copper took forever to heat. Water was drawn from a well and carried to the house in buckets made from kerosene or benzine tins, and there were always two or three buckets of fresh water outside the back door. When the garden needed water it was drawn from the well or carried from the river in buckets. Bread was baked in the wood range, as were the cakes and puddings. Jessie made her own yeast, rolling little worms of yeast dough and storing it in tightly corked bottles on a shelf above the stove.

Every now and then one would pop, a sound the family was used to but they loved it to happen when there were important visitors.

The children were shy with strangers, but totally at home in their wilderness of bush, swamp and estuary. Their games were simple, willow sticks for horses when they were younger, broader sticks for cricket bats as they grew. At night they would play by the fire, using dried beans for counters, soldiers or horses, an old tin tray for a battlefield or a farmyard. Bill had a Meccano set which he treasured, everyone had cork pop guns and Nelson and Ralph had an air rifle which was wrapped up and exchanged between them at Christmas and on birthdays.

Nelson loved the outdoors

They were all envious of Nelson, whose birthday was the day after Guy Fawkes night. They never celebrated Guy Fawkes, but there were always crackers among Nelson's birthday parcels and there was big excitement when they were let off.

Mavis had two white rabbits, Bib and Bub, and a china doll she called Janey May with blue eyes. She had a doll's house too, and in the end Fred gave her a padlock for it so she could keep her younger sister from messing up her carefully-arranged treasures. Muriel had a rag doll, the love of her life until she left it out in the rain one night, and a slip of earth came down and buried it. Miss Goodwin at the Takaka gift shop would help with birthday gifts, and over the years she got to know the family well enough to make suggestions and choose the most suitable things to send back in their order.

The children loved Jessie to read to them from the few treasured books on her bookshelf. *The World of Wit and Humour* was one of their favourites. It was a huge volume, blue with gold writing on the spine, and it was illustrated with black and white drawings and sketches. Their mother had won it as a school prize at Johnsonville in 1891 and it seemed far bigger and grander than anything that had ever come out of their little school. There were poems and stories, yarns of the Yukon goldfields, tales of Irish blarney. Ralph loved a story called the Spelling Match, because the hero was called Ralph too. Muriel liked the poems, Nelson and Bill liked the stories by Mark Twain. Later they found an even more exciting book at Meadowbank, their Uncle Evered's army drill manual, and they practiced sloping and presenting arms, positioning sentries and forming up to advance on the enemy.

Jim Perrott became ill and Fred and Jessie invited him to come and live in the little whare behind their house. By now he was a very old man, shortish in stature, with a white beard stained yellow with tobacco juice from the pipe he loved to smoke. Fred and his brothers and sisters had grown up knowing Mr Perrott. He was their link with the past, a well-read man with a lively mind, whose stories were always fascinating. He knew the Maori history of the area as well as the more recent events, and had been called on from time to time to act as interpreter for various government officials. Among his special friends over the years had been William Hadfield, Will, Christiana and George Winter and Florence Knowles.

Jim had retired from his labouring work years before and now he collected a government pension. He loved to fish and he kept a good garden, and he still had a dinghy he rowed around the inlet. When the Hadfield children were away he would go up to Big River to feed their rabbit for them. He knew all the native trees and plants and would gather leaves, roots and berries for medicinal purposes, sending seeds away to people who needed them.

He was always interested in new things and was as excited as everyone else when he saw his first aeroplane, an Avro 504L seaplane which flew low over the inlet on 1 December 1921. The little plane was on a barnstorming tour of the country and worked out of Nelson Harbour for a several weeks, flying joyrides up and down the coastline. When it circled Awaroa the watchers could make out the advertising slogans on the fuselage, and marvelled at the double wings and the narrow floats underneath.

Mr Perrott wrote and received a lot of letters, and kept in touch with people like the Gibbs, the Pratts, the Sigleys, the Thompsons and Ella Flower. In 1925 he exchanged telegrams with Walter Nash, then secretary of the Labour party, later to become Prime Minister. He kept a diary, noting who came to visit and who passed along the track by his whare, and he was always on the lookout for vessels coming over the bar. He spoke fluent Maori and his diary was kept in a mixture of his two languages.

"Kua tae mai a Essie Thompson...." he would write. "Mr Manson and I went to the rocks..... Kua patua he poaka.... He tonga kino.... Will Winter and Will Hadfield came with books....posted reta to G Winter and Flossie..."

He noted the weather, the movements of boats like *Venture, Oban* and *Old Jack,* and the cycles of planting and harvesting, recording when his drumhead cabbages were planted, when he put his net into a drum to tan it, and when he went over to Meadowbank for lemons or onions.

Jim Perrott had a lot of visitors and in latter years it became a tradition for people who came to Awaroa for their holidays to make an expedition to Silver Point to pass the time of day with him. Jack Ricketts, the McLarens and Cunliffes, Bob Allen, Mr and Mrs Sixtus all visited him regularly. The new Takaka constable, Canning, made a courtesy call in 1923, and when Floss left for Auckland and again when she got home she paid special visits to him.

Mr and Mrs Samuels were his closest neighbours and were good friends who kept writing long after they moved to Nelson, and he also saw a lot of the Browns who lived at Waiharakeke. Whenever his many Maori friends from Riwaka or Motueka came up to Awaroa to go eeling or gather flax they would stop in at Silver Point.

The children used to visit his whare where he would serve them mugs of cocoa and homemade bread and butter liberally sprinkled with white sugar. Muriel remembered his beloved Silver Point as a home for cicadas fiddling shrilly in the manuka scrub. The ground felt crisp and dry, covered with coral moss and heath.

"I remember a particularly nasty thorny bush which my father called South African Devil or some such nasty name. The seed pods looked exactly like milk chocolate, a rare luxury to us children."

Jim had other sweets to offer though. He would give the children black prince apples, darkly crimson outside, white flesh tinged with pink in the middle. He grew long thin grapes, called ladies fingers, and with every offering there was a smile and a story. If they were lucky he would tell them about the old days in the inlet, before their grandfather's time.

One of their favourite stories was about the day he stole the peaches.

"My mate and I were camped nearby, squaring logs," he told the enthralled children. "We were always short of food, in those days, and this time we were down to our last handful of flour and right out of sugar. You know, sometimes when you get a craving for something sweet it just eats at you until you think you'll go crazy if you don't get a taste."

They nodded solemnly, knowing exactly how that felt and awed that even grownups could be hungry for sugar.

"What happened, Mr Perrott?" Ralph asked.

"Well, I'll tell you. You see, there we were just hankering for something sweet to settle the worms in our stomachs, and there just across the river was Spanton's orchard, all the fruit you could imagine, and ripe for the picking. It was a full moon, you see, and the more we thought about those peaches just hanging there, the more we were tempted to get some."

Their eyes always grew wider as he described the way he and his mate had rowed across the inlet, watching out for any sign of movement on Spanton's bank, and how they had snuck quietly up to the trees holding their breaths so Spanton's dogs wouldn't bark, how they had filled their hats with peaches and hurried away again, too nervous to even snatch a taste until they were safely back in their camp.

"Well, those peaches weren't as ripe as we'd thought," he told the young Hadfields. "In fact, to tell you the truth they were green and hard, and my teeth weren't as good as they should be even way back then."

Muriel always darted a glance at the old man's mouth at this point, fascinated by his shrunken gums and the few broken teeth that remained, stained yellow by years of strong tobacco.

"We found an old iron cookpot under the trees there, and we scoured it out with a bit of seawater and a handful of sand, then rinsed it in the river to get rid of the salt. It was still a bit rough and brown looking on the inside, but my mate thought it would be all right, so we cut up those peaches and stewed them over a nice fire until they were all soft and mushy."

"And then you ate far too much," Mavis prompted.

"Aye, that's right, and we lay down in our bunks and went to sleep, until the whole mess turned rotten in our stomachs."

For the next 24 hours, he told the children with a cackle, the two paid the price for their theft. The unripe fruit reacted with the iron of the cookpot and gave them both crippling stomach pains they remembered years later.

Jim Perrott had been goldmining in the Wakamarina, Collingwood and the Tablelands and he had hunted in the Riwaka Valley. Over his many years he'd sat around many smoky campfires and yarned with many of the district's older identities. He was a mine of information and a fund of good stories, and when he and the children were alone he would tell them about their grandmother Adele in her young days, how she and their grandfather built Meadowbank together, and how she used to hang her white sheet on the dog tree when she wanted him to row over the bay.

JIim Perrott ended his days in this whare at Big River.

When the day came for Mr Perrott to leave his Silver Point home Fred brought him around to the head of the inlet by launch, and he lived in the whare and had his meals with the family. The men would talk about old times and laugh together, and they were fond of good-natured debate and argument. Jim left the table in a huff once, the children wide-eyed and fascinated with the discussion which was about whether or not men were descended from the apes. Jim was a convinced supporter of Darwin's theories of evolution but Fred firmly believed in the Bible's version.

In 1925 Jessie's brother Bob Winter died in Nelson. Christiana was over at Big River staying with the Hadfields, but Bob had a job as porter at the hospital and he was alone in their Emano Street house when he got the flu. He took to his bed, warming it with hot bricks, and in his feverish state he burned himself badly. He had little natural resistance and the illness soon turned to pneumonia. An urgent message came to Jessie and Christie at Big River to say he was in hospital, but he died a few days later.

"Your aunt Chrissie will come to live with us now," Jessie told the children after the funeral. Fourteen-year-old Mavis looked around the crowded room with dismay.

"But where will she sleep?"

"In her tent, the same as she always does. But perhaps Father will build her a little room of her own soon?" Jessie suggested softly. She knew that her sister was finding the winters harder each year, and even though she piled her little bed high with blankets and rugs and the household cats snuggled up with her for warmth, the tent was not really a long term solution, especially in June and July. Christie was 40 now, her lame leg giving her a lot of pain and trouble, and she spent more and more of her time sitting or lying down.

The little two-bedroomed house at Big River was bursting at the seams with six children and two adults living in it and now Mr Perrott in his whare and Aunt Chrissie in her tent. Fred had never finished the verandah along the front, and sometimes when the rain kept pounding down relentlessly and the washing had to be aired and dried in the kitchen it seemed as if they were literally living on top of one another. There was no room for tensions and tantrums though, and Jessie found she was grateful for her sister's help, especially with the children who went to her for stories and games as well as help with their lessons.

Their brother George Winter had gone to Australia to be a missionary. He had always wanted to work with Maori in New Zealand, but after making himself fluent in the language and training in missionary work at Rotorua he found there was no place for him outside of teaching, and he had little aptitude for working with children. He had spent a few years in Wellington where he became interested in the trade union movement, and his letters home were full of stimulating reports and ideas. Jessie, Christie and James Perrott all wrote to him regularly and all three of them looked forward to the Australian letters in their mailbag. George and Jim Perrott corresponded in Maori, and George often wrote of Aboriginal arts and culture.

Jim had always been close to the Hadfields and now he was part of the family. Christiana made him a velvet smoking cap which he treasured, and he bought her some rug wool to hook into a rug for his whare. He kept his few possessions in his old wooden sea chest, and he would sit at the door of the whare and read for hours in his little round spectacles, his tin of tobacco and his favourite pipe near at hand. He was the last of the Awaroa pioneers, an old man who had been a runaway sailor and was now the only surviving link between those 19th century immigrants and their New Zealand-born children.

Muriel sometimes carried his cup of tea to him - the pleasant late afternoon tea was a ritual before milking and the evening chores.

"Sometimes Jimmy let me look at the dozen or so Christmas cards he kept in a chocolate box - I read the verses over and over again and remember one in particular, a pretty one with roses and forget me nots on a celluloid cover," Muriel remembered. The box of cards was later given to her and she always treasured it.

Fred and Jessie Hadfield's home at Big River, Awaroa.

Lynette Wilson photo

Jim used to go for a walk each day of about two miles, resting at a comfortable spot where manuka brush and heather made a soft sofa on the outside of the road and he could look down across his beloved inlet. One day Muriel reported that Mr Perrott had not come back from his daily walk. Fred went looking and found the old man had suffered a severe stroke, one side of his body paralysed.

Fred got the gig and they gently lifted him onto a mattress and blankets, making him as comfortable as they could for the hard journey home. He couldn't speak to tell them where he kept the key to his sea chest and the men had to break into it with an axe to get his good clothes out for him. The next morning he was loaded onto the gig again to go down to the Sawpit Point where Alf Gibbs was waiting with his launch to take him out to Nelson.

The family gathered in silence to watch him leave, Fred walking at the horse's head to guide it on the journey.

It was too much for gentle Jessie. There were seldom displays of affection even between husband and wife in the Hadfield family, but when she saw the poor frail old man leaving his beloved bay for what everyone knew would be the last time she ran after the gig, climbed on the step and quickly stooped to kiss him on the forehead.

The last pupils at Awaroa School - Ada, Ralph, Nelson, Frank, Muriel and Joan Hadfield, This photo was taken in the late 1920s by their teacher, Mavis Hadfield.

Mr Reilly was popular with the children, especially the boys who even took him pig hunting with them one day. He would stride down the road singing "When Irish Eyes Are Smiling," and the ladies all found him charming.

The school inspector Mr G Overton wasn't quite so impressed. The seven children on the roll displayed uneven abilities, he said. "Half the pupils appear to be producing good work, the other half showed considerable weaknesses, and rapid improvement should be looked for."

There was a fine garden, however, and teacher and pupils deserved credit for the attractive appearance of the grounds.

Bill gained his proficiency certificate that year and left school to work around home for his father. There were only six children left at school now, all Hadfields, and Mr Reilly was the last outside teacher to be appointed there.

Jessie taught sewing at the school while Pat Reilly was the teacher, and one morning they waited a very long time for her to arrive. She had worn a narrow skirt and misjudged her leap into the dinghy to cross the river. She was soaked to the skin and had to run home and change her clothes before she could go to school. There was no sewing machine in the classroom and she and the girls sat in a little sewing circle with needle and thread, darning socks, sewing buttons and button holes and learning to stitch a neat hemline.

Laura's children usually went home for lunch, but on wet days they would take lunch with them to eat in the school porch, and sometimes when there was a sudden shower Welby or Laura would bring lunch to the school house to save the children getting wet.

They were puzzled to see their mother arrive one gloriously fine morning and hang a cloth bag of fresh-baked pies on the peg in the porch, but they stayed at school that lunch hour as she obviously meant them to, enjoying the extra time to spend playing with the others. When they got home that afternoon nothing was said, but their cow lay contentedly right outside their kitchen window licking a wobbly newborn calf. Such things were not seemly for children to watch.

On 17 June 1929 the earthquake hit. It was a fine frosty morning and Mavis who was now eighteen was teaching the six of her siblings and cousins still at school. Ralph, Nelson, Muriel, Ada, Frank and Joan were outside with their lessons when Mavis appeared at the door of the schoolhouse, her face white with fear. They ran to a clear space, and they held each other tightly as the trees and grasses waved wildly and the chimney rocked from side to side, bricks flying from one side and then the other as it settled down into a peculiar bulbous shape.

The violence of the movement forced them to their knees in the grass, and as soon as it subsided they made their way home, Ada, Frank and Joan running to their mother who had headed to meet them. Ralph and Nelson rowed the other two girls across the river and when they got home they saw their mother busy putting their most treasured possessions out on the ground in front of their house. Christie had been sitting out in the sunshine writing letters when the earthquake occurred. Bill was skinning a sheep in the yard and Jessie had been indoors, fortunately with the fire nearly out.

"Thank goodness!" she cried when she saw the children coming. "I was going to come and look for you. I was frightened the chimney had fallen."

"The fire wasn't going," Mavis assured her. She looked from her mother to the big clock, its glass front still intact, looking strangely incongruous on the front path where the hens and a couple of weka were investigating busily. Inside the house was a mess, jars of jam and fruit fallen from the cupboards to be smashed on the floor. It was too late to save the marble fire surround which had come with the Winter family from Abergavenny in 1888. The uprights were still intact but the smooth marble shelf had fallen and shattered. Every cup on the shelf had smashed, although many of the handles were still hanging from the cuphooks where they had been swung against each other.

Little Joy was sobbing with fear in Christie's arms as the aftershocks continued, and Jessie banned the younger children from the house, calling Mavis to help her as they made a make-shift lunch and took it outside to eat on the grass. Then they lit the copper behind the house and began the heartbreaking job of cleaning up broken glass and china, spilt food and damaged possessions.

There were violent shocks through most of that day and the family waited anxiously for Fred who was away working on the road. Jessie wouldn't let the boys go to look for him for fear of another big quake, although Bill was sent a little way along the track and he came back reporting slips and fallen trees. It took Fred many hours to get back home, leading his horse carefully around the many slips and crevices in the newly formed roadway, and Jessie and the children flew to greet him as soon as he appeared.

The earthquake was centred at Murchison and Awaroa got off lightly compared with other districts. It was still a major catastrophe in that isolated little settlement, where summer preserves were part of winter food supplies and the smashed crockery and ornaments could not easily be replaced. That night Jessie's family had baked potatoes in their jackets for tea, a rare treat indeed, and the grown-ups drank their tea from tin mugs while the children waited for their turn.

The telegraph poles were brought down by slips but the wires were still taut and unbroken for the next few days. One of the most amazing events was the arrival down the wires of a cablegram from Hugh Oliver, who had heard about the earthquake on his wireless set in Detroit, Michigan. He sent an urgent reply-paid message asking if there was anything he could do.

"Is all well? Anxious. Earthquake. Reply. Do you need assistance. Love Hugh."

Fred fingered the telegraph form over and over until he knew the words by heart, and he repeated them in wonderment to everyone he talked to. That Hugh Oliver had heard of their earthquake in America, that he had been concerned enough to telegraph and that the message had got through when all their other communication routes were closed and the earth was still rumbling and trembling beneath them seemed to be beyond comprehension.

The inlet bubbled and hissed for days afterwards, the normally golden sands black with churned up mud and with little geysers and whirlpools as the ground gradually subsided again. It took longer for the animals to settle down, and when the immediate jobs were tidied up and the two families had their homes in order again, they were amazed at what had happened around them. The earthquake had caused dramatic changes to the landscape. The track through to Canaan, cut years before when Joe Sixtus brought his cattle down to Awaroa,

Bill and Mavis would go out to Takaka dances on his motorbike.

was completely cut off by trees and slips and many of the other tracks and pathways through the bush were impassable. Trees and branches had come down everywhere and the hillsides had cracked and slipped so that with the next heavy rains the whole aspect of the countryside changed. Fred lost valuable river flats and so did Welby, and both farms were even less viable.

That year Bill Hadfield got his first motorbike, a 1928 AJS which he bought from Nalder and Biddle in Nelson and rode down to Big River. It was only a year old and had been the shop bike, used by young Jack Flowers who was the boy in the workshop. Bill went off looking for work up the Motueka valley and at Dovedale. He got a job wiring houses for electricity, working with Norm Steele who taught him what to do as they went along. Bill also worked for Fred Gibbs at Stanley Brook and went on to help with the tobacco harvest. Eventually he came back to Takaka where he worked for Birdsall Motors.

In 1930 Welby and Laura left the inlet with their family and moved to Riwaka where Welby and the boys got work in the hop gardens. Frank and Joan went to Riwaka school but they hated it, too shy to mix with the other children and bewildered by the noise and bustle. Before long it was clear that Welby's health would not allow him to keep up working for wages, and the family returned thankfully to Awaroa. They went back up the river to their old leasehold farm, which had been left abandoned, and lived off the land.

Fred's brother Bill Hadfield came home from the sea to marry Nellie Redfern from Picton, and the two made their home in Nelson. Their first daughter, born in 1934, was named Adele after Bill's mother.

The Awaroa school closed for the last time in 1931. Muriel passed her proficiency and she and Joan gave up lessons altogether, leaving Joy to work at home by correspondence.

Ray Fry grew tobacco at Awaroa, on Winters' old farm, but it was not very successful. The Spanish heather originally planted by Harry Hadfield around his house had gone wild and taken over the flat plain, and it was hard to keep it clear. Tobacco was also grown at Totaranui, where the older Hadfield children found work in the sheds, but the growers had trouble getting contracts and eventually they were forced under. Hops were more successful, but the real money was in hop poles, another traditional source of income for the Hadfields. Fred cut hop poles and shipped them out for sale around Riwaka, just as his father had done 40 years before.

For the young Hadfields the bush was their home and their playground. In November they would search for the kiekie vine and eat as many as they could, enjoying the sweetness of the fruit. They would climb all over the fallen logs in the swamp, looking at the leaves and water ferns. Welby would bring home delicate white orchids for his wife, telling the children he had split logs open to get at the flowers growing inside them.

A big flat edible fungus grew on the rotting trunks of fallen pukatea trees, and the children thought they looked like elephants' ears. Welby, Bert and Jim would go for miles through the bush gathering them by the sackful to sell to the Chinese people living in Motueka, who prized them as a delicacy. It was an old family tradition. Adele had helped her boys gather the same fungus from the same bush a generation earlier

Welby and Fred taught their children how to recognise the different woods and how to use axes and other tools, and they all knew how to choose the best firewood. Their knowledge was passed on from William and Harry who had learned from boatbuilders like Amos Ricketts and Dave Gilbertson.

Totara was inferior timber, used only for piles and fenceposts, and white pine was used for boatbuilding, rata for the knees and joints on dinghies, rimu and matai for fencing and flooring. Matai was known as red pine, although later rimu was sometimes also called red pine. All the Hadfield men were accustomed to working long hours in the bush, gathering timber which was their fuel, their building material and often their income.

Then there was a terrible accident. Welby and Laura's son Bert was killed by a flying log. He and his cousin Frank Nicholls were cutting fenceposts in bush high above the river, using a wire flying fox to bring the logs down. They were both experienced bushmen, but it was dangerous work and it took only a moment's inattention for the fatal mistake to be made. A heavy post was sent down the wire when Bert was working underneath it, and in spite of a warning shout the river drowned out the sounds and he was hit and killed instantly.

For Laura and Welby, the loss of a second child at Awaroa was a dreadful blow. Jim, their eldest, was away from home now, and they had only Ada, Frank and Joan left. Jessie was away when the accident happened. Laura and Welby were at Meadowbank and Ada was up at Big River keeping Muriel company and helping to look after the household. Jessie hurried home for the funeral, held at Awaroa on a beautiful clear day with the police, the minister and the families in attendance.

Little Eva's grave was up the river, but Bert's funeral service was at Meadowbank. They took his coffin down the river on the high spring tide in Fred's boat, the few other mourners who had come in by road following in other boats, and he was buried under the holly tree beside his grandfather William and his uncle Evered.

There was joy as well as grief that year for Jessie and Fred. Mavis, their eldest surviving child, turned 21 and was the first of the new generation of Awaroa Hadfields to marry. Her husband was Wilfred Bradley, whose uncle had run a sawmill at Awaroa and whom she had met at her Auntie Floss's house at Riwaka, and her wedding at the Motueka Anglican Church was a simple ceremony with only a few members of the Bradley family as witnesses. They settled at Green Tree Road, Riwaka, where they lived close to Floss and her husband.

Christiana became very ill in April 1933. Jessie did what she could for her sister, but she was too ill to ride in a vehicle over the rough road to Takaka, nor could she cope with a long boat trip. Jim Perrott whose traditional Maori remedies had been useful in the past was long gone and there was no one else in the bay to call on for help. Christie took medicines and herbal remedies sent by well-meaning friends, but her body was retaining all fluids and her condition deteriorated rapidly. Jessie telephoned to the doctor in Takaka, describing her sister's internal problems as best she could, while Muriel sat by her aunt in the annex and bathed her red swollen face with a flannel. Fred tactfully left the house so his wife could talk more freely.

"He said to give her warm baths," Jessie said wonderingly when she'd rung off. "Best stoke up the fire and fill all the kettles, girls. I don't know what else to do."

Jessie and Muriel dragged the big tin hip bath into the tiny room beside the sick woman's bed, while Joy kindled the fire and got the water boiling.

When Laura came down from Meadowbank that afternoon she found Christiana seriously ill, feverish and bloated, and her sister exhausted with worry. Laura sat with her for a while to give Jessie a spell, but soon after she got back home one of the boys came across the inlet to fetch her again. Christie Winter was dead, her lively mind stilled for ever.

Fred telephoned the doctor this time, to report the death and Constable Berthelsen made the trip down to Big River from Takaka to carry out the formalities. He found a grieving family. Muriel acted as his hostess and presided over the teapot while her mother sat drained and silent.

"I hope the next time I see you it will be under happier circumstances," the policeman told Muriel gravely as he left the house. Muriel hoped so too. She was fifteen years old, and she had already lost a baby brother, two uncles, her dear Mr Perrott and her cousin Bert. Now her dear Aunt Chrissie was dead too, her body ugly and swollen and her sweet smile gone.

Muriel and Joy took care of the chores while their mother and their aunt Laura began the now-familiar rituals. They washed Christiana's body and laid her out in her best flannel nightie, and then while Fred built her a coffin out in the shed the women began baking, cleaning and preparing for visitors.

Christie was buried over the river near Welby and Laura's old house, beside little Eva Mahala Hadfield. It was an appropriate grave for Christiana Winter. Big River had been her home as Meadowbank had never been, and she had always felt closest to the children.

It was months after Christie's death before the last of her regular letters stopped coming. She'd taken art classes from England and religious instruction from London, and had correspondents in Africa and the United States. When she died, bookseller and publisher A H Reed of Dunedin wrote condolences to Jessie, who with her sister was a regular mail order customer. His letter was one of many from people all over the world who had been touched by Christiana Winter's lively mind.

In time Fred bought a wrought-iron railing to protect the little plot where Christie and little Eva were buried, and family members kept it tidy while the bush grew back all around it and the fantails and bush wrens fluttered near.

With her sister's death Jessie inherited the Emano Street house, which was kept tenanted for years and eventually the section was passed onto her daughter Muriel and sold. It was almost 50 years since the Winters had first come to Awaroa and now Jessie and Will, who had both married Hadfields, and Bessie Connor down at Karamea were the last of the family.

There were only ten Hadfields left at Awaroa, Fred and Jessie at Big River with their three younger children, and Welby and Laura who had moved to Meadowbank with theirs.

Awaroa School in the 1920s. Fred and Jessie Hadfield's farm can be seen across Big River. Christiana Winter and Eva Hadfield were buried near Welby and Laura's house, near the track to the left of the picture between the school and the river.

CHAPTER THIRTEEN : ADA, JOAN, LYNETTE
1932

IT WAS ADA AND JOAN'S IDEA to farm Meadowbank again. Their father was confined to a wheelchair most days now, and Laura spent her time looking after him. Bert was dead and Jim had moved away to run a fishing boat out of Riwaka, so there was no one left to earn an income. Their lease at Big River was abandoned in the early 1930s, the property sold up and the family moved down to Meadowbank, renting the homestead and surrounding land from Welby's brothers and sisters who still jointly controlled the estate.

The old homestead had been empty since Will and Ivy Winter left the bay and it was showing signs of neglect, the orchard and garden overgrown and the house weathered and faded. Fred had done his best but it was too far away for him to do more than basic maintenance, and although families like the McLarens came to stay there in the holidays there were long periods of time when it stood dark and silent.

Ada was nineteen, Frank sixteen and Joan fourteen when they moved back down near the mouth of the inlet. Frank would soon have to leave the inlet to look for work, but the girls knew that with hard work and determination they could be self-sufficient and support their parents on Meadowbank's seventeen acres, and they set about proving it. They loaded what they could of their possessions into the punt and the sledge and then Ada and Joan walked down to the old homestead carrying what was left over.

They were excited as they walked through the double wooden gate in the boxthorn hedge, planted by their grandfather William and left unkempt and wild for all those lonely years since he had gone. Ada and Jim could dimly remember their grandfather, but to Frank and Joan he lived only in their parents' stories of the old days. Meadowbank was the place where their father had grown up, and as they ran excitedly through the rooms he and Laura reminisced about their aunts and uncles and their childhood adventures, stories that had been told over and over whenever the families got together. There was Bert's grave too, and Laura and Welby took comfort in knowing they were close enough to put flowers on it, or to sit under the big tree in the cool of the evening and remember their son. .

There was plenty of work to do to bring the old house alive again. Windows were flung open and their curtains washed and aired, chimneys were cleaned out and the stove was lit again, hedges and lawns were trimmed, soil was dug over and new vegetables seedlings were planted. Welby fixed the cowshed and the girls tidied the orchard, and soon there were cats at the back door, calves in the paddock and hens scratching in the dirt once more.

The girls lived in the upstairs room at the gable end of the house. It was a pretty room, with violets on the wallpaper. Downstairs there was a sitting room with a neat blue fireplace, sharing a common chimney with the open fire in the dining room behind it. Their dining table was cedar, and the sitting room ceiling was whitewashed.

The kitchen was at the back of the house, and the big brick oven Adele had built in the back yard nearly fifty years before was soon back in use for the weekly baking. It stood about four feet high and five feet long and a corrugated iron roof was built over it to keep the rain off. Laura had baked in a brick oven for most of her life and was acknowledged as the expert, her skills learned from her father the pastrycook. There were always bundles of manuka, neatly tied, and then finely chopped wattle ready to stoke the fire once it was alight. The bricks were heated for hours with a good hot fire, then the ashes were scraped out and the food put in, bread at the back, then meat and then cakes, and the entranceway sealed with wet cloths around the wooden door. Meadowbank had a good wood range too, and after the boys left home she baked in that.

They did their washing outside, boiling the clothes in the big copper and then wringing them out to hang on long lines propped up in the middle with manuka poles. All the girls at Awaroa had been used to standing with their skirts kilted up around their bare legs on washdays, wringing the heavy sheets over the grass by holding each end and twisting them around, trying to ignore the sandflies that swarmed around their ankles. It was heavy work, but at Meadowbank there was a a miracle of labour-saving technology, a hand wringer on the tub.

"I've changed the beds," Ada called cheerfully one Monday as she headed out the back door with her arms full of bundled sheets. Her mother nodded, busy with her broom and duster. It was a glorious spring morning, and the big cherry tree dripped with blossom which turned hazy as smoke and steam billowed up from the copper. Ada's face was soon red and sweaty as she stirred the clothes with a well-worn stick.

It wasn't until after dinner that Laura realised her ring finger was bare. Her hands were gnarled and roughened with work and she often slipped the worn gold engagement ring off and put it up on the shelf in the kitchen, or under her pillow...

"Oh no," she whispered, and ran to check. The ring was gone, lost in the crease of a sheet or pillowcase and shaken out under the cherry tree.

They searched for ages, but the ground was thick with lush spring grass and white petals, trampled by their feet as they'd braced themselves to lift the heavy sheets and wring the water from them. The little band that Welby had given her so long ago and she'd worn so proudly was never seen again.

"I wish I could buy you another one," Welby said softly when they sat out on the porch late that evening. "I've not given you much in the end, have I?"

Laura looked up at the bright stars in the night sky, and at the pathway the rising moon made on the dark still water of the inlet. It was high tide, and the steady flash of the Farewell Spit lighthouse was the only movement around them. Then a fish jumped close to the shore, and sparks of phosphorescence winked for a moment and were gone.

"Awaroa diamonds," Laura laughed. "What more could a woman need?"

Welby went back to his old craft of boatbuilding. He'd learned from his father and built his own boats in his turn, and now he was ready to pass his skills on. They all knew the basics because they'd been brought up to boats and the sea, and William Hadfield's handiwork was all around them, from the *Venture* to the big model boats he'd built for his grandsons in the last few years of his life.

Welby taught the girls to recognise and handle timber, supervising them as they built their own dinghies. He was confined to his wheelchair most of the time, but that didn't stop him from planning and overseeing the work. He would send Ada and Joan off to find rata for the knees and then show them how to frame the hull and shape the planks.

They had several boats in the latter years at Meadowbank. The *Wave* was a cabin launch and Laura and the girls would take her around to Bark Bay to pick grapes in the late summer. Later they built the *Breeze*, a large open boat they eventually decked in. Welby arranged with Fred and the boys to have *Venture* towed back down to the little creek where she had been built, intending

Meadowbank came alive again in the 1930s when Welby and Laura Hadfield moved in with their three younger children. The land around the homestead was farmed once more, bread was baked in the oven Welby's mother Adele had built, and fruit harvested from the trees his father had planted.

Laura Hadfield (on jetty) with her daughters Ada and Joan and their cousins at the Awaroa wharf. Ada and Joan built several boats at Awaroa under their father's guidance and vessels like the *Breeze*, built by the two women in the 1930s, are still afloat today.
"Dinghies were easy, launches took a little longer,"Joan said.

to do her up after years of neglect, but the project was too ambitious and she was left to rot quietly in the tide.

Soon after they moved to Meadowbank the ship *Antonio* dumped its timber dunnage in the sea off Awaroa because it could not offload it at the port. It was a welcome windfall for the Awaroa families. Most of it floated ashore and Welby, Frank and the girls spent weeks gathering it from the beaches and towing it behind the dinghy or sledging it back home. They used it to supplement timber from their old home up the river, and they did up the little wharf and boatshed down past the dog tree. They found they had enough left over to build a little two-roomed cottage beside Meadowbank.

Under Welby's supervision the little cottage took shape very quickly. It was built for Laura's parents the Cunliffes and other family members to stay in and it served its purpose for years. Flowers were planted around it and the big cherry tree dropped its blossom over the roof every spring, turning the cottage into a picturesque little holiday home.

Ada and Joan were both good at handling animals, and they had learned to work harness horses from a very young age. Both could hunt and fish as well as any man, and when they moved down to Meadowbank they learned how to farm cows and sheep. The used horses to plough the paddocks. They kept goats, caught wild in the hills and tamed, and would harness them sometimes to haul smaller loads. One little black goat would be taken down to Sigley's orchard, and a sugarbag split down the middle and tossed over her back to be filled with apples. She would make just enough fuss to toss a few out so she could eat them, and then would carry the rest of the load home. The sisters were happy to butcher the farm animals for meat, but had trouble killing them, so when it was time to kill a sheep Ada would put it in a wheelbarrow and take it back up to the house for her father to cut its throat.

Later they had a tractor, and would kill their own cattle beasts by shooting them and hoisting them up with the tractor to skin and butcher them. Joan was a crack shot as her mother had been before her, and she and Frank would roam the hills hunting for wild pigs. They cured the best of them for bacon, using a dry salt method, but the wild pork was never as good as their own domestic grain-fed pigs.

Ada looked after the dogs, and once when they were hunting their fox terrier, Rata, was gored by a pig which put its tusk into the dog's shoulder and throat. It was the sort of injury the girls were used to dealing with and there was no question of getting a vet. Ada tended the half-dead animal until the wound healed itself, and the little dog was soon back chasing pigs again.

Life at Meadowbank was more isolated for Ada and Joan than it had ever been in their parents' day. The sawmills were gone now, the scows no longer working in and out, and there were only a few isolated households between Kaiteriteri and Totaranui. There were a few boats working up and down the coastline, carrying coal from Puponga and cement from Tarakohe, but only an occasional fishing launch came over the bar and into Awaroa.

Supplies came in by road and seldom as far as Meadowbank, so one of the girls would have to go up to Big River once a week to get the mail, taking a boat if the tide was right or riding over the mudflats. Bill and Nelson had put a telephone in to Meadowbank when Fred took over the post office and the lines, and it became an important link between the two Hadfield families who were now too far apart to see each other very often.

One day in June 1934 Laura heard the black telephone on the wall ring with her code, and she wiped her floury hands on her apron before she answered.

"I'm a grandmother at last," Jessie announced. "Wilfred has just telephoned us with the news, and mother and son are doing fine."

"I'm so glad,"Laura said softly. "The first of the new generation."

"They've named him Ian. Mavis was hoping for a son."

"And I'll bet Fred hoped for a grandson. Congratulations to both of you, and all my love to Mavis."

But Laura was thoughtful as she went back to her kitchen and poked at the fire. She knew her old friend and sister-in-law well enough to know there would be quiet tears up at Big River, and when the last batch of biscuits was out of the oven and set to cool she tidied the kitchen and packed the best ones into a basket.

"I'm going to Jessie," she told Welby. "The girls will see to your lunch."

Laura rowed up to Big River on the rising tide, her strong arms moving rhythmically as her mind wandered down through the years. There at the mouth of the inlet she and Jessie had spent carefree summers with their brothers and sisters, laughed and joked with the Hadfields and the Cracknell boys. She wondered where the years had gone.

Jessie was out in the garden, her gentle face shaded as always by a big straw hat even though the winter sun had no strength in it. She smiled her gratitude as she went down to take the painter and help Laura out of her boat.

"Hello Grandma," Laura said. "That sad face isn't for Mavis or little Ian, is it?"

"How did you know?"

Laura linked her arm through her friend's and they walked back up the paddock towards the little house in silence.

"Clifford was my first child," Jessie said in a low voice. "Our first son, and he was so precious."

"As they all are," Laura said. "I remember the day he was born."

"You were such an expert, with your two."

"Bert would have been 25 this month, and Clifford would be 24."

"And Colin would have been thirteen if he had lived. And your poor little Eva." Jessie's eyes brimmed with fresh tears. "Three sons and a daughter we've lost between us, Laura, and the first is always so precious. I can never forget my little Kiwi, even after all this time."

"But now here's little Mavis, grown up and with a son of her own. Be thankful, Jess, and leave the dead with God."

Jessie squeezed her arm gratefully. "I'm glad you're here. And glad Mavis is in good hands, with a midwife and a doctor and a husband and an aunt all clucking around her. It wasn't like that for our first ones, was it?"

"I remember when our Jim was on the way," Laura grinned. "I didn't know what was wrong with me when I started feeling ill every morning. I had no idea how babies happened, and Welby had to explain. I don't know which of us was more embarrassed."

Jessie blushed. "And now we're grandparents, and you're a great aunt."

"I do my best," Laura laughed as they reached the house. "And here's Aunty Joy, doing her lessons."

The little girl looked up, delighted. "Am I really Aunty Joy, Mother? Will the baby call me that?"

"When he's old enough to talk, dear. Wilf said they might bring him down for Christmas so you can practise being an auntie then." Jessie moved to the stove and poked the fire up under the big kettle. "Now clear that table off for little Ian's grandmother and his great aunt. We're both old ladies now and we deserve a cup of tea."

By the late 1930s both Frank and Nelson had gone off to find work, leaving Fred and Jessie up the river with Muriel and Joy, and Laura and Welby at Meadowbank with their two girls. Mr Avery lived alone at Awaiti, and there was no one else around.

The sisters grew close, dependent on each other and shy with strangers. Ada handled the dogs and the cows, Joan ran the garden, did the hunting and looked after the goats, and they worked together on the heavy jobs like sawing wood to keep the stove and the fires going. They seldom left the property, and for nearly twenty years they lived with their parents in a very self-contained family unit.

If there were visitors, Laura and Welby did the honours, and more often than not their daughters would stay out of the way. They had their goats, dogs and horses for company and they weren't very confident with people.

When she was still a child up at Big River Joan had an accident which left her permanently lame. Two young teachers took her up onto a horse with them to go for a ride, and the one in front was holding her by her clothing when she fell heavily down onto the road. Her pelvis was crushed with the impact, and although she was taken to the doctor there was little to be done to ease what would be a permanent hip injury. Her disability didn't stop her getting about in the hills, although for most of her life she suffered aches and pains in her hip.

Joan became very fond of young Edgar Sixtus, whose family lived up at Canaan. He and his father knew the Hadfields well because they had farmed at the inlet, cutting a walking track between Canaan and Awaroa so they could drive sheep up. Edgar bought a sixteen-foot boat from Welby and had it fitted with an engine at Riwaka, and he used it to get up and down the coastline with timber and other loads. For a while Edgar was a frequent visitor at Meadowbank, helping out around the farm and going out fishing with the girls. They would go off for picnics on Sundays, and sometimes on expeditions into the hills or along the coastline.

Welby soon realised their relationship was deepening into something more than friendship, but he could not spare Joan from the farm. He discouraged Edgar's visits and the family accepted his ruling, little knowing the relationship would endure long after they had all left the inlet. Edgar went off goldmining and became a good friend of Floss and her husband, who in 1940 introduced him to his future wife Mona Downing, and the couple spent their working life together up at Canaan.

Moving back down to Meadowbank meant the girls were a lot closer to the sea and in tune with the tides again. They fished regularly, using a spear or a knife to get snapper and netting for moki and herrings. Snapper had always been speared at the inlet. The technique was to row up the harbour until they saw a tail sticking up, then chase the fish with a spear or harpoon at the ready.

"You jump out of the boat and they turn around and go for you, and if you're nervous you jump out of the way and lose them, but if you're not they come right up to you and veer away at the last minute and then you can get them," Ada explained to one of her Nelson cousins. Joan and Frank had been

A Christmas party at Meadowbank, December 1930. From left back: Nelson, Ralph, Fred and Mavis Hadfield, Betty McLaren, Bert and Welby Hadfield, Nina McLaren, Nellie (seated) and Bill Hadfield, Mr Hermanson (owner of the *Waitohi*) and his sister, Evered McLaren, Mabel Gray (Nellie's neice), Lake Holyoake (obscured), Keith Goodman. In front: Laura McLaren, Edgar Sixtus, Jessie, Muriel and Joy Hadfield.

chasing snapper through the rushes up at Little River, getting them with the axe. "It's cleaner than the harpoon. That's too heavy and it makes too much of a mess of the fish."

The sisters were also keen whitebaiters and kept up the Awaroa tradition of looking forward to each whitebait season and sharing their catch around the family. Although they worked in the mud and muck of the farm they wore skirts all the time, right up until they left the inlet. Women never wore trousers at Awaroa. They would ride in skirts, their legs chaffing on the saddle, and would tuck them up into their bloomers when they were scrambling through the bush to get firewood.

Like their mother, aunts and grandmother before them, they would wade out to launch dinghies or clear fishing nets with their bare legs turning blue and purple in the icy winter sea, but their skirts were shorter now, and in summer they fashioned swimsuits out of large handkerchiefs and would swim in them when the men were away.

They were wary of stingrays, called stingarees, which would chase the boats in the inlet. Welby found it hard to believe until one day Ada rowed him across the inlet to see some big wild pigs rooting on the hillside. On the way home she said quietly "Look out the back, Dad," and sure enough there were

302

four stingrays behind the dinghy, following in its wake. The girls had always known to steer clear of them, because their behaviour in the water seemed deliberately aggressive.

They would row and motor up to Totaranui and like their grandfather before them they were always watchful, always aware of the the tides and the weather. So was Welby, and as he became more and more crippled he would sit for hours in front of the homestead looking out to sea. When Ada and Joan took one of the boats out across the bar he would watch them until they were out of sight, often with a sigh of envy, and look out for their return.

One afternoon Laura was alarmed to hear him shouting and banging his stick against his seat.

"Whatever is it?" she demanded. "Are you all right?"

In answer he pointed up towards the hills.Out of a cloudless sky a black storm rolled over the horizon, the clouds moving fast. Already they could feel the wind whipping up. Laura looked out to sea, where the little white-painted *Wave* was already turned to follow the coastline to Totaranui, directly in the path of the storm which the girls could not possibly have seen yet.

"They'll never get to shelter before it hits them," she breathed.

"Call them back," Welby said. "Signal them. A sheet, anything. They must turn and glance behind them sooner or later."

Laura ran up the stairs and flung the bedroom window open, her thoughts racing as she watched the launch moving across the still-calm water. A flash of sunlight on the top of a wave gave her an idea and she snatched the mirror from its hook on the wall and leaned out of the window as far as she could, turning it to catch the sun and flash it out across the bay. Down below she saw her husband out of his wheelchair now, agitated, staring at the toy-like boat in the distance as if he was willing it to turn.

For several minutes Laura flashed her signal out across the water, and out of the corner of her eye she could see the storm clouds roiling over Awaiti and moving over the hills towards the sea. A flash of lightning behind Mount Alma told her there was substance to the black front, although the sky above Meadowbank was still as blue and innocent as before.

"They've seen it!" Welby shouted, and to her relief she saw the little white boat falter and begin to turn. She hung the mirror back on the wall and hurried to get the washing in. The storm hit half an hour later, just as the Breeze came in over the bar, and by the time the girls had tied their boat up and secured it they were drenched with the driving rain that whipped around the inlet and ducking their heads against the thunder that rolled across the sky.

That afternoon while Ada sat out in the little cowshed milking, and Joan fed the fowls and goats and tied the dogs up, Laura slipped out to the graves under the big magnolia tree. She placed a sprig of daphne on Evered's grave, taking a minute to remember the boy she'd known so well. Evered had drowned because he hadn't heeded the weather warnings. Her girls were safely home because the lesson had been well learned since.

Strange things happened at Meadowbank while Laura and the girls lived there. Steps were heard on the stairs at night, and twice when they were coming home across the water in the dark they saw the dim light of a candle in the upstairs window when no one was in the house. The cat stiffened in alarm one day and looked towards the empty stairs, and once Laura felt a chill breath on the back of her neck as she worked at the kitchen bench.

Ada and Joan slept in an upstairs bedroom under the gable, and visitors were put in a tiny bedroom across the hall. Once when a cousin came to stay she woke in the middle of the night, sensing that someone had stood at the foot of her bed, and she fled to the girls' room in terror. The presence was strong at times but never malevolent, as if a sad spirit still lingered to revisit the old house, walk the rooms and wonder at what fates had befallen the family.

There was an older, stronger presence at the Sawpit Point, where Maori artefacts had been found in shell middens and there were still oven stones, rounded and blackened from ancient fires, washing out of the bank. The young Hadfields all learned to walk well clear of certain areas where they were made to feel uncomfortable and uneasy. They followed their own instincts, respecting something they didn't understand but didn't question either.

Once Ada and Joan moved to Meadowbank they seldom saw their cousins from Big River. Muriel would go down to visit but she would have to set off on the falling tide and leave again for home before the tide got in again, as her grandmother had done before her. If they were late the children would have to run and wade, and sometimes swim, to beat the tide and Fred would always be watching out for them.

When Muriel was old enough she went out to work for a season in the hopfields with her Auntie Floss and her two young cousins. Like Welby and Floss she became a Salvationist, making her declaration for God at a meeting in Motueka in 1936.

"Picture the hall, hard forms, the band rather loud. What wasn't solder was brass, according to the bandmaster, and of course he had to play as well as conduct...There was Mrs Anderson, confined to a wheelchair, and the little widow lady who wheeled it in. Dulcie Anderson played the old organ, wearing a large bonnet and an old-fashioned 'speaker' uniform... Joyce, her sister, was in the band, and she wore a modern tunic-type straight uniform with pleats from the shoulders and band epaulettes..."

Her first Salvation Army meeting was an inspiring event for the shy young eighteen-year-old from Awaroa, but she was thoughtful and sincere when she made her personal commitment the following week. She went back to the inlet a lone soldier, and was soon a member of the recently-formed Takaka Corps of the Army. Her Auntie Floss was a dynamic and powerful influence, and Muriel soon found herself part of a large family of Salvation Army friends in Golden Bay, accompanying the officers when they delivered the *War Cry* in Collingwood, Bainham, Rockville and Puponga. She would bicycle long distances around the Bay to attend meetings.

Back at Awaroa she started a bible class, persuading her older brothers, sisters and cousins to join her. Welby helped them out, and the first Sunday afternoon Captain Ingerson, her senior officer and mentor, biked all the way from Takaka to Awaroa to get the group started.

When Muriel was old enough she went to live with her aunt Floss and work for her as a maid. They were both regular members of the Motueka meetings, and before long Muriel was off to Wellington to work fulltime for the Salvation Army. She began in the kitchens of the People's Palace in Cuba Street and she took to the life and enjoyed it. The discipline was hard but she found it rewarding and satisfying work, and after serving her time as a uniformed "lassie" she went to the Salvation Army College to train as an officer.

Will Winter had been working at the Tarakohe cement works since it first began, but now he went up to the Upper Anatoki, supervising the goldminers who worked on the government's employment schemes. He ran a large camp, keeping the men fed and the records straight, and as he explored the mountainous back country with them he wrote long letters home to his sister Jessie.

"Monday 28, Labour Day, continuous rain," he wrote in 1935 from the Upper Anatoki camp. He told her he was reading the *Times Literary Supplement,* the *New York Times* book review pages, *London Punch* and *Literary Digest* from a bundle Bess sent up, finding the papers a welcome change from his routine work with time sheets, forms and requisitions. He had to write reports on everything that went on up at the camp, and he described to Jess how he had even had to act as camp doctor when a man injured his leg.

"It turned out to be a poisoned knee which one of his mates had operated on with a razor. I sent up lint and bandages, also peroxide but was anxious to see how he was, as such bush surgery is liable to cause blood poisoning when applied without antiseptics....the whole thing started out as a carbuncle which though painful was less dangerous than the operation."

Will Winter spent the Depression years at this goldminers' camp at Anatoki.

Will Winter - poet, woodcarver, botanist and Wainui Hill roadman

Will described a recent trip out on the ranges.

"The rain set in before noon and continued all night with snow. Twelve hours out, and came down a different ridge which proved a series of ghastly precipices and bluffs, the worst of which, having negotiated by a hair's breadth, you wonder whether the next one will be a sheer impossibility. However I got out before dark pretty well sodden - hardly a pleasure trip. Large masses of snow on the tops 3ft deep and more, sometimes it will bear, but often one goes through it; once I went through into a creek and got boots full of water. Some deer about, but didn't get a shot; it is hard to approach them in the bush.

"The mountain mingi or neinei is very beautiful on the timberline, its crooked limbs crowned with heads; broad leaves, dark green at the base shading off to red, in the mass giving a purple effect. I regretted leaving the camera on account of the weather being dull, I could have got one or two snaps there....."

They exchanged books on botany, and Jess obtained a microscope which she and the children used to study native plants and ferns. When she first spotted a strange chrysalis in her garden early in 1937 Jessie sent it to the Cawthron Institute, who identified it as pteromalus puparum, a parasitic wasp recently introduced from England to control the cabbage white butterfly. She pored over scientific texts as enthusiastically as she pored over the *Yates Garden Guide* and the seed catalogues which came in the mailbags. She grew pansies and polyanthus, and planned gardens of bright colour.

Will sent specimens and sketches down from the mountains, and his letters were read carefully and treasured. After the work schemes finished he often returned to the hills behind Golden Bay to fossick for gold, and he sent detailed reports to Jessie with equally detailed sketches scattered through the pages as he described what he had found.

"...I was up the Waikoromumu a fortnight or so back," he wrote one day. "Went up for a sample of a red marble which is mentioned in Dr Bell's report. 2500ft up, the P of W feathers (Lodia Superba) grows in thousands. Fronds as long as your arm! A great sight, and the land snail (paryphanta Hochstetter) is very plentiful. I should have liked to carry on but had to get back before dark, having no grub or blankets. I got the marble, it is a beautiful stone..."

Another letter was even more evocative.

"I made a trip to the Wainui, left here Saturday 5pm carrying tucker and a coat to sleep in, also prospecting tool, dish and a scraper I made for crevicing from a shear blade. Arrived at the hut on top 1680ft in time to get a stock of wood before dark. Fortunately I found some spuds and a spare billy and frypan and was not long in preparing a feed, bacon, spuds, toast and of course tea.

The Hadfield family with visitors at Awapoto. From left: Richard Gaskell, Jeff Shallcrass, Bill, Gordon, Vena and Elaine Hadfield, Mrs Terepa Shallcrass. In front Howard, Donald, Lester, Diane (Nancy behind her) and Fred Hadfield

Photo by Jeff Shallcrass senior

Returned soldier Ralph Hadfield (centre) welcomed home by Will Winter and Bill Hadfield. Ralph and his brother Nelson both came home safely from World War Two

Now the opportunity was there for the original farm to come back into the family. When Nelson came home from the war Fred and Jessie's eldest son Bill, grandson of the original William Hadfield, returned to the inlet with his wife Vena and their family and settled on the Little River property.

A new generation was growing up around Awaroa. Laura McLaren and her children had always come and gone from the inlet, staying at Meadowbank, and now her grandchildren were coming and going from Awaiti, where her daughter Bethany was a frequent visitor.

Betty had been brought up with her mother's stories of Awaroa, and had spent her own summer holidays at Meadowbank or at Fred and Jessie's house. She was the same age as her cousins Bill and Ada, and like them she remembered her grandfather William, and Auntie Ivy who had been strict with all the children, and Uncle Will who had been charming and made them reed whistles with his pocketknife.

Betty was left a widow after her husband disappeared from Tahuna Beach one night, and she and her children were part of Bill's family, spending the summer holidays with them and helping out on the farm.

Mavis's daughter Lynette was born in 1940, and from the time she was a little girl she looked forward to her Awaroa visits. She grew up with the family stories and her grandfather told her more. He pointed out the graves of all the people who had been buried at Awaroa, Evered, her great grandfather and Bert at Meadowbank, the Ricketts boy at Big River, baby Eva and Christiana Winter over near the school.

When she was eight years old they rode down to Meadowbank together, the little girl perched in front of Fred on the big plodding bay horse. The tide was ebbing and the gritty golden sand was still waterlogged.

"Did I ever tell you about the time I found the shipwreck at Totaranui?" Fred asked.

Lynette shook her head. It seemed strange to have her grandfather's voice coming from behind her back, and she was a little nervous about being so far up from the ground, her dress tucked up around her thighs and the feel of the horse's warm hairy shoulders against her bare legs. She risked a look ahead to Meadowbank, still a long way away across the shallow estuary. There was a plume of smoke rising lazily from the kitchen, and on the beach in front of the homestead a flock of black and white oystercatchers gathered like a congregation spilling out from church.

"When I was just a lad, it was. There had been a terrible storm and we hadn't been able to get over and get the mail for days. That was before we had a post office at Awaiti."

"Did you have to go to Totaranui to get the mail? Where was the post office?" Lynette asked. "Was it up at the big house?"

"Aye, but not that house. There was a grander one before it, but up the same avenue. There were lots of buildings there once. Did you know there was tobacco grown there, and your uncle Billie went over to work in the sheds tying it up for drying?"

He laughed at her expression of disbelief. "Oh yes, there were lots of things going on at Totaranui. There was a school there too, and once a long time ago there was a little spastic girl who had terrible fits, and she was kept in a padded room with a special nurse. But I'm telling you about the sailing ship, and I wish I could remember where it was. I looked and looked for it afterwards."

"But I thought you saw it?"

"I came around the point from here and I saw something on the beach, or I thought it was on the beach. It was a ship, and as I rowed closer I realised it was a bit higher up and had been there a long time. I went ashore and had a good look over it."

Lynette screwed up her eyes against the sun and tried to imagine the bare bones of a sailing ship rising out of the sand. The picture grew more vivid as her grandfather talked about the rusted iron fittings, the hardwood pegs in the deck, the peeling shreds of green copper still clinging to the hull. Ropes and sails had long since rotted away but a mast still lay spiked in the sand, disappearing into a dune beside the hulk.

"I climbed all over it but I couldn't find a name anywhere, or what had happened to it. She was a schooner, about seventy feet I guessed, and the storm had swept the sand off her all down one side. She could have been buried there for thirty or forty years, and as far as I know she's still there."

"Didn't you dig around her and get the timbers? There could have been treasure inside or anything."

"That's what I thought too." He chuckled. "After an hour or so I remembered what I was there for and took off up to get our mail. The tide was on the turn because I'd mucked around for so long, and so I had a stiff row home I can tell you. I didn't say a word about the wreck up at the homestead because I could see she'd just been uncovered and I thought with a bit of luck I'd be able to get Welby and Roy back up with me to have a good fossick over her before anyone else beat us to it."

"So what happened, Grandad?"

"Nothing. Nothing at all. We were flat out with lambing and it was a couple of days before we could get back up. We bought an axe and a shovel and thought we'd have a go at the mast, but we never found it again. I knew where it was but the wind had blown the sand back up over that wreck and buried it deep. The beach was as clean as if it had never been there at all."

"What did Uncle Welby say?"

"He wasn't very pleased with me, I can tell you." The old man shook his head. "I never saw that ship again, and neither did anyone else from what I heard. Nature showed her to me, and nature hid her away again, and as far as I know she's under there still."

The little girl looked out at the froth and foam of the summer sea beyond the bar. What terrible storm had forced the ship ashore, she wondered, and what had happened to the survivors? A launch moved slowly along the coast and in her mind it was transformed into a two masted schooner, white sails billowing as the sailors leaned into the wind, shouting at each other above the sound of the sea.

Meadowbank was always wonderful, with the sun streaming in the windows and Auntie Laura presiding over a proper afternoon tea. There was a hand embroidered cloth, white with pink and blue daisies, and the milk and sugar was in dainty china jugs. There was a gingerbread cake, and pikelets with thick strawberry jam, and against the walls the big wooden chests full of Uncle Welby's shell collection. The shells had become his hobby, a part of the sea that he could enjoy from his wheelchair, and he had big cabinets with sliding drawers, each filled with shells from all over the world carefully arranged and labelled. Welby wrote to other collectors, swapping shells and learning more about them, and he always showed them to the children who came to visit.

After tea the grownups sat and talked. This was the part Lynette loved, the time when old Uncle Welby turned his big cane wheelchair to face the sea again and her grandfather sat beside him with his hands folded loosely in his lap and his eyes on the distant horizon, and the time seemed to stand still and their low voices merged with the sound of cicadas in the manuka as she escaped outside to play by the creek and the mulberry tree.

Sometimes there would be a new litter of kittens, or a playful young goat to feed with crusts of bread from Auntie Laura's kitchen, and sometimes Ada or Joan would take her into the garden and let her pick raspberries or plums to take back home to Big River. There were always flowers, and blackcurrant bushes and tomato plants and the rich smells of the earth and the sea.

They stayed at Meadowbank too long that drowsy afternoon, and when Fred came to find her there was urgency in his voice. Joan held the horse and Ada lifted Lynette up, and they set off briskly down the track to the boatshed and Sawpit Point, a bag of provisions and gifts slung over Fred's shoulder. The horse farted richly and the smell wafted around them, and Fred clucked impatiently and urged it into a faster gait.

The tide was rushing in and the first deep creek was well up the horse's legs. They took the fastest route they could, sticking to the edge of the water and the hardest, driest sand they could but now the sea was creeping around them like an octupus, its tentacles slipping past and ahead of them from several directions. By the time the got to the top of the inlet they were in the reeds and rushes, the horse's progress slowed by black, gnarled elbows of wood bedded into the muddy creek bottoms.

They swam the river, Lynette twisting the coarse black hairs of the horse's mane through nervous fingers as the cold frothy water crept up around her knees. As always, she glanced across towards the Awapoto valley, deep in the blue shadows of late afternoon. Whenever she went to Uncle Bill and Auntie Vena's house she always imagined her great-grandparents living there in their old-fashioned house under the brooding hills.

There were seven children at Awapoto now, and Uncle Bill had built a little schoolroom for them to do their correspondence lessons. Sometimes Lynette envied her cousins their splendid backyard and their isolation, and at other times she felt sorry for them for never going to town or to the pictures and never having any friends except each other.

Then they arrived back at her grandparents's house, where the yellow climbing rose Stella Gray almost covered the little shed out the back. It was hard to imagine Fred and Jessie and Auntie Floss all younger than her mother was now, living in a tiny one-roomed hut out there. That first building was long gone but further away in the paddock the old whare that had once been a schoolroom was still standing, empty now. Lynette could see in her mind's eye old Mr Perrott sitting on the porch in the sun, and Auntie Muriel as a little girl bringing him tea.

Outside the back door of her grandfather's house there was a row of kerosene tins filled with fresh water from the well, and inside a big jug of milk stood on the kitchen table covered with a circle of white net weighted down at the edges with little glass beads. There were cats everywhere and the smell of last night's mutton made her nose wrinkle. Auntie Joy was trimming rhubarb stalks to make a pie for tea, and Grandma was busy with her seedlings.

Over the whole river flat the shrill hum of a thousand cicadas vibrated the air, as it did all through the long hot summers.

Another afternoon Lynette went with her grandfather to feed the fowls and tie the dogs up under the big fig tree.

"There's a man buried over there," Fred told her, pointing across to the foot of the hill where the chestnut trees marched in a row. "Long before my time, it was, but Jim Perrott told me."

"Who was he, Grandad?"

"No one knows. Jim thinks he must have jumped ship and come to work with the sawyers in the bush. It was all bush here once, a long time ago."

"When Mr Ricketts lived here?"

"Yes, they were the first to clear the trees, and they cut a lot down. But then after they went, other men came in to cut the timber. My father was one of them, and so was Jim Perrott. This poor soul had an accident with a tree, and no one knew his name or where he came from, so all they could do was bury him here by the river."

Lynette looked across the peaceful grassy bank, littered with fallen chestnuts, and tried to imagine a time before her grandfather had been there. She felt sorry for the man with no name, but glad there had been someone to bury him and remember.

She went down to Awaroa as often as she could, usually with Uncle Ralph who would come home from his shearing jobs in Cheviot to stay in the little army hut behind her parents' house. They'd set off together in his little blue Morris Minor, his rifle in the back seat in case he had a chance to go pighunting, a box of food tucked in with Lynette's clothes so she could last out the long days when her grandparents didn't start their dinner until late.

Sometimes they stopped in at the Pohara Hall where there was a dance going on and they'd mingle with all the other locals. Ralph would melt into the corner with the men, to talk about shearing and stock sales and eye the ladies and whirl out onto the floor every now and then with a laughing woman in a swirling dance dress. Lynette would sit with the girls on the long narrow benches, eyeing their hairstyles and waiting for a chance to practice the steps her class learned on the tennis courts at school. Now and then Uncle Ralph would swing past her and wink, or appear as her next partner in the long chain of men in the Gay Gordons.

Then the long trip over the hill in the dark, to Wainui Bay and then into the deep hills and winding down through the trees, headlights flashing yellow on the clay road ahead and lighting up the glowworms in the clay banks.

Crossing the Awapoto - Donald Hadfield comes home with fresh-trapped possums. He and his brothers dried and sold the skins to earn a part-time income.

This bridge across the Awapoto was the only road access to the Hadfields'farms when Bill arrived there with his Graeme Paige car and trailer. Passengers always got out to walk across the bridge.

They'd get to Little River and Uncle Ralph would toot the horn at Uncle Bill's, or stop in with messages and plants and packages.

"I'll come over tomorrow," he'd shout and they'd head off again very slowly, Lynette walking ahead in the darkness over the precarious little bridge to her grandparents' house. There'd be a cup of tea and hugs and soft words in the flickering kerosene light, and Grandad would shake her hand formally as he always did, and then Grandma or Joy would send her off to bed in the little room beside the kitchen. She loved waking up there, seeing the washstand with its old fashioned bowl and jug painted with roses, the crude home-made wooden dresser where her mother had kept her hair ribbons and treasures. Hard to imagine three girls in that room, and a teacher too sometimes, and the three boys noisy in the porch as they ran up from the whare where they'd slept, and Auntie Christiana Winter in the sleepout where Auntie Joy lived now.

Ralph and Bill would spend hours tinkering with cars and motorbikes over at Awapoto. Their father had never owned a car, but Bill had worked at Birdsall's Garage in Takaka and bought his first motorbike in 1929. He was inventive and mechanically adept, and he had set up a Pelton wheel to provide power to his house and run a refrigerator. At Big River his father still used an old wooden fluming to run water to the cowshed, while the house supply was drawn up from the well in buckets as it had always been.

The Awaroa families always got colds and diseases when they went out or had contact with other children, because their natural immunities were developed to suit their environments. They lived without conveniences like refrigeration, their meats kept in a safe and their milk in a bucket, and they thrived on food that was often prepared and kept unhygenically by town standards, but they had no defences against colds, flus and measles.

Bill's sons grew up knowing how to hunt and fish and how to improvise around the farm. The children played in the bush, creeks and rivers and swam in the sea, their childhood marked by collections of shells and other Awaroa treasures. Vena did most of the teaching in the little schoolroom and her eldest daughter Elaine stayed at home to help around the house after the others had all left home. Like Adele before her, Vena never got used to the enclosing and brooding hills and the weeks and often months of isolation from other women. For Bill, the Awapoto valley was a paradise, and he never understood why his wife and children felt lonely on the farm.

Lynette Bradley grew up and left school to work in the little gift shop in Motueka and she chose birthday and Christmas presents for her grandmother to send off to her family.

"I thought the little blue vase for Auntie Vena and the framed text for Auntie Muriel," she would write, and she would picture Grandma Jessie sitting at her window handling each little trinket and rewrapping it carefully to send out again in the next mailbag. Then there would be another pot of tea made, another spoonful of sugar added to the cup, and her grandmother would sit at the table dreaming, her hands around the earthenware teapot as if to draw its warmth out while she thought about her children and grandchildren.

The old people seldom left the inlet now, but every few years Jessie would come out for a holiday and visit all her family in turn. She stayed with Floss once or twice, and she visited Mavis at Green Tree Road where she sat on the porch and dozed through the hot afternoons, her legs propped up to ease the pressure on her veins, her eyes on the tide as it frothed in to fill the mudflat.

Cars had been driven in to Awaroa since the 1930s and the boys had used motorbikes to get in and out, but Fred still rode a horse with the mailbags slung across the front of his saddle. In later years the saddle had been patched and repatched with an old woollen suit jacket stitched over the leather, and more often than not Fred walked along the track leading his horse rather than adding to its burden. He always came down the hill track to the Robertson's farm at Wainui, past the little schoolhouse on the corner, and would call in for a cup of tea and a chat by the coal range before heading home again in the late afternoon.

Welby, Laura and the girls left the inlet in 1949 and went to live at Central Takaka where Ada found work milking cows on Brownie Baigent's dairy farm. Bill helped them widen the passageways of the new house so Welby could get around it in his wheelchair, but by now he was a severely crippled old man, the arthritis having taken its toll, and on 4 August 1950 he died.

It had broken his heart to leave his beloved Meadowbank, but he had never owned the property and there had been increasing pressure from his brothers and sisters who felt their families had a right to enjoy their Awaroa heritage too. Welby and Laura had always wanted to live out their days at Awaroa and they left sadly, bitter at the fighting and scrapping from siblings they felt had never shared their deep love for the land.

Ada and Joan found it just as hard to leave. The inlet had always been their home and they had grown up in tune with the cycles of the seasons and the tides. They always hoped they could live there again, perhaps at Cave Hill or Silver Point or on their old land up at Big River. On their last trip from Meadowbank across to the roadend at the head of the inlet, Ada spotted a snapper tail sticking up out of the water. She grabbed the axe and jumped out of the dinghy after it, only to find the water wasn't as shallow as she'd thought.

She got her snapper though, and made quick work of cleaning it up with the knife that was always in the dinghy.

"Our axe was sharp for once," Joan told her mother. "Jim always used to say that Hadfield axes were always blunt so we wouldn't cut our toes off when we were doing our jobs."

The snapper was a delicious farewell meal, and as always the sisters laughed at the minor inconvenience of soaking wet clothes.

They hated giving up their animals but they didn't have enough land at the new place to keep very many. They milked for the Takaka factory and raised calves to sell, and managed to keep a couple of pigs and a few hens as well. They left their sheep behind for Fred to shear and farm, and when their favourite cow Tui calved they offered her to their uncle Fred rather than sell her. Over the years they gradually pulled their old house at Big River down and took the timber out to reuse in Takaka.

Meadowbank was left empty again, the family still undecided nearly 30 years after William's death about how to settle the estate which was still owned jointly between the eight siblings. Some wanted the house cleaned up and rooms allocated for each family to use, another wanted it subdivided and titles allocated to each family, others wanted it sold and the money shared out.

The work and worry devolved on Fred as it always had, and he found himself negotiating with Welby's widow Laura for her possessions still at Meadowbank, and with his own brother Bill who made a strong bid to buy the property. Welby's estate was administered for Laura and her daughters by the Public Trust and Fred found himself reporting to them once again.

In 1952 the last dissenter finally agreed to the terms proposed by the other surviving family members and the first steps were taken towards subdividing the land and winding up the estate. Sections were to be allocated to each family and the rest of the land sold, but it was not yet on the market, because the family could still not agree on its value. It was suggested that lots be drawn for the choice of sections, and the title with the old homestead on it should be valued at £100 more. The Park Board was keen to acquire Cave Hill and Silver Point and so were various family members, and the future of the little cemetery became an issue again.

Fred was in his seventies now and a grandfather, and he had spent his whole life at Awaroa as a farmer, shipowner, contractor and labourer. He and Jessie still lived simply in the house he'd built for her on the banks of Big River, and their needs were few. They drew their water from a well, baked their bread on a coal range and ate the meat, fruit and vegetables from their own land. Their youngest daughter Joy stayed at home to care for them, and Bill helped when he could from Awaiti.

Fred Hadfield carried the mail from Wainui to Awaroa for 50 years. It was this publicity photograph, published in the *New Zealand Free Lance* 9 July 1952, which enabled his half-brother Reginald to trace the family 46 years after their mother Martha Adele Knowles was murdered by Reg's father in Palmerston North.

NZ Post photo

Fred sat down at the table one evening and made a list of everything he owned in the world, from the sea chest he'd inherited from his father to the wellworn old axe that stood outside the back door. His inventory filled less than two handwritten sides of the page.

Then one wet morning in 1952 a bombshell was dropped in his lap. When he opened the mailbag there was a letter from his half-brother, Reginald Knowles.

Fred had last seen the boy in 1906, when he had travelled to Palmerston North to collect Evered after Adele had been murdered. He remembered as if it were yesterday that fateful day in the Salvation Army house when Evered had held little Floss and refused to go without her. Acting on an impulse Fred had brought the girl back to Awaroa, but he had obeyed his father's instructions and left his half-brother to be adopted out. Although he had replayed the scene many times in his mind, he had been sure it was the right thing to do, and he had never expected to hear of Reginald Knowles again.

A few months earlier Fred had played host to a reporter who had taken his photograph for the *Free Lance*, a news magazine circulated all over New Zealand. The magazine still had pride of place in their home, where Jessie teased him about his handsome good looks and his long white beard and moustache. He sat astride Polly, mailbags slung over the front of the saddle, and the story claimed him to have the longest rural mail round on horseback anywhere in New Zealand.

Now it seemed Reginald had been looking for his family for some time, and when he saw Fred's name and photograph he wrote to ask for help in tracing Adele's family.

It was a worry for Fred, who brooded for a week before breaking the news to Florence. His mother's divorce, second marriage and tragic death were never discussed, and the new generation of Hadfields knew nothing about the skeleton in the family closet. Fred had kept his mother's memory sacred and secret, concealing his own feelings for nearly fifty years and he had never even talked to Floss about it. On 5 September 1952 he wrote to her, warning her that what he had to say would come as a shock.

"Somehow he has a number of birth, marriage and death certificates and has been trying to work out matters for himself. He says he remembers the terrible day when he was a small boy and has memories of his wee sister Flossie and has often wondered what had become of her, and has prayed that some day he would find out and meet again.

He has had rather a sad time altogether but from his letter seems to be a real good fellow and a Christian..."

"....Reginald asked for you to write to him. He will be watching for your letter as I told him in the letter I am sending him today that I was writing to you. His memory of you is as a little sister. I would not say too much about it as there may be some who remember enough about the past to say unpleasant things.

"His present name is unknown to any except of the family and I would not let the other name come into it at all. Trusting you are all well I am in haste, Fred J Hadfield"

Floss had no hesitation about her response. She sent a telegram to Reg immediately. "Just heard wonderful news, greetings and love, writing immediately - Sister Flossie."

Her long-lost brother responded with a telegram of his own.

"10th September 1952. God Bless You little sister, he has watched over us both 45 years. Love. Reginald."

Over the next few months they wrote constantly, filling in the gaps for each other. Reg's adoptive parents had split up when he was seven, putting him back into Salvation Army care at Eltham. Four years later his adoptive father turned up and reclaimed him and the two led a nomadic life, following the bush gangs around the middle of the North Island.

By the time Reg was in his teens he was on his own again, finding work on farms and in labouring gangs and fending for himself. He married young, and had to ask the Postmaster to consent to his marriage because he had neither parent nor guardian to take responsibility.

It was a rocky beginning but Reg made a good marriage and had seven children. As they grew up he began to wonder more and more about his natural parents. He delved into the records and slowly discovered that his nightmarish memories of the day his mother died were all true. Her death certificate showed that she had been married before, and that Evered whom he had always believed was his brother was in fact a half-brother. He also discovered he had a sister, her name and whereabouts unknown.

Reg tracked down and talked to his aunt May Violet Slyfield in Wanganui, who still had in her possession the Snow family Bible and who told him what she knew of the Hadfields.

"My sister Laura Smith and I used to sit and knit together and wonder about what had happened to Adele's little Reggie," May told him. "You were never forgotten, but lost, or should I say mislaid?"

When Reg discovered that Fred had taken Flossie home to Awaroa and brought her up with the Hadfields he was overjoyed.

Adele Hadfield's son Reginald, born at Haven House Nelson and adopted by a Salvation Army couple in Palmerston North when he was four years old.

He spent many years trying to trace his family and was 50 when he was finally reunited with his sister Florence Knowles.

"Fred, the Good Shepherd put a very heavy load on your capable shoulders at an early age, and you have done it most capably. God be praised that you didn't let Flossie out of your sight," he wrote. He met Darcy and Rita in Auckland, and soon after he and Floss made contact she travelled to Auckland to visit him and fill the gaps in her long-suppressed family history.

Reg remembered the day Fred took Floss and Evered away. He said he'd been promised lollies but the man never came back with them. He remembered Evered very well, and that he was good to the children. His mother had a scrubbing bucket on her arm when she answered the door to William Knowles that fateful morning, he told Fred, and he even remembered the building she used to clean, a dentist's rooms where Reg used to go with her and play with the false teeth.

His adoptive father had remarried and had not mentioned Reg anywhere on the marriage documents, effectively disowning him although it was a legal adoption. It had always been a great sadness to Reg that he had no family to call his own, and when he finally found his sister Floss it was a joyful reunion. Neither were Hadfields, but both were Adele's children, sharing the Newth and Snow family heritage with the Hadfield family. Their relationships with their half-brothers and sisters were always to be constrained by what was known as the family tragedy, the shadowy figure of their father always there between them and the Hadfields.

No one ever found out what had happened to William Knowles. He was released from prison and was thought to be living in Wanganui, but in later years those of his grandchildren who searched for information were unable to find any record of him and it was assumed he had changed his name.

There were rumours, and when the story began to come out after being buried for so many years there were memories of an old man who had knocked on doors around Nelson asking about the family. He was an itinerant artist, a landscape painter, and was living near Stratford, he told one of Laura McLaren's married daughters when he tracked her down. He asked for information about the Hadfields, but she was frightened and sent him away.

"If a man comes to the door selling paintings, Mum, you look at him. He looks exactly like the photo they had of Grandma and him. He knew a lot about Awaroa too. I'm sure it's the chap Knowles," she told Laura. "He told me ever so much about the inlet and about the Hadfields, and people don't tell you those sorts of things for nothing."

The sisters suspected that their Auntie Olive knew where he was all the time, although she never told anyone about him. Once Betty plucked up the courage to ask her point blank.

"Oh, I know where he is, all right," she was told, but Olive didn't enlarge on it very much. Auntie Olive never enlarged on anything.

The McLaren girls managed to piece some of the story together. Knowles had stayed with the Salvation Army, living in an isolated home between Stratford and Wanganui. He was reputed to have two daughters from his first marriage. Towards the end of his life he met a man who became his constant companion, and he would spend long periods of time painting and then travel around selling his work.

Knowles may have traced his daughter in the end, although he never met her. Her children remember her being very upset and agitated when an old man arrived at Riwaka on the service car and asked for her. She refused to see him, and the children were kept indoors. In the end he left the district again.

When Reg and Floss finally met each other they were both grandparents, Reg 50 years old and his sister two years younger. Their meeting filled a gap both had felt all their lives, and by the time he came down to visit the Hadfields in Riwaka, Takaka and Awaroa he was ready to claim his place as a family member and a friend.

It was an emotional pilgrimage. Finally Reg and Floss stood together at Evered's grave, their arms around each other and the tears flowing freely for their mother as well as the half-brother who had watched over them.

There was a much larger reunion at Little River in 1958, a formal get-together for the whole Hadfield family. For some, like Darcy, Laura, Roy and Ivy Hadfield, it was a nostalgic gathering. For those of the next generation it was a homecoming and a chance to bring their husbands, wives, sweethearts and children to the place where their New Zealand history began.

Fred, Jessie and Joy still lived at Big River and Bill and his family were at Little River. There were fifty people gathered for the weekend, and the talk was of cherries and whitebait, rowing in the inlet and hunting in the hills. Fred was harvesting flax again, over on Bill's farm, and there were lots of stories about the old flax cutting gangs. Now Donaghies Rope and Twine merchants in Dunedin were paying £95 a ton for top, scutched fibre and as always Fred was keen to try another income earner from the inlet.

The grandchildren were told the old stories and shown the heart Evered and Eileen had carved in the cabbage tree at Meadowbank - EH loves ES 7/1/ 16. They saw the hulk of the *Venture,* now rotting quietly in the little tidal creek where she was launched more than fifty years earlier.

The Reverend Keith Hadfield, grandson of Harry Roodhouse Hadfield, led a thanksgiving service outside the old homestead at Little River. His theme was appropriate and timeless.

"I will lift up mine eyes unto the hills, from whence cometh my help."

One of the congregation was young Lynette Bradley, now 18. As she wandered along the tideline in front of Meadowbank with the others and listened to her aunts and uncles reminiscing, she already had her own store of childhood memories, the hills and the broad stretch of inlet as familiar to her as her own home in Riwaka. Over the years she would be drawn back again and again, not yet realising the influence the events of the past would have over her future.

Hadfield family reunion at Little River, Awaroa 1958. *From left back* :Charlie Hadfield (standing), David Lankshear, Gordon, Laura McLaren, Elaine, Wilfred Bradley, John Wilson, Lynette Wilson (obscured) Mavis Bradley, Rita, Minnie, Vena, Marcia, Nelson, Kathy, Bernard, Keith, Ralph and baby Gillian behind. *Seated:* Jim, Fred, Bill senior, Roy, Darcy, Betty Lankshear, Joy, Bill, Jessie. Children: Howard, Paul, Rex and Suzanne Lankshear, Nancy, Donald.

Fred and Jessie didn't go to Lynette's debutante ball in 1957, nor to Mavis and Wilfred's silver wedding in August that year, but they added the photographs to their crowded mantelpiece. At the family reunion they met and approved of Lynette's future husband John Wilson, a young carpenter who was a good friend of Laura McLaren's grandson Darryl in Nelson. John's parents had died young and he had lived with his grandparents. Like the Bradleys, his family had been in New Zealand since the early days of European settlement.

Both John and Lynette loved the sea and ships, and they made their home in Green Tree Road on the bank of the little tidal estuary opposite the Riwaka wharf. It was only a few doors from Lynette's family home, and as John built their house Lynette was already planning and planting her garden.

Jessie and Fred turned eighty in 1959 and celebrated their golden wedding. Their lives were quiet and content, their days gentle. Fred spent long evenings at the dining table as he always had, doing his business, writing letters and worrying about the roads. He still wrote in pencil a lot of the time, drafting his business letters out on the backs of the *Nelson Evening Mail* wrappers before writing a neat copy to post.

He protested to the parks board when they began closing the roads again. Land access to Awaroa had been surveyed in 1899 at the request of the settlers, he pointed out, and his father had been one of those who raised three quarters of the money for the first horse track. They had petitioned the government for a road through to Marahau long before the Takaka road was in place.

"I'm not asking for big expenses, just some smoothing and clearing and a new bridge," Fred told the council, and he begged them to retain control of the road because he felt the parks board would want to control access.

Letters from children and grandchildren tumbled out of each mailbag, with news of weddings, christenings and mumps, promotions at work and holidays around the country. Muriel was up at Roto Roa Island near Auckland with her husband and children, and she wrote describing her trips to the mainland on the launch *Lady Roberts II*. As Jessie read her descriptions of the seats in the glassed-in wheelhouse, and the two berth cabin below decks where Muriel retired to feed the baby on the journey she was reminded of her own trips back and forth to Nelson on the *Lady Barkly*.

Jessie's garden had always been her great love, and many of the letters painted pictures of other gardens, seeds that had been exchanged and cuttings taken. She traced the stories of her children and her children's children through their descriptions of roses, sunflowers, pansies and autumn leaves.

Fred and Mavis with her Bradford van at Awaroa - her parents never learned to drive.

When Bessie's daughters went home to Wales to trace their origins they wrote descriptions of Abergavenny, and of the people who still remembered Houlson the photographer whose sister who had gone off to New Zealand.

Fred read the *Nelson Evening Mail* from cover to cover, keeping his wife and daughter up with world affairs. At night they would listen to the world news on the wireless, and on Sundays to the church service, enjoying the old Sankey hymns.

Jessie moved slowly and dreamily, spending more and more time sitting contentedly in the big wicker wheelchair her sister Christiana had bought forty years before. Her blue eyes still twinkled and her skin was still soft and white under the big sunhats she had worn all her life. These days her hair was white too and her smile was sweet and gentle.

The estate had still not been settled and the old homestead at Meadowbank was crumbling quietly away. Family members came and went, camping in the tumbledown rooms and wandering through the orchard as they passed on their stories and memories to husbands, wives and children. When Ivy Winter died in 1961 her son Henry Roberts inherited her share and there was a fresh round of discussion about Meadowbank.

The new generation was more mobile and they treasured their holidays at Awaroa. "Have you had any whitebait this season?" they would ask the old folk.

There were dried flowers and pictures from their grandchildren for Jessie's birthday, pots of melon and cape gooseberry jam from their daughter-in-law and fond cards and messages from the wider family that year of 1965. Jessie was the last of the Winters, and now it was her turn to reap the gentle love and affection she'd always shown to others.

She died peacefully in hospital, her Dear Boy by her side.

In the 1970s Fred finally saw the Meadowbank property subdivided. It had taken nearly 50 years of discussion and debate between the heirs to William Hadfield's estate, but in the end the seventeen acres around Meadowbank was divided into eight lots, one for each of William's living children and their descendants. New baches and cottages sprang up along the edge of the beach and the old homestead was left to blend comfortably in with the trees. Family members still went down for picnics and camped in the orchard, and sometimes Fred would go down there himself to sit on the bench overlooking the inlet, his long white beard wisped in the wind as he talked about the past.

For those who knew the stories it was easy to see the shadows of those who had gone before, to imagine the laughter of the children as they left for school and the swish of Adele's skirt as she hung a white sheet on a branch of the dog tree to summon Mr Perrott from his whare on Silver Point.

Lynette and John Wilson had three sons, and then in 1972 she gave birth to a daughter, a little scrap of a girl with her father's red hair and her mother's laughing eyes. Fred was staying with Mavis in Green Tree Road, and after the child was born he visited Lynette. He was courtly and formal in his jacket, shirt and tie, with a gift of flowers. The boys were playing out on the lawn and he watched them for a long time before turning to his eldest grand daughter.

"I have something I want to ask you, Lynette," he said gravely. "Would you consider naming the little girl after my mother?"

Lynette looked at him curiously. "You've never talked about her, Grandad. She died quite early, didn't she?"

"I was 27 when she died," Fred said simply. "And you're quite right, I've never talked about her, but I've never forgotten her either."

He sat down at the kitchen table, his old eyes soft with memory.

"Her name was Adele."

THE FAMILY OF FRED AND JESSIE HADFIELD (UPDATED TO DECEMBER 2004)

WILLIAM WELBY HADFIELD and MARTHA ADELE ANN SNOW

Their eldest son

FREDERICK GEORGE HADFIELD and JESSIE WINTER
9/10/1879-11/1/76)   1879-1965

married 1909

CLIFFORD FREDERICK
15/3/1910-20/3/1917

MAVIS JESSIE
21/7/1911- 18/6/1993
m Wilfred **Bradley**

— Ian 24/6/1934-29/12/2003
m Helen Rawiri
Anne Marie 19/9/1957

Lynette Wynsome
23/9/1940
m **John WILSON**

Darryl John 21/12/1961
m Colleen Spencer
Michael John 27/3/1989
Amy Adele 22/8/1993

Mark Ian 26/9/1964
m Jenny Carter
Liam Martin 23/7/96
m Claire Kelliher
(Sabastian Kelliher)
Jack Campbell Louis 19/10/2002
Molly Jessie Evelyn 3/3/2004

Craig Bradley 14/10/1967

Julia Lisa Adele 12/2/1972
m David Howarth
Opi Joe 19/1/97
Finn Pasquale 21/5/2000
Poppy Cerys Anne 9/7/2003

WILLIAM ROGERS
8/3/1913 - 17/1/2004
m Vena Langford

- **Elaine**
- **Gordon**
- **Lester**
- **Donald**
- **Diane**
- **Howard**
- **Nancy**

RALPH GORDON
19/3/1915-19/9/1995
m Edna Mary Riches
13/10/1956

- Elizabeth Anne 29/6/1960
- Norman Richard 23/12/1964
- Gillian Mary 21/12/1957

NELSON IVAN
6/11/1916 - 14/6/2002
m Marcia Roberts 1952

- Miriam
- Leann
- Neville

MURIEL CHRISTIANA
8/7/1918 - 25/6/2002
m Arnold Dalefield 8/1/1955

- Raewyn Dorothy Jean 8/3/1956
- Carol Evangaline 13/7/1957
- Roseanne May 23/1/1959

COLIN HOULSON
3/1921 - 20/11/1923

DOROTHY JOY
8/1922 - 3/8/2002

EPILOGUE

1976

FRED HADFIELD DIED in the Joan Whiting Memorial Hospital in Collingwood in January 1976. He was 98 years old and he had become a legend, an old white-haired man whose eyes had seen the history of the whole district unfolding. He had been born when New Zealand was still a young country and had grown up knowing those first Europeans to settle its shores. He was survived by six of his eight children and now his son Bill was an old man, the last of the Hadfields of Awaroa.

In his last years Fred did go back to the little house he had built on the banks of Big River. He spent some time sorting through a lifetime of papers, looking at old photographs, and re-reading letters from family and friends now long gone. In the evenings he wandered down to the river, much closer now than it had been before erosion ate into the banks. There was still no front verandah to sit on, although the piles were still there where he'd started to build one more than sixty years earlier.

There was one letter Fred kept with him all through those last years, and after his death it was found in his pocketbook, the paper worn thin where it had been folded and carried near to his heart. It was dated 22 October 1896, and it was the first letter he ever received from his mother.

"Meadowbank, Awarua, Totaranui. My dear Boy, I hope you have arrived all safe and well. We got your letter from Nelson. What a shame you used some of Miss Winter's money to pay Cross, you should have kept it for what I gave it to you for....Laura Cunliffe says you had on your patched trousers when you went there to see them. I do hope no one else saw you in them....Mrs Cunliffe came home on the Thursday, the *Transit* got here on the Wednesday, the *Comet* came in too and stayed all night....We have had no meat since you left till tonight. They went out pig hunting three times and saw no tracks.....I wish I had the money to spare. I would be there for a trip too. What job have you got and how do you like it? You must write a lot to me. Have you shaved yet and did Uncle Howard know you? Tell me what you think of everything ...”

The little house on the banks of Big River was left just as Fred and Jessie had lived in it, the door closed against the weather, the pictures still on the walls, the books on the shelves and the earthenware teapot still on the table.

Now their son Bill and his family were the only Hadfields left at Awaroa. Fred's dog Joe settled in happily at Bill's farm, although it took him some time to get used to sleeping in a kennel instead of in his master's back porch. Much of the land around Awaroa was now incorporated into the National Park, and hunters and trampers were more frequently through the area although the pigs that had once been plentiful were much harder to get.

Bill and his family had their own grief to deal with. Bill's third son Donald worked on the farm and earned money trapping possums and skinning them, and one stormy night not long before his 21st birthday in 1967 he was found dead from cyanide poisoning. He had been in the farm shed across the river tacking skins out to dry, and when he didn't return home his older brothers went to look for him. They brought the body home, and Donald Hadfield was buried at the Kotinga cemetery, near his mother's family.

Vena never recovered from her son's death. She spent her last years in the Joan Whiting Memorial Hospital in Collingwood, and when she died she was buried beside her son. Their children grew up and left the inlet, but Bill stayed on alone at Little River.

Venture slowly fell to pieces in the creek, but a new boat came in over the bar. John and Lynette Wilson launched their motor launch *Matangi* at Riwaka in 1969 and one of their first trips was to Awaroa. It was an auspicious launching. John built the boat himself and named it in memory of his grandfather who had been donkeyman on the ship *Matangi* many years before. The original *Matangi* was eventually broken up at Wakatahuri in the outer Pelorus Sound.

Matangi was launched in the estuary near the Wilson's house, and the bank had to be scraped out to allow her to go into the water easily. To John's delight a greenstone adze emerged from the earth when they widened the bank. He saw it as an omen of good luck for *Matangi* and for all her passengers.

*Abel Tasman Explore*r stands off the Awaroa beach after dropping Keith Hadfield off on the land his grandparents Harry and Annie Hadfield farmed last century.
Gilbert Hadfield photo

John's grandfather was a seaman who crossed Cook Strait more than ten thousand times. His father and uncles had been seafarers too, sailing from Wellington to the Chatham Islands to fish for cod from the *Miro,* a former gunpowder boat of 70 feet which was eventually sold as an oyster boat in Bluff. The *Miro* is still afloat and one of John Wilson's dreams is to see it restored it to its original condition with a bowsprit.

The Wilsons operated a regular passenger service up and down the coastline, and as the Abel Tasman National Park developed so did their business. They replaced *Matangi* with larger vessels, *Ponui* built in 1907, *Waingaro*, and *Abel Tasman Explorer,* built by John's father's best friend Jack Guard. A Torrent Bay bach left to Lynette by her father was turned into a tourist lodge, and as their family grew Lynette and John turned more and more towards the park for their livelihood.

Lynette honoured her grandfather's request and named her daughter Julia Lisa Adele Wilson. Julia was the tenth Hadfield descendant to carry Adele's name and the first of the new generation. The tradition was carried on down when her brother Darryl's daughter was named Amy Adele.

When Julia was twelve she was handed down the big silver locket from the Winters of Abergavenny, given in turn to her grandmother and mother as the eldest daughters of their generation, and when she was married the ceremony was at Shoreditch in England, within metres of the place where her ancestors Frederick Brown Hadfield and Anne Wyan Welby had been wed. Julia married a Welshman and her wedding ring was of Welsh gold, made from two worn wedding rings found in her great-grandmother Jessie's black japanned jewellery box. She didn't realise it at the time, but her wedding day was on the anniversary of her grandmother Mavis Hadfield's marriage to Wilf Bradley.

Like her brothers, Julia grew to love the inlet and learned to retell the family stories to the tourists and visitors who came to Awaroa.

Joan Hadfield was finally married to her old childhood sweetheart Edgar Sixtus. While she and Ada farmed at Meadowbank he and his first wife Mona Downing had lived high above them at Canaan, and their life together had been richly satisfying. Edgar had developed an interest in rocks and minerals early in his life and he became an authority on the geology of the area, his collection well known and respected. They celebrated their 50th wedding anniversary shortly before Mona's death in 1990.

Edgar, Joan and Ada had always been friends and when he became a widower they began to see more of each other. He proposed to Joan in front of a busload of retired friends when he was 83 and she was 74, and a few weeks later they were married at St John's hall in Motueka.

Their wedding on 30 June 1992 was to be a quiet ceremony but the guest list grew to 80. Joan wore deep pink with pink and white flowers in her hair, and her new husband told guests he thought she looked gorgeous.

"It was a lovely day for me," Joan said afterwards. "The good bit was when Edgar said I do. I was rather hesitant, but I did too."

Edgar, Joan and Ada lived quietly together in Motueka, content with their cats and their garden, until Edgar's death in 1999.

The two sisters inherited their mother's love of painting and in their later life they both took lessons and developed their talents. Now their own Awaroa and Golden Bay scenes hang on their walls beside Laura's work, and they can be reminded of their beloved inlet and the blue shadowed hills that surround it.

The old homestead at Meadowbank was pulled down, the timbers piled up in the blackberries and gorse where the cowshed had once stood, but in 1994 Lynette and John Wilson built and opened Homestead Lodge, a luxury accommodation house modelled on the original Meadowbank.

Meadowbank, built by William and Adele Hadfield from pitsawn Awaroa timber in 1884, stood by the sea for nearly a hundred years.

Part of their property was an inheritance from Mavis who had died the year before and left Lynette her share of the original family title. Olive's family inherited the piece of land where the old homestead had stood, and they asked Lynette and John to buy it from them as they wanted to see it kept in the family.

The big two-storeyed lodge was built on the original house site, fitting snugly among the trees planted by William, Adele and their children. The high gabled roof is a mirror image of the old house, and the view across the inlet is the same as it always was.

As they battled the elements and the tides to bring in building materials by launch, Lynette and John Wilson were often reminded of William and Adele's building project a hundred and ten years earlier. There was still no electricity at Awaroa and no road access to Meadowbank, but four-wheel drive motorbikes had superseded the horse and sledge and they had a generator and power tools to do the work that had once been done with a crosscut saw. Takaka rugby team members carried the waterpipe through fern and gorse and dropped it across gullies where Lynette's grandfather once hunted pigs, and where her aunts Joan and Ada used to search for their missing stock.

The Wilsons run guided walks and kayak trips through the Abel Tasman National Park, with overnight stops at Awaroa and at Torrent Bay. For the guides and chefs employed by the company the park is their summer home and many have family associations going a long way back. They're steeped in the natural and social history of the park and keen to share it.

Meadowbank Homestead - Awaroa, built by William and Adele Hadfield's great grand-daughter Lynette Wilson and her family as a tourist lodge on the site of the original homestead known as Meadowbank.

Lynette's family also owns the Old Cederman House at Riwaka now, and she has lovingly refurbished it the way it would have been when Adele and young Fred stayed there in 1884, and when Jim Perrott worked for the Cederman family before he and Adele ever met. When Lynette polishes the stair rail she is very aware that her great grandmother's hands were on it before hers, and in the garden she plants old lavenders and roses to recreate the atmosphere of colonial days.

At Awaroa these days, gourmet meals are served at the lodge, now called Meadowbank Homestead - Awaroa. Guests relax in a living room furnished in flowered chintz and ornamented with black and white photographs from the past. The old piano stands in the corner but today it's only an ornament, the wooden frame warped by years of damp air. In the bedrooms there are more photographs of the Hadfield family, and through the windows come the scents of sea air and old roses.

The dog tree still stands, and so do the trees Roy and Fred brought back from the coast for their mother. An old fig tree weeps where the orchard was, and every spring there are snowdrops, granny bonnets and old-fashioned daffodils on the lawn.

William's and Adele's first home still stands at Little River, back up at the head of the inlet under the brooding hills. Over the years the farm gradually went back, but sheep still roam the hills and Bill Hadfield still has an old dog to sit with him on the porch and bark at approaching visitors. The old homestead is back to its original size, the additions built on by the Campbells and the Hunters pulled down over the years, but the rhododendrons planted by Bill's grandfather William Welby Hadfield still flower in the spring. The oil paintings that once graced the sitting room at Meadowbank look down over Bill's plain wooden table, his crowded bookshelves and the bits of rock, whittled wood and other treasures, and in the shed his old Graeme-Paige estate car is buried under fifty years of memorabilia.

The house that William Welby Hadfield built at Awapoto in the 1870s, as it was with the two-storeyed extension built on by the Campbells. William and Adele lived there with their first three children Fred, Welby and Ivy. Their son Bill lived there for a while early this century, and their grandson is living in the house today.

The history of Awaroa is the history of the Hadfields. Down at Meadowbank a sixth generation plays on the beach now, and thousands of visitors from all over the world read the memorial plaques in the little cemetery behind the lodge. The inlet belongs to other families too, and years of launch trips and picnics and snapper fishing expeditions and long lazy days in the summer sun have been captured in their photo albums and in their memories.

Today Lynette's husband and sons skipper their boats up the eccentric granite coastline William and Harry knew so well more than a century ago. Visitors are told how the New Zealand Company's immigrant fleet sailed down this coast in 1841, looking for flat land to establish the settlement of Nelson.

The three ships *Whitby, Arrow* and *Will Watch* were six months from England, filled with the advance party of fit young men bursting to feel their new world underfoot and a sharp axe in their hand, and among them were Mark Newth and William Snow, Adele Hadfield's two grandfathers. Lynette Wilson is descended not only from these two but from James Bradley who was also on board *Whitby,* while his wife and children came out on the *Lloyds* with Ann Newth and her family.

Their ships anchored at Astrolabe, named and charted by Dumont d'Urville in 1827 and where the little brigantine *Jewess* had been only a few months before. Sails were still a rare sight along that coastline, where Abel Tasman and James Cook had passed in previous centuries.

There were earlier footsteps in these sands. Guides point out kumara pits and shell middens, and the places where eels were trapped, kiekie berries and pingao gathered. Over 800 years of occupation can be traced through the surviving legends and place names.

There were refugees here, dispossessed tribes fleeing to the hills, villagers harvesting their crops and others visiting to gather food and pass on the news of political alliances and coups. Ngati Rarua succeeded Ngai Tara and Ngati Tumatakokiri, the names evoking images of waka gliding along the eccentric granite coastline and grounding on the beaches.

The coastal walkway is a gentle one, through wetlands rich with raupo, flax and manuka. Granite blocks and giant kanuka distract the eye from the tiny bush orchids and insect-trapping sundew plants or the cicadas, mantis and dragon flies which share the bush with fantails and fernbirds.

The spirits of the past linger at Awaroa. When trampers emerge from the Torrent Bay track in bright sunlight they skirt Venture Creek where the last bones of the old scow lie rotting in the mud. It's easy to catch glimpses of history there, to imagine an axe ringing in the silence or the laughter of children carrying their schoolbooks through the forest, and to see the solid canvas sails of a flat-bottomed scow, her decks loaded with timber, flax, wool or granite for the Nelson market.

Sometimes in the amber glow and deep shadows of dawn you can almost catch a glimpse of a long salt-stained skirt kilted up above bare legs as a young woman wades out to float a dinghy.

Sometimes in the late afternoon the deep green of the bush by the old sawpit turns cold and shadowy and you hurry by the place where warriors once gathered, where shards of argillite and ancient greenstone lie buried with the shells.

And sometimes in the night the seabirds cry, reminding you of the loneliness of the place, the strange booming of the underground waters of Canaan, the richness of songs and music rolling from lighted windows, the shouts of men who rowed out into the darkness to meet the steamers, and the thin desperate cries of those who never returned.

In the old house there was sometimes a door opened unexpectedly, a cold breath on the back of a neck or the soft footfall of someone unseen, and even in the new Meadowbank the spirit lingers, to catch family members unawares with happenings that cannot be explained. Adele Hadfield's portrait hangs at the foot of the stairs, her proud grey eyes watching over the house and everyone within it.

At night the stars hang heavy in the sky and the moon reflects in the water. You can hear the tide when it turns, and the moreporks as they call from the hills. At dawn the shadows are long and golden, the sands vast and textured with trickles of clear water. The godwits and oystercatchers make delicate patterns among the shellbanks and the scoops of sand hollowed by the wind, and if you're lucky there are no other footprints.

That's how it has always been at Awaroa.

The *Venture* lies quietly at rest on the Awaroa mudflat.

To Awaroa

These things bring with them sadness
strangely sweet -
The blue of distant hills
bush clad, late afternoon,
the tang of wood smoke.
The wistful scent of bush flowers
and wild honeysuckle -
cicadas shuttling in the long, dry days.

The river gurgling over stony falls;
The high-pitched jangle of a gramophone.

And lonely graves -
where echoes of voices, long-stilled by death
yet keep on echoing within my heart.

These are the scents, the sounds, the scenes
the Spirit of the Place
where I was born.

- Muriel, nee Hadfield
1999

Photo - The Nelson Mail

LYNETTE WILSON is the great-great granddaughter of Frederick and Ann Hadfield who brought their family to New Zealand from England in 1858. Lynette was born and brought up at Green Tree Road in Riwaka where she and her husband John raised their own family in turn.

Lynette has always had a love of gardens, a love she inherited from her great grandfather William Hadfield, and she maintains the gardens at Homestead Lodge and Torrent Bay Lodge as well as at the Old Cederman House and her own home in Riwaka.

From her grandmother Jessie she has a love of painting and a flair for design, and she puts both to good use at Awaroa and at home.

Lynette and John share a fascination for small boats, especially the sailing scows and other coastal craft that traded along the coastline between Nelson and Golden Bay.

Gathering and researching the history of the Hadfields has been an absorbing and rewarding task that has taken her many years and reinforced her love for the inlet where she and her family now have the Homestead Lodge.

Photo - Ian Garrod

CAROL DAWBER is a Picton-based writer who has over the years tramped and sailed the Abel Tasman coastline and walked the golden sands of Awaroa.

She worked in collaboration with Lynette for over two years researching the background and helping to assemble the jigsaw puzzle of letters, diaries, memories and photographs that together made up the story of the Hadfields of Awaroa.

Carol has worked as a journalist, publisher, editor and scriptwriter. Awaroa Legacy is her fifth book.

Goat Bay

ABEL TASMAN NATIONAL PARK

Waiharakeke Bay

o

Awaroa F

Cave Hill

a *q* *e*   *i*

Awapoto River

Sawpit Point

c *h*

d

Awaroa Inlet

p

f

j   *g*   *r*

l

k

n

Awaroa River